And There Was No Poor Among Them

And There Was No Poor Among Them

Liberation, Salvation, and the Meaning of the Restoration

Ryan D. Ward

Greg Kofford Books
Salt Lake City, 2023

Copyright © 2023 Ryan D. Ward
Cover design copyright © 2023 Greg Kofford Books, Inc.
Cover design by Loyd Isao Ericson

Published in the USA.

Cover image: "Christ on the Cross between the Virgin and St John," by Michelangelo

All rights reserved. No part of this volume may be reproduced in any form without written permission from the publisher, Greg Kofford Books. The views expressed herein are the responsibility of the author and do not necessarily represent the position of Greg Kofford Books.

ISBN: 978-1-58958-787-8
Also available in ebook.

Greg Kofford Books
P.O. Box 1362
Draper, UT 84020
www.gregkofford.com
facebook.com/gkbooks
twitter.com/gkbooks

Library of Congress Cataloging-in-Publication Data

Names: Ward, Ryan D., author.

Title: And there was no poor among them : liberation, salvation, and the meaning of the restoration / Ryan D. Ward.

Description: Salt Lake City : Greg Kofford Books, 2023. | Includes bibliographical references and index. | Summary: "While The Church of Jesus Christ of Latter-day Saints has expanded many fundamental Christian doctrines, salvation is still understood as pertaining exclusively to the next life. How should we understand salvation and what does the timing of the Restoration reveal about God's vision of salvation for a suffering world? To answer these questions, author Ryan Ward traces the theological evolution of salvation from the liberation of Israel from oppression to the Western Christian development of salvation as an individualistic, transactional atonement. This evolution corresponded with the shift of Christianity from a covenant community to an official state religion aligned with imperial power structures. Ward also explores the economic and social movements in the centuries leading up to the Industrial Revolution, which solidified the power of propertied elites at the expense of the poor, plundered entire continents, and killed millions. Synthesizing these theological and historical threads, And There Was No Poor Among Them: Liberation, Salvation, and the Meaning of the Restoration asserts that the Restoration is God's explicit rejection of social and economic systems and ideologies that have led to the globalization of misery. Instead, Ward shows how the Restoration and the gospel of Christ is an invitation to a participatory salvation realized in Zion communities where "there are no poor among us.""-- Provided by publisher.

Identifiers: LCCN 2023006870 | ISBN 9781589587878 (paperback)

Subjects: LCSH: Church of Jesus Christ of Latter-day Saints--Doctrines. | Salvation--Church of Jesus Christ of Latter-day Saints. | Salvation--Mormon Church. | Salvation--Christianity--History of doctrines. | Zion (Mormon Church) | Mormon Church--Doctrines.

Classification: LCC BX8643.S25 W37 2023 | DDC 230/.9332--dc23/eng/20230412

LC record available at https://lccn.loc.gov/2023006870

For Bea:
Whose brazen self-identification as a "citizen of the world" began to open my eyes to humanity to which I had long been blind.

The glory of God is the poor person who lives.
— Oscar Romero

Contents

Foreword: Liberation Theology and the Modern Church, by Robert A. Rees	xi
Acknowledgments	xix
Introduction: Two Salvations	1
1. The Old Testament: Liberation and Salvation Remembered	11
2. Jesus and the Reign of God: Salvation as Covenant Community	43
3. Christian History: Salvation Turns Personal	83
4. The Calamity Which Should Come: The Restoration in Historical Context	109
5. The Book of Mormon: Liberation and Salvation Retold	137
6. Zion: And There Was No Poor Among Them	189
Conclusion: Toward Restoration	213
Bibliography	225
Scripture Index	237
Subject Index	241

Foreword

Liberation Theology and the Modern Church

Robert A. Rees,
Co-founder and Vice-President of the Bountiful Children's Foundation

I: Salvation Restored

Ryan Ward's *And There Was No Poor Among Them: Liberation, Salvation, and the Meaning of The Restoration* may be the most important book I have read in the past three decades. That's not hyperbole. I read lots of books and find wisdom, inspiration, guidance, and even delight in many, but this book gives me all those things and, in addition, calls me to repentance in a way that, as a believing Christian, I not only can't dismiss, but truly recognize as necessary.

Ward's book, written in the spirit of the promise of restoration, is *that* good, *that* true and, in the way it awakens the words of Christ to a fallen and failing world, even *that* strangely beautiful. I can think of no other book that I've read during the past thirty years except for the scriptures that has challenged my mind as deeply, opened my heart as fully, and awakened my soul as profoundly as Ward's does in calling us to follow Jesus in creating a society in which there are truly no poor among us. We tend to think of this as an idealistic, spiritual utopia that is beyond our grasp, beyond our means and beyond our time, but modern revelation suggests that such a society is ours to envision and establish, not at some future time and place, but here and now. Further, Ward contends we are under a covenantal obligation to do so. In his Conclusion, he asks an ultimate question, "The world cries out for salvation. Who will answer?" Who indeed?

My response upon reading Ward's book reminded me of how Herman Melville's felt when he first read Nathanial Hawthorne's *Mosses from an Old Manse*, a collection of stories that helped inaugurate the imaginative flowering in the New World we know as the American Renaissance. Melville said he experienced "a shock of recognition," by which I think he meant the revelation of some fundamental truth. *Recognition* or *re-cognition* (from the Latin verb *recognoscere*) means "to know again," or "to recall to mind," or it could mean to know something for the first time and intuitively recognize its truth from all the other truths one has known or should have known.

II: A Community of Revelation

Ward's deep scholarship, his broad knowledge of scripture and history, and his spiritual insights and thoughtful ponderings confirm the fact that the Restoration is not something that happened, but rather something that *is happening* and *will continue to happen* as we are called to be part of what I call a "community of revelation": called to be anxiously engaged in the vertical and horizontal unfolding of light and truth which flow from both heaven and earth—and will continue to do so until the Savior returns and the restoration is fulfilled. In other words, within our own lives and spheres of influence, we are called to ask for, receive, and share light as it is given us regarding this and other sacred callings. This is precisely what Ward's book does.

It is exhilarating to acknowledge that what Ward has written is revelation, revelation that challenges me to do what I have covenanted to do many times—covenanted, I believe, both in the heavens before I was born and in this world when, as a ten-year-old boy, I was baptized in a bronze basin in the Mesa Temple, covenanted in modern temples over the course of my life, and covenanted when partaking of the sacrament nearly every Sunday for the past seventy-seven years—covenanted to keep Christ's commandments, including ministering to the poor, the disabled, the dispossessed, and all of those with whom Jesus identifies (and asks us to identify) as the least among us.

I know all the reasons, explanations, and excuses for not doing this because I have given them myself, many times. I am familiar with the political justifications, the institutional rationalizations, and the religious guises that keep the poor ever with us, but Ward leaves me convicted and convinced that I have not done enough to address the problems of poverty, inequality, and injustice among my fellow beings; that "because I have been given much, I too must give," both much and *more*; and that even though I might consider myself poor, by comparison with most others, I am indeed rich, especially in light of my old professor Hugh Nibley's definition, "To be rich is to have more than you need."

III: A Secular Witness

While it may be just a happy coincidence, I find it truly affirming that contemporaneous with the publication of Ward's book is Pulitzer Prize-winning author Matthew Desmond's *Poverty, by America* (Crown, 2023). Desmond's is an affirming and secular witness to Ward's conclusion that poverty exists (including in the Church) primarily as both a conscious and subconscious choice by those who do not live in poverty. Both authors argue persuasively that poverty in (and *by*) America (and other developed nations) exists and persists because we choose to make it so. The partial and often temporary victories we have won in the various national and international wars we have waged against poverty over the past century demonstrate that if we truly wished to, we have the ability and resources to significantly diminish and even eradicate poverty.

Wishing to do so means acknowledging such realities as the following:

- The richest 1% of Americans own 40% of the nation's wealth.
- The wealth of the fifty richest people in the United States is equal to that of the poorest 165 million.
- Globally, 1.2 billion children live in poverty.
- Globally, 719 million people (9.2%) live on less than $782 *a year*.
- Annually, three million children die of hunger and its related causes.

Addressing poverty and its related conditions and consequences (such as illness, early mortality, lower education, lower earning power, higher crime, and incarceration rates) means abandoning the myths about the poor that we harbor defensively, including that the majority of the poor are so by choice, that they tend to be lazy and irresponsible, that they deserve their station, and so forth. Concomitant myths are those about the rich—that, as opposed to the poor, they are responsible and industrious citizens who have earned and therefore deserve their wealth and status. Some of these myths are vestiges of our Puritan past and its belief in the visibly elect and the Gospel of Wealth, which suggest that wealth is both a sign of a person's righteousness and a validation of God's favor and blessings.

IV: The Call to the Church and to Individual Latter-day Saints

It is clear from the Doctrine and Covenants that obeying the commandments and realizing the promises of the Restoration are expected of both individual members and the corporate church. Latter-day Saints who pay tithes and offerings and make charitable contributions to other humanitarian causes, are, on average, more charitable than most Americans. In fact, according to a study done at the University of Pennsylvania, "When it comes to being generous with time and money, Americans who are not Mormons can learn from Americans who are."[1]

One could argue that, because of our understanding of the Law of Consecration and the specific commandment to have no poor among us, we might take greater leadership in sharing these divine concepts: first, by doing all we can to ensure that there are no poor among us and, second, by showing the world how doing so is possible. Thus, as Ward says, "the law of consecration can be viewed within a larger context of God's justice working to overcome inequality throughout the world." Were the church able to eliminate or at least significantly reduce chronic poverty among its members worldwide, it would be in a powerful position to help other churches and nations to do the same.

It must be noted that the Church does have a significant international humanitarian outreach with programs devoted specifically to emergency response, clean water, immunization, maternal and infant care, and hunger, and that it makes generous donations to the United Nations, the Red Cross, and similar organizations. In 2022 the church gave more than a billion dollars' worth of aid and support to humanitarian causes. Some contend that with its vast wealth (estimated to be more than one hundred billion dollars) the Church could give much more, including to the poor.

While the Church has been largely successful in addressing poverty among its members in developed nations, it has been less so among members in developing nations, a conclusion based on the work my colleagues and I in the Bountiful Children's Foundation have been doing for the past fifteen years in addressing malnutrition among Latter-day Saint and other children. In the twenty countries in which we work, a number of faithful Latter-day Saints live in poverty, some in extreme, intergenerational poverty and thus suffer many of the ills that plague the poor elsewhere, including death. Thankfully, this is something the Church is just beginning to turn its attention and resources to address in a systematic, coordinated way.

Latter-day Saints are thought to have an influence beyond what their numbers would suggest. In business, politics, education, and other areas of society, they tend to demonstrate leadership. Poverty is a serious global

---

1. Jill DiSanto, "Penn Research Shows That Mormons Are Generous and Active in Helping Others," Penn To-day, April 17, 2010, https://penntoday.upenn.edu/news/penn-research-shows-mormons-are-generous-and-active-helping-others

problem to which the Church and its members have the potential to make a major contribution. As Ward states, "Zion is to be a light to the world—to show the world how to be God's people—and the defining characteristic of Zion is that there is no poor among them." This suggests that if the Church were to seriously work toward establishing a Zion culture among its members, it could show other societies and nations, especially poorer nations, how to do the same.

V: Jesus's Last Great Message

To those who find Ward's call to eliminate poverty unrealistic or even fanciful, I respond that it is in perfect harmony with Jesus's last, great teaching—both to his original disciples and to us—which is a powerful affirmation of how deliberately, how consciously, and how often he linked having no poor among us with our being of one heart and one mind, which clearly at present we are not. That teaching, found in the twenty-first chapter of John's Gospel, suggest how seriously the Lord considers, and expects us to consider, the primary focus of his ministry, which was:

> to proclaim good news to the poor. . . .
> to proclaim freedom for the prisoners
> and recovery of sight for the blind,
> to set the oppressed free. (Luke 4:18–19)

This final teaching takes place on the shores of the Sea of Galilee where, while his disciples were spending a night of fruitless fishing, he had been preparing breakfast for them. What an amazing scene: the Lord of all creation fixing breakfast for his friends! After helping them fill their nets with an abundance of fish, he called out, "Bring some of the fish you have caught. Come and have breakfast" (John 21:11–12). After they had eaten, he turned to Peter and asked, "Simon, son of John, do you truly love me more than these?" When Peter affirmed that he does, Jesus simply said, "Feed my lambs." He asked the same question a second and third time, and with each subsequent affirmation, he responded similarly, "Feed my sheep."

What does Jesus mean by his question, "Do you love these more than me?" Scholars have puzzled for centuries over the antecedent of the ambiguous "these." Perhaps the most logical answer is, "Do you love me more than you love these things—including this meal and extra fish I have just provided for you—or perhaps even the world itself?" I think he referred specifically to the great abundance of unconsumed fish that remained after his disciples had their fill. Having earlier seen him perform the miracle of feeding the five thousand, I believe he is challenging them to take these fish and feed them to the poor, which is why, after his exchange with Peter, he said simply, "Follow me"—meaning to do what you have just witnessed me doing.

What Peter seemed to have missed, and what I think many of us in his church miss, is Jesus's implied statement, "Peter, I have just fed you and I have provided enough fish for you to feed many others. What are you going to do with all this fish?" Peter, having had his own hunger satisfied, seems to have forgotten the bounty with which he and his fellow disciples have just been blessed. He doesn't ask, as we might expect he would after watching Jesus's ministering to the poor for three years, "Lord, to whom shall we give these extra fish?" Apparently, he is no longer even aware of this bounty.

To those of us living in the modern, developed world, Jesus is saying something similar: "I have blessed you with enormous wealth. Many of you live in houses more spacious than you need and often some of your bedrooms lie empty; you drive cars and pass by the poor on roads and byways. You eat three meals (or more) a day and your larders and pantries are fully stocked. You have enormous freedom of movement and choice. You have more of everything than you need and have more luxuries than any previous generation in history. What do you intend to do with all these things? Do you love me enough to follow me and give generously to the poor?"

Of course, some of us not only do not think of sharing our abundance with others beyond what the Church asks in tithes and offerings, we somehow think we deserve that abundance and may believe that much of what we enjoy is the result of our own industry and reward for living righteously. We forget that in our time the Church has added a fourth essential mission to its *raison d'etre*: "To care for the poor and needy." Many of us have the other missions (to preach the gospel, to redeem the dead, and to perfect the saints) written indelibly in our hearts, unaware that the third cannot be fully possible without the fourth. Ward asks hard and even uncomfortable questions about our priorities as a church and people. But they are necessary questions that we must answer with honesty and love.

What we seem not to have internalized is that with us God is neither ungenerous nor parsimonious. To those who are thirsty, the Lord does not just offer a drink of water; to land that is parched, he does not send just a little rain; and to souls in need of blessings, he does not speak just a few perfunctory words. As he says to Israel, "For I will pour water upon him that is thirsty, and floods upon the dry ground: I will pour my spirit upon thy seed, and my blessing upon thy offspring" (Isaiah 44:2). "To pour" means "to stream or "flow continuously or profusely."[2] Such gracious, abundant overflowing is characteristic of God's gifts to us. As the poet Robert Herrick expresses it:

> God's hands are round and smooth, that gifts may fall
> Freely from them and hold none back at all.[3]

As God's children, I believe he hopes we will do the same.

In his October 2014 conference address titled "Are We Not All Beggars?" Elder Jeffrey R. Holland states,

> Down through history, poverty has been one of humankind's greatest and most widespread challenges. Its obvious toll is usually physical, but the spiritual and emotional damage it can bring may be even more debilitating. In any case, the great Redeemer has issued no more persistent a call than for us to join Him in lifting this burden from the people. As Jehovah, He said He would judge the house of Israel harshly because "the spoil of the [needy] is in your houses."[4]

Those of us in the modern church, members as well as leaders, need to imagine Jesus's questions to Peter as directed to us, individually and collectively: "Is the wealth with which I have blessed you and the Church truly being given to the poor and needy in as great a measure as possible? Are there any malnourished children among you? Are there any brothers and sisters who go to bed hungry night after night? If so, are you feeding them? Are there any naked among you? If so, are you clothing them? Are you providing shelter for the homeless?"

Once again, I am grateful for Ryan Ward, a fellow saint who has written so powerfully and persuasively to remind me of what my heart knows to be true. Even though as a child of the Great Depression I grew up in both spiritual and temporal poverty, I have been blessed beyond measure. Ward's concluding paragraph reminds us that "the good news of the gospel points us toward a salvation realized and fulfilled through participation in the love of God, manifest as the struggle for and liberation of humanity and creation. Toward a new day and new life for the crucified people of the world. Toward restoration of justice. Toward restoration of equity. Toward restoration of community. Toward restoration. . . ."

Amen!

---

2. TheFreeDictionary.com, s.v. "pour."

3. Robert Herrick (1591–1674), "God's Hands."

4. Jeffrey R. Holland, "Are We Not All Beggars?," The Church of Jesus Christ of Latter-day Saints, October 2014, https://www.churchofjesuschrist.org/study/general-conference/2014/10/are-we-not-all-beggars.

Acknowledgments

I am grateful to all of the liberation theologians who have shaped this work. Their theology was not merely an intellectual exercise. It was developed to provide comfort and support to people suffering under horrific historical circumstances. This dire need required them to search, struggle for, and seek out a means of providing both the assurance of and the "hope for things which are not seen which are true." This work, I hope, does justice to their ideas and to the nameless millions whose suffering required them and still requires them today.

I owe an enormous debt of gratitude to Deborah Brunt. She has contributed to this work in ways both large and small. She has read, reread, edited, and commented on many drafts, pointed me to books and articles, discussed and shared enlightening and insightful views on many of these ideas, and pushed me to be more expansive, inclusive, sensitive, and generous in my writing and my own perspectives. If this work succeeds in some small measure, it is in large part due to her contribution and influence.

Thanks also to my father David Ward for reading and providing feedback, discussion, and encouragement on much of this work, and to my kids for putting up with Dad's obsession with "Jesus books" these past few years.

I am also grateful to Loyd Isao Ericson for his essential support of this project. His enthusiastic response from the moment I proposed this idea has reinforced my own feeling that this was an interpretation worth developing and sharing, and his suggestions and contribution have added depth and perspective to the finished work.

And lastly, thanks to my wife Bea for her endless support and love.

Introduction

Two Salvations

The gospel is literally translated as the "good news." What's so good about it? For those of us who are members of The Church of Jesus Christ of Latter-day Saints, the question gives pause. Well, maybe not so much pause as incredulity. We know what's good about the gospel. The good news of the gospel is, for us, in a nutshell, the Plan of Salvation. This is our understanding of our Heavenly Parents' plan to shepherd us through this mortal existence and provide a way for us to return to their presence, to live with them and our families for eternity by participating in and receiving the ordinances of the Church.

Growing up in Southeastern Idaho in the 90s in the middle of the "Mormon Bible belt," this was my understanding. The good news of the gospel was that because of Jesus Christ, some day in the future I could return to live with Heavenly Father. So I grew up with this more or less constantly in the back of my mind. Going to church was a weekly reminder that I needed to watch out and be careful. Why? Because as bad as God wanted me to come back to live with Him, Satan wanted to claim my soul for his own. Why? Because he was so miserable that he wanted everyone to be as miserable as him.

Satan was everywhere, and he used everything to try to get at me. Satan was in the TV, in the radio, in the tapes and CDs I listened to, in the girls that walked past me in the mall. Satan was in the nonmembers at school, even in my fellow church members who weren't on their guard as much as I was. If I wasn't careful, Satan would get me to do horrible things, like listen to heavy metal or gangsta rap, watch R-rated movies, drink coffee or alcohol, smoke cigarettes, or be too close of friends with nonmembers. For the girls, he might even get them to wear a sleeveless shirt or a skirt that didn't go all the way past their knees. All of this would lead one day to the worst of all possible outcomes; not being worthy to go to the temple, go on a mission, or be sealed for time and all eternity to my wife.

But it was okay, because God had foreseen all of this stuff. And had provided a way for me to be able to repent and be cleansed from my sins. Because of Jesus, salvation was possible if I felt bad enough for the sins I committed and remembered them all so I could repent. And because of Jesus, I could sleep well at night, confident in the knowledge that lingering a bit too long on that music video on MTV or sneaking a peak at the Victoria's Secret store in the mall wasn't going to be the end of me.

Or in my less comfortable, more guilty moments, I could take an exhaustive inventory of my life to try to figure out which of my many sins might keep me from heaven, which forgotten mistake would be displayed widescreen for all to see at the day of judgment. Was it the aforementioned MTV, listening to Snoop Dogg or other CDs with Parental Advisory stickers (which I got my eighteen-year old friend to buy for me and hid in my scripture case so my parents wouldn't find them), skipping seminary to go joyride with my friends, writing my mother's checks out for an extra twenty dollars when I filled the car up with gas, taking some of the food we were supposed to throw away at my job at McDonalds home with me at the end of my shift, cheating in school, or noticing the changing shapes of the girls around me during adolescence and feeling something stirring?

To a teenage boy growing up in the early 90s in white middle-class Idaho these were my concerns. Well, these were my concerns when I thought about church stuff. Mostly I wanted to hang out and cruise around with my friends, listen to music and buy CDs, go out to eat, and play Nintendo, basketball, and baseball. I wasn't really too concerned with salvation as something that had relevance for me in my daily life. As long as I did what I needed to and didn't mess up too bad in this life, God would take care of it for me in the next. That was the good news of the gospel for me.

Meanwhile, at the same time I was growing up in rural potato country, three thousand miles away in El Salvador, a country that I wasn't really aware of, people hoped for a different kind of good news. Since 1979 (I was two years old) the country had been involved in a civil war. The military government, which came to power in a coup, had been fighting guerilla groups for control of the country. The government represented the interests of the wealthy landowners and corporations who strenuously resisted any reforms to the current agrarian economic system. They relied on forcible eviction of peasant farmers or terrorizing them into leaving their land in order to expand their land ownings, increase their profits, and "keep in existence an almost feudal system of exploitation."[1] Any resistance was condemned as a communist threat to national security.

---

1. Oscar Romero, *Voice of the Voiceless: The Four Pastoral Letters and Other Statements*, 3.

Not surprisingly, the peasants did not take kindly to being exploited and abused by the wealthy landowners, and so they aligned themselves with the guerilla groups that were trying to overthrow the government. The military ruthlessly cracked down in a campaign of terror and repression, targeting civilians and peasants. Some seventy-five thousand people, mostly civilians, were killed over the next twelve years (an unknown number "disappeared"). The United States, concerned about the advance of communism during the Cold War and protecting its own corporate interests, sent millions of dollars in military aid and weapons and provided military training for the Salvadoran government who then used the money to fund and train security forces and operate "death squads," military groups who killed and terrorized villagers.

On March 18, 1981, several days after a military sweep—a government operation that raided villages and summarily executed any civilians encountered—between four thousand and eight thousand villagers, mostly women and children, waded into the waters of the Rio Lempa river, attempting to flee into Honduras to escape the government death squads. Caught between the Salvadoran military on one bank and Honduran troops (under orders by US superiors) blocking their escape on the other, they were bombed and strafed with machine-gun fire by military planes. Hundreds were killed. Later that year in December, in one of the most infamous instances of violence in the civil war, the Atlacatl Battalion (a special unit trained by US military advisors) occupied the village of El Mozote and massacred over one thousand unarmed men, women, and children.

Given the repression and terror carried out by the government against civilians, some of the clergy of the Catholic church sided with the peasants and civilians. This turned the government against the church. They began targeting clergy who were speaking out against the military government atrocities, accusing them of siding with the rebels. They targeted priests, volunteers, and people who had come from abroad with humanitarian agencies. These organizations ran food banks, provided social services to the displaced, and offered relief and healthcare for the poor. Human rights and labor leaders were also targeted. Anyone suspected of antigovernment sympathies or collaboration was at risk of abduction, torture, and death.

On March 24, 1980 (one month after my third birthday), Archbishop Oscar Romero was assassinated as he performed mass for his congregation.[2]

---

2. Romero had become increasingly and vocally critical of the government in his three years as archbishop. The day before he was assassinated he pleaded with the National Guard, police, and military: "Brothers, you come from our own

At his funeral a week later, government snipers and covert bombers killed forty-two people and wounded scores more who were there in mourning. On December 2, 1980, members of the National Guard abducted, raped, and killed four Catholic women from the United States (three nuns and a lay worker). On the morning of November 16, 1989 (I had been ordained a deacon earlier in the year), a government death squad, trained only hours earlier by members of the US military, entered the campus of the University of Central America, dragged five Jesuit priests from their beds, forced them to lie face down on the grass in the courtyard, and shot them in the head. They searched the compound, found another priest and killed him, and then they shot and killed the housekeeper and her daughter who were huddled in terror in a corner of their bedroom.[3]

In this climate of fear, repression, and horror, what does the good news of the gospel look like? What does salvation look like? Can these innocent women, men, and children afford the luxury of a personal inventory of their sins? Does such an idea even make sense for them? Can the mother who does not know where her children's next meal is coming from think about the eternal state of her soul? Can a child who watches their parents murdered in front of them think about such things? Will a person dragged from her bed in the middle of the night to an undocumented government torture center consider whether the dress she is wearing is too short, or shows her back or shoulders?

I dwell on these scenes not to be morbid or sensationalistic, but to highlight the very real difference between the historical context in which I grew up and the one taking place in this small Central American country. For me growing up in Mormon Idaho, salvation meant something very different than for these poor Salvadoran villagers. For me, salvation

---

people. You are killing your own brother peasants. . . . In the name of God, in the name of this suffering people whose cries rise to heaven more loudly each day, I implore you, I beg you, I order you, in the name of God: stop the repression." Oscar Romero, "The Church Serves Personal, Communal, and Transcendent Liberation."

3. This horrific act of violence led to international outrage and eventually helped to turn the tide of the Salvadoran civil war towards peace talks and an amnesty between the government and rebel groups. The names of these eight Salvadoran martyrs are Ignacio Ellacuría, Ignacio Martín-Baró, Amando López-Quintana, Juan Ramón Moreno-Pardo, Joaquín López y López, Segundo Montes Mozo, Elba Ramos, and Celina Ramos. Their colleague Jon Sobrino was coincidentally out of the country and so escaped assassination.

was something pushed off many years in the future that would take care of my bad choices and foibles. For them, it meant literal saving from exploitation, starvation, rape, torture, or death. It meant liberation from an oppressive government. The difference could not be more stark. That difference is the focus of this book.

I suggest that the idea of salvation needs to be rethought in the Church. No, not just rethought. Radically expanded in light of horrific and tragic scenarios like that in El Salvador, one of scores throughout history and in the world today. *Whatever it means for the next life, salvation cannot leave behind those in this one.* I suggest, and I believe that history and scripture bear this out, that God's work in the world has much more to do with affecting the salvation of God's children from the kind of horrors the vast majority of them suffer on a daily basis than in tying down loose ends for the next life. I will refer to this as temporal salvation, or liberation.[4]

This distinction is not semantic. The way we define salvation tells us not only what is required of those who claim to be God's followers and disciples of Jesus, it also reveals to us the structure of reality in the world and how God feels about that structure. If salvation is about returning to live with God in the next life, it doesn't really matter much how the current world is structured. But if salvation is about liberating people from oppression and the things that make them unable to live *this* life to its fullest, including in relation with God and one another, then we have to seriously question the structure of the world. Not just question—we have to work to change the structure of the world. We have to work to change the economic and political systems that exploit and oppress the vast majority of humanity and creation. It is crucial for us as a church to undergo a paradigm shift to this end—or we risk being left behind while the work of God commences around us in the world. Our insistence on a separation of the spiritual from the temporal has blinded us to the reality

---

4. This theological approach to understanding the good news of the gospel is known as "liberation theology." The term was first used by Gustavo Gutiérrez in his seminal 1971 work *A Theology of Liberation*. In his later book *We Drink from Our Own Wells: The Spiritual Journey of a People*, Gutiérrez defines liberation as "an all-encompassing process that leaves no dimension of human life untouched, because when all is said and done it expresses the saving action of God in history" (p. 2). See William Cosgrave, "The Theology of Liberation," 506–16, for a brief introduction. See also Alfred T. Hennelly, *Liberation Theologies: The Global Pursuit of Justice*, for a survey of the many approaches to liberation theology that have been worked out globally.

of the need for justice and liberation around us. This work, the work of justice and liberation, the work of building community, *is* the work of God. Moreover, I suggest that this work, and the dire need for it in the world today, was the fundamental purpose and vision of the Restoration.

This book is an appeal to center liberation and justice in our definition and conceptualization of salvation. Salvation has played a fundamental role in Judeo-Christian religious tradition for all of biblical and modern history, but what is meant by salvation has changed throughout that history. This book attempts to trace the evolution of this term throughout history, with a special focus on the role of the Restoration and what its timing and vision tells us about the ways in which we should view salvation and what that means in practice. Once we center liberation in our view of salvation, the way we view and interpret other aspects of our faith tradition is reoriented. This book aims to paint a picture of one such possible reorientation.

Chapter 1 describes the understanding of the idea of salvation throughout the history of Israel in the Old Testament. We will examine how temporal salvation was a central concern of Israel and was formally codified in God's covenant with them. God's salvation very much meant deliverance and liberation from political powers of oppression and occupation, and the law God gave to Israel contained specific economic and social codes and prohibitions designed to maintain justice and equity in their communities specifically for the poor and marginalized. Within the kingdoms of Israel, a primary focus of prophetic activity was to highlight when the ruling powers were ignoring or actively exploiting these vulnerable groups. As the voice of God, prophets called those who oppressed the poor to repent. A primary goal of such prophetic activity was to reveal the specific nature of the systems of oppression and exploitation and to show the people the way towards a new type of reality, a community of relationship with God and one another.

Chapter 2 explores the ministry and mission of Jesus of Nazareth, with a focus on the historical context in which he lived. We will see that Jesus came into the world at a time of great political and religious upheaval in which the Jews were under three layers of oppression: two layers of political oppression and a further layer of religious oppression. We will see that this historical context played a critical role in the mission of Jesus—both how he viewed his mission and the logistics of the way it was carried out in the lives of his followers; from the people he ministered to, to the parables he told, all culminating in his death at the hands of the Roman authorities as a political criminal. We will also discuss what the resurrection might mean in light of Jesus's mission and ministry understood in this context, and we will explore how the poor and suffering in the world can be particularly identified with the suffering of Jesus and how this changes our view both of Jesus and "the crucified people of the world."

Chapter 3 will discuss the way the concept of salvation changed from the idea of liberation, physical deliverance, and covenant community to a legal transaction between individual humans and God. We will examine a number of social and historical factors that contributed to this shift, including the theological idea of purgatory, the advent of the guilty conscience with Augustine, the increased focus on death and the afterlife that followed the Black Death in the Middle Ages, the institutional and doctrinal changes introduced by the Catholic church that focused salvation more on individual piety and penance, and the changes in orthodoxy that accompanied the Protestant Reformation. Throughout, we will see that shifting ideas about the meaning and mechanism of Christ's Atonement play a critical role in the way that the Western church interprets salvation. We will also reexamine the interpretation of Paul that was so crucial to current Protestant ideas of salvation in light of the "new perspective on Paul" that attempts to place Paul in his proper historical context. This allows us to situate Paul's work and ministry squarely within the framework of expanding the covenant community to the Gentiles, an idea at odds with the Protestant interpretation of salvation as an individual justification through Christ.

Chapter 4 will survey the specific state of the world at the time of the Restoration. My position is that the Restoration was God's direct response to the philosophical, economic, political, and social movements that accompanied the Industrial Revolution and the rise of unfettered capitalism. The social and legal changes that took place resulted in wealth (in the form of lands and the means of manufacturing) being transferred to a wealthy elite. The common law that peasants had relied on for centuries was revoked via enclosure movements, and they were forced into wage labor. Colonialism and imperialism plundered entire continents in the Americas and in the East, and visited death on tens of millions through genocide, slavery, and disease. While this inequality and human and planetary exploitation has only widened in the two hundred years since the Restoration in the United States and other Western countries, it has heartbreakingly expanded even more in the Global South. What does the Restoration mean against this backdrop? Hearkening back to a historical, temporal, and liberative view of salvation is, I suggest, the key to understanding both the timing and the prophetic vision of the Restoration.

Chapter 5 will examine the seminal scripture of the Restoration, the Book of Mormon, through the lens of a liberation view of salvation. We will see that the overarching narrative is that of a cautionary tale about the fate of a civilization that privileges wealth and accumulation over just and equitable treatment of its people. This undercurrent runs through the entire narrative, and the familiar Church concept of the "pride cycle" that leads to epochs of prosperity mixed with decline and destruction is critically dependent on the way that people are treated in society, with a key indicator of a diseased society being the presence and exploitation of poor and marginalized people. Whatever the Book of Mormon reveals about the nature of God's plan, humankind's role and eternal destination, and the role of Jesus Christ, it all takes place against a backdrop where temporal salvation is key. The covenant relationship we enter into with God, symbolized by the baptismal covenant, is at its foundation a promise to enter into community with one another. Throughout the Book of Mormon, prophets remind the people of the importance of "remembering the captivity of their fathers," positioning their messages firmly within a liberative context.

Chapter 6 will look at temporal salvation as envisioned by the early Church, specifically focusing on the idea of the Zion community and how this was understood as a new community that would live a consecrated life. We will see how Joseph Smith's prophetic activity was intended to open the saints' eyes to a new reality and understanding of the nature of God's relationship and covenant with humanity and creation. In addition, we will examine several key passages of Restoration scripture and Church history which suggest that, far from being an idealistic idea of a utopian society that was abandoned early on in Church history, the covenant Zion community was actually a founding principle on which the Church was established and for which the Restoration took place. This idea of a Zion community is in stark opposition to the political and economic systems of today, and it offers a new vision of community based on principles of love, justice, and equity. The establishment and expansion of this community constitutes the ongoing historical fulfilment of the "new and everlasting covenant."

As a boy growing up in Idaho, my view of salvation differed drastically from the view of salvation understood and needed by those civilians suffering through the Salvadoran civil war. The main premise of this book is that we have focused on this individual view of salvation to the detriment and abandonment of those who need communal, liberative salvation in the Salvadoran context and others like it. This need is enormous, and I believe that the neglect of the poor and oppressed by Western Christianity, and the approval and support of political and economic systems which depend on and produce massive exploitation and inequality, is what the Lord refers to when he says that the world "lieth in sin" (D&C 49:20). This is a travesty. It is outrageous. It is counter to everything we claim to believe in as Christians. It is the true face of the Satanic in the world. The world does not need salvation at some unspecified point in the future, after this life. The world needs salvation now. The tears and blood of millions cry out from the earth for justice. For liberation. For salvation! Our own religious tradition is perhaps uniquely positioned to claim this mandate of salvation-as-liberation as a birthright, but we have carried over too much theological, doctrinal, and cultural baggage from our own peculiar American-Protestant heritage for this vision to be fully recognized or realized.

My hope is that these pages will awaken within the reader some sense of the urgency with which I have come to feel convinced (and convicted) of this responsibility so that we may work together to bring to pass the vision of the Restoration God has for the world: To build Zion communities. Communities of love and divine relationship where all may flourish and where "there are no poor among them" (Moses 7:18). This is salvation. These are the very real stakes. Until we are all saved on these terms, none of us can be.

Chapter 1

The Old Testament: Liberation and Salvation Remembered

Israel knew God above all in relation to the real historical life of its people.

— Jon Sobrino

Understanding the evolution of conceptual and theological ideas about salvation in the Christian tradition must begin with the Hebrew Scriptures, the Tanakh or Old Testament. This collection of narrative prose, prophetic pronouncements, and poetry was edited and compiled during the period of the Babylonian captivity. Throughout, the authors attempt to make sense of Israel's place in history and of God's relationship and promises to them as a people. Reading the Old Testament, however, can be challenging, if not confronting. The god of the Old Testament can seem harsh and retributive, a god who takes any possible opportunity to visit the people with destruction or who commands and aids in horrific destruction perpetrated by the people.[1] The familiar miraculous stories of deliverance do not sit well with the divine and human violence, especially by those who are portrayed as being favored of God.[2] In addition, the lack of context that modern-day readers have for understanding ancient beliefs and sociocultural practices makes it very difficult to wade through the specifics of the narrative and prophecies. As a result, we usually gloss over a great deal, focusing on the Plan of Salvation narrative touchstones and passages that are interpreted as prophecies of the coming of Christ and his mission.

This is a shame, because in the Old Testament narrative, despite the nationalistic and violent god depicted by the writers, we can perceive the

---

1. This depiction of God is even more disturbing and jarring given the widely accepted view that the premortal Jesus Christ, or Jehovah, is the god of the Old Testament.

2. John Dominic Crossan, *God and Empire: Jesus Against Rome, Then and Now*, 65–74, suggests that this disconnect reflects the fact that the Bible (and I would say all scripture) presents two parallel visions of divine reality: a god of violent retribution and a god of nonviolent distribution. Our challenge as Christians is to decide which vision of God we will adopt and which reality we will create.

continual struggle of the Hebrew people to see God's salvation in their history. In these stories, God acts to save without any prerequisite. God saves because "that is the kind of god [God] is."[3] The acceptance of and gratitude for God's salvation is shown in the safeguarding of human relationships, particularly as they concern the poor and vulnerable, the marginalized and oppressed. Prophets are sent to warn the people when the societies they build do not provide means for subsistence for all people or place burdensome religious restrictions on participating in God's freely given salvation. Prophets warn that a focus on wealth and the resulting inequality eventually always leads to societal collapse and trauma. They invite the people to repent, or to turn back to God and recommit themselves to God's ways.

Any attempt to understand the biblical witness of salvation in terms of liberation must address the elephant in the room: the fact that much of the writing in the Bible reflects the patriarchal and other contexts in which society in antiquity was steeped.[4] As a result, although God's vision and goal for the people is justice and equity, due to the social, historical, and cultural context, the narratives and codes of ethics as recorded in the Old Testament are often far from egalitarian and just. Certain groups, most clearly women, are not treated justly under these codes, as is clear from the sexual purity codes and lack of property or inheritance rights for women in the Mosaic law.[5] We might also ask how the Hebrews justified slavery, having themselves just been liberated from bondage? The language that prophets use to describe Israel and its relationship with God is often

---

3. Ted Grimsrud, *Instead of Atonement: The Bible's Salvation Story and Our Hope for Wholeness*, 43.

4. See Gerda Lerner, *The Creation of Patriarchy*; Rosemary Radford Ruether, *Sexism and God-Talk: Toward a Feminist Theology*; and Elizabeth Schüssler Fiorenza, *Bread not Stone: The Challenge of Feminist Biblical Interpretation*. See also Elizabeth Schüssler Fiorenza, *In Memory of Her: A Feminist Theological Reconstruction of Christian Origins*, for a discussion of the influence of patriarchal culture on the New Testament portrayal of Christian origins.

5. An extreme example of this is the "rape codes" in Deuteronomy 21 and 22, which reduce women in sexual encounters to the question of whether or not they are captives, virgins, betrothed, or married. Although some have interpreted the forcible marriage of a virgin woman to her rapist (Deut. 22:28) as ensuring an inheritance and livelihood for the woman, this viewpoint utterly dehumanizes and strips the woman of self-determination, as do these codes in general. See Susanne Scholz, *Sacred Witness: Rape in the Hebrew Bible*, 109–16, for further discussion.

heavy with misogynist and sexually violent metaphors and imagery.[6] What are we to make of the fact that God supposedly orders the genocide of the Canaanites—women, men, and children, even animals? Can any attempt to square these and other atrocities with a god of liberation and justice who sides with the poor and oppressed be successful?

Any honest attempt to read and understand the Old Testament in our current day and age must grapple with these problems and contradictions. They show both that the arc of God's liberation in history is continual and that human systems of oppression and domination can prevent the full liberative purpose from being realized. Intersectional injustice along the lines of sex, gender, race, class, and so forth slows the realization of the full liberation God desires for humanity and creation. Only by wrestling with these issues and applying the biblical witness anew to the injustices of our own day will we be able to discern the totality of God's liberative purpose that at times struggles to surface through the limited and biased worldview of the biblical writers and our own narrow interpretive lenses.[7]

Our study of salvation in the Old Testament must also take into account the fact that the Hebrew religious tradition did not have a developed sense of the afterlife. Israel believed in a place where all spirits went after death, both wicked and righteous, known as *Sheol*, but there was no real sense of what awaited these spirits or of how or if they were rewarded or punished.[8] Salvation in the Old Testament, therefore, is not about the afterlife and instead has a particularly temporal character. It has to do with the stuff of lived experience. This becomes clear if we examine the Hebrew word from which salvation is translated: *yeshu'ah*. It indicates saving or deliverance from physical, mortal danger, or political enemies. It is translated in various places in the Old Testament as salvation, help, deliverance, and health.

God's motivation to act in this saving capacity towards creation is made clear in the short verse that caps off the creation story: "God saw

---

6. Scholz, *Sacred Witness*, 1–5. The first few chapters of the book of Hosea are some of the most explicit and difficult examples of such imagery.

7. Fiorenza, *Bread Not Stone*.

8. See Glenn S. Holland, *Gods in the Desert: Religions of the Ancient Near East*, 239–40. The idea of an afterlife which included hell and the devil as the preparator of it likely developed during Israel's exposure to Persian religious tradition during their exile. The still-developing theology of an afterlife is highlighted by the debates between the Pharisees and Saduccees over resurrection in Jesus's day.

everything that he had made, and indeed, it was very good" (Gen. 1:31).[9] This pronouncement shows not only that God is pleased with the aesthetic beauty of creation, but that God views it with affection. To say that creation is good indicates that it was, and that it is worth tending to and shepherding through continued existence. God continually acts in history to save and heal creation and humanity through grace and love, inviting us to respond in kind one with another. Ted Grimsrud sums up this liberative context for understanding salvation in the Hebrew Bible:

> The Old Testament begins with a portrayal of creation at peace. However, after the beginning, the Bible presupposes disharmony and brokenness—and focuses on the struggle for salvation. Salvation results in healed brokenness, restored health and wholeness. The Bible presents salvation on three levels: (1) salvation as liberation from powers of brokenness, (2) salvation as restoration of harmony with God, and (3) salvation as restoration of harmonious human relationships. The Old Testament story places priority on salvation in the first sense (liberation). The other two follow from and depend upon the first. Because God acts to deliver, people are then freed to respond to God and restore harmony in their relationships with God and to live in harmony with one another.[10]

The Exodus

God's covenant with Abraham promised him both that his descendants would be numberless as the stars and that through their family God would bless all of humanity. As we know, through a series of events, Sarah and Abraham's posterity came to reside in Egypt. Jacob came with his eleven sons and their families to flee starvation during the famine. They were rescued by their brother Joseph, who had been previously sold into slavery but then eventually won Pharaoh's favor.

After several generations, the Israelites "multiplied and grew exceedingly strong, so that the land was filled with them" (Ex. 1:7). Worried that the Hebrews were becoming too powerful, Pharaoh enslaved them. Worried still that they would pose a formidable threat to Egypt's power if they joined with an invading army, he told the Hebrew midwives to kill all newborn Hebrew boys. Moses was born under this standing death sentence, but was spared by the courageous and subversive acts of the Hebrew midwives, led by Shiprah and Puah, as well as his mother Jochebed, sis-

---

9. Unless otherwise specified, Bible citations are from the New Revised Standard Version.

10. Grimsrud, *Instead of Atonement*, 28–29.

ter Miriam, and Pharaoh's own daughter, who refuse to honor the edict of genocide.[11] Moses is forced to flee Egypt for his life after killing an Egyptian overseer who is beating a Hebrew slave. He settles in the land of Midian, becoming married and raising a family there while his people toiled under fierce oppression in Egypt.

> After a long time, the king of Egypt died. The Israelites groaned under their slavery, and cried out. Out of the slavery their cry for help rose up to God. God heard their groaning, and God remembered his covenant with Abraham, Isaac, and Jacob. God looked upon the Israelites, and God took notice of them. (Ex. 2:23–25)

It was during this time that God spoke to Moses out of the burning bush as he was shepherding his father-in-law's sheep:

> I have observed the misery of my people who are in Egypt; I have heard their cry on account of their taskmasters. Indeed, I know their sufferings, and I have come down to deliver them from the Egyptians, and to bring them up out of that land to a good and broad land, a land flowing with milk and honey. (Ex. 3:7–8)

God's determination to liberate the Israelites from their oppressors was, however, not just an act of mercy. As Bruce Birch explains,

> God has not only freely taken initiative but has done so in relationship to human suffering and need. God's "seeing" and "hearing" are not generalized expressions of omniscience, but focused divine regard for oppression and suffering. Divine response is attuned to and mobilized by human cries of pain. Perhaps the most remarkable self disclosure in this verse is in the phrase "I know their sufferings." The Hebrew verb used here (*yada'* "to know") indicates something broader than cognitive knowledge. It indicates a participation in and experiencing of that which is known. Thus, God indicates a divine choice to enter into and experience Israel's suffering.[12]

To emphasize the seriousness with which God takes this covenant solidarity with Israel, God's name is revealed to Moses. The exact interpretation of this name, usually translated as "Yahweh" or "YHWH," is unclear.[13] What is more important for the present discussion is what the giving of the name signifies:

---

11. We must acknowledge how this entire episode turns on the courageous action of five women, a contribution that is far too often minimized in this story.

12. Bruce C. Birch et al., *A Theological Introduction to the Old Testament*, 111.

13. This name has variously been translated as "I am who I am," "I will be who I will be," and "I will cause to be what I will cause to be."

> The act of revealing the divine name is itself remarkable. In the ancient world, the giving of one's name is an act of intimacy that establishes relationship. It is related to vulnerability as well, for to know God's name is to have access, communication, and relationship by those who name the name. To know the name of God opens the possibility of honoring God more deeply in relationship, but for God runs the risk of abuse and dishonoring of the divine name as well.[14]

In this simple but stunningly intimate act God affirms the central importance and risk of entering into divine relationship with humanity. God has entered, according to Walter Brueggemann, into a dialogue with Israel "that is potentially transformative for all parties . . . including God."[15] It is a risk taken in full knowledge and in absolute solidarity with Israel—and by extension of the covenant relationship, with all creation.[16]

Moses and his brother Aaron returned to Egypt with the good news of deliverance, relaying God's message to them: "I am the Lord, and I will free you from the burdens of the Egyptians and deliver you from slavery to them. . . . You shall know that I am the Lord your God, who has freed you" (Ex. 6:6–7). But for the suffering, enslaved Israelites, this declaration is beyond comprehension. Even with this exciting news, they "would not listen to Moses, because of their broken spirit and their cruel slavery" (v. 9).

So God concocts with Moses and Aaron a miraculous plan to liberate Israel. Following the plagues, the Israelites leave, or are rather driven out, of Egypt. As if the plagues and deliverance were not enough for the Israelites to remember who had liberated them, one final showdown is set up between Israel and Pharaoh, in which God decisively and miraculously delivers Israel again in spectacular fashion, parting the Red Sea and allowing them to walk through before sending it crashing down on the armies of Pharaoh. This final act of deliverance seals the liberation of Israel, offering a repudiation writ large of Egypt and her values.

God's deliverance of Israel reveals God's character in heretofore unknown ways. First, God acts to liberate Israel in response to their suffering. This tells us that God is not a dispassionate god only concerned with honor and holiness. God acts of God's own accord, but this action is in response to human suffering. Second, God acts for liberation against

---

14. Birch, *Old Testament*, 113.
15. Walter Brueggemann, *An Unsettling God: The Heart of the Hebrew Bible*, 11.
16. For an extended and thoughtful treatment of the implications of this relational view of God, see Walter Brueggemann's *Old Testament Theology: An Introduction* and *An Unsettling God*.

bondage and in opposition to the powers of domination and oppression set up by corrupt human institutions. God is shown to be specifically and unequivocally on the side of Israel, in opposition to the wealth, power, and oppression symbolized by Pharaoh. God is a god for the oppressed, as opposed to the gods of Egypt, including Pharaoh, who are the gods of the wealthy and ruling class.[17] Lastly, the imagery of natural plagues and the final defeat of the Egyptians via the seas, earth, and air indicates that it is not just God who opposes systems and structures of oppression, but that creation and the created order itself is antithetical to unnatural systems of domination set up and perpetuated by humans. Furthermore, catastrophic natural consequences can result when creation is warped and exploited by human greed beyond its intended purpose.

When the reality of their liberation sinks in, the prophet Miriam takes up her tambourine and leads the women in song and dance: "Sing to the Lord, for he has triumphed gloriously; horse and rider he has thrown into the sea" (Ex. 15:21). The enemy vanquished, the Israelites are liberated, and they know how it has been done and who has liberated them. The joy of liberation, however, fades quickly, and soon the Israelites are complaining repeatedly to Moses in the wilderness. But as many times as they complain, God provides a way forward. In further acts of salvation, God makes the water at Marah potable (Ex. 15), delivers manna from heaven and quail (Ex. 16), and water from a rock (Ex. 17). At last they reach the land of Midian and are welcomed by Moses's father in law, Jethro.

Establishing Community

Israel, now free of bondage, must build a society and community for several hundred thousand people from the ground up. Having played such a decisive role in their liberation, Moses finds himself now in the unenviable position of arbiting the social and tribal problems that crop up with increasing frequency. He sits in his tent day in and day out, hearing their cases and rendering judgment (Ex. 18:13). Already, power politics and unjust treatment are creeping into the lives of the people. The purpose of God's liberation is in danger of being frustrated.

At this time the people had no formal code of laws or ethical standard to guide them; so, God gave such a code to Moses on Mount Sinai. The Ten Commandments and other laws provided by God predominantly deal with relationships in the community. They are not arbitrary edicts from a

---

17. Birch, *Old Testament*, 110.

god who is worried about honor being offended by disobedient humans. They are far from the idiosyncratic and burdensome legal sanctions we often take them for. Most importantly, the laws codify a system of society and community that would ensure the Israelites do not lapse into systems and structures of domination and oppression—as is wont to happen in human society.[18] As Ted Grimsrud writes, "The law provides social structure for the delivered slaves to sustain the effects of that deliverance."[19]

The progression of stipulations is from the most general to the more specific.[20] From the outset, however, God shows concern for the vulnerable by emphasizing justice, or the equitable and fair treatment of people, while making special provision for those who might be taken advantage of. Having themselves been liberated from Egyptian bondage and oppression, James Cone explains that "Israel must now live as Yahweh's liberated people, becoming the embodiment of freedom made possible through the freeing presence of God. The covenant . . . requires Israel to treat the weak in their midst as Yahweh has treated it."[21] Thus, those who have been enslaved for payment of debt (usually the children of the debtors) are to be set free every seven years without debt (Ex. 21:2). People who kill accidentally are to be given a safe haven, away from those who wish to do them harm in retribution (v. 13). Recognizing that miscarriages of justice or abuses are more likely when those seeking redress or who are being ac-

---

18. Many of the stipulations in these laws, such as forgiveness of debts and periodic returning of land to original owners, are similar to the "restoration" edicts of the Babylonian kings. These edicts, which were often made upon the ascendance of a new king, were intended to restore balance to the social and economic systems in the kingdom in order to stabilize the king's tax base; see Dominique Charpin, *Writing, Law, and Kingship in Old Babylonian Mesopotamia*, ch. 6. The code given to Israel suggests that Yahweh was concerned not only with periodic restoration of equity, but with setting up a system that ensured perpetual justice. The usage of the term "restoration" in reference to this establishment of justice has profound implications for our understanding of our own restoration tradition.

19. Ted Grimsrud, *Instead of Atonement*, 34.

20. See Richard A. Horsley, *Covenant Economics: A Biblical Vision of Justice for All*, chs. 2–3, for extended treatment and discussion. Horsley shows how many of these laws are critically involved in protecting the intergenerational family as the main economic unit of production and reproduction. Families provided the labor and resources for subsistence, and a breakdown of the family unit had specific and direct economic consequences. The social relationships in the community were also critical for survival and well-being, hence many of the direct protections for them.

21. James H. Cone, *God of the Oppressed*, Kindle, loc. 1391 of 5313.

cused are not of a privileged group, God warns the people not to side with a wicked majority in cases brought to trial, to not kill the innocent, and to not oppress non-Israelites in the community (Ex. 23:9; Lev. 19:33–34). As some of the most at risk within a community, widows and orphans are given special protection (Ex. 22:22–23).[22] In addition, strict controls are established around procurement and accumulation of land, ensuring no one is taken advantage of or left in ruin due to the seizure of their land or means of subsistence (Lev. 25).

Within the Law, it is clear that God is particularly concerned with the welfare of the poor. This is evidenced by the institution of the sabbatical year, in which fields, orchards, and vineyards are to be left fallow every seventh year "so that the poor of your people may eat" (Ex. 23:11). God forbids the adding of interest to money lent to the poor and makes provision for them during harvest, commanding the people to leave areas of their fields unharvested, to leave the gleanings, and to not collect the fallen grapes in their vineyards (Lev. 19:9–10). God's feelings for the poor and needy are summed up with the following blanket injunction:

> If there is among you anyone in need, a member of your community in any of your towns within the land that the Lord your God is giving you, do not be hard-hearted or tight-fisted toward your needy neighbor. You should rather open your hand willingly lending enough to meet the need, whatever it may be. . . . Since there will never cease to be some in need on the earth, I therefore command you, open your hand to the poor and needy neighbor of your land. (Deut. 15:7–8, 11)

Solemnizing and Safeguarding

If the law set up a social and legal structure under which people could live in justice and equity, what was the purpose of the sacrificial practice?[23] Looking back with our individualistic twenty-first-century eyes

---

22. These codes would have been crucial, as the Hebrew cultural tradition, dominated as it was by patriarchal rights and authority, had no provisions for widows. A woman who lost her husband and had no sons would have been in an especially precarious position, and would have been forced to take extreme measures to maintain a subsistence and livelihood. The extremity to which many women must have been forced is illustrated in the earlier story of Tamar (Gen. 38) and the later stories of the daughters of Zelophehad (Num. 27) and Ruth.

23. Sacrifice was practiced ubiquitously in the ancient world, although the purpose and specific methods vary widely across groups and regions. See Daniel C. Snell, *Religions of the Ancient Near East*; Sara Iles Johnston, ed., *Religions of*

and understanding, we might say that the purpose of these sacrifices was to cleanse individuals from their sins. But we have to remember that God has always referred to Israel as a collective. They are God's people. God is concerned with them as a group and the covenant faithfulness of the group is what matters.

Sacrifices offer a way for the people to solemnize their commitment on a continual basis, to recognize and remember the hand of God in their continued salvation as experienced in their lived community relationships. Of the litany of sacrificial rites specified in Leviticus, only a few are for sin offerings (Lev. 4–6). In the case of such offerings, one kind is made for sins of which the person or Israel as a group is not initially aware but is made aware of later. In the case of knowing sins of abuse against another individual, restitution must be made *before* the sacrifice (called a trespass offering) is offered, thereby allowing the offering to affirm the reparation of the relationship and recommitment to God.[24] Thus, sacrifice seems to play a much more complex and nuanced role than simply being a means for individuals to cleanse themselves and restore divine favor.[25] Ted Grimsrud clarifies:

> Sacrifices are not theologically central to Old Testament salvation, though they are commonly practiced. In numerous instances forgiveness and, even more, deliverance, do not depend upon sacrifices. The basic dynamic, on Yahweh's side, is the decision to save simply because that is the kind of god Yahweh is. The basic dynamic, on the human side, is repentance and trust. The sacrifices then follow, as the means to concretize the reception of the gift.[26]

But this cannot be the whole story, because the handbook of sacrificial rituals in Leviticus speaks repeatedly of atonement and forgiveness. But if community, if relation, is foremost in God's eyes, what can be going on here if these sacrifices do not provide a way for individual cleansing from sin?

In the ancient world, the two most common ways of creating, maintaining, and restoring relations were by giving a gift and sharing a meal. This was the cultural framework through which Israel viewed sacrifice. Marcus Borg and John Crossan explain

---

the Ancient World: A Guide, 325–48; and Glenn S. Holland, *Gods in the Desert: Religions of the Ancient Near East*.

24. John H. Hayes, "Atonement in the Book of Leviticus," 5–15.

25. See James A. Greenberg, *A New Look at Atonement in Leviticus: The Meaning and Purpose of Kipper Revisited*, for a review and in-depth treatment and discussion of Israel's sacrificial rites.

26. Grimsrud, *Instead of Atonement*, 43.

> How, then, did people create, maintain, or restore good relations with a divine being? . . . Again, they could give a gift or share a meal. In sacrifice as *gift*, an offerer took a valuable animal or other foodstuff and gave it to God by having it burned on the altar. . . . In sacrifice as *meal*, the animal was transferred to God by having its blood poured over the altar and was then returned to the offerer as divine food for a feast with God. In other words, the offerer did not so much invite God to a meal as God invited the offerer to a meal.[27]

Thus, in addition to providing an ongoing way to remember and recommit themselves to God's salvation, another purpose of sacrifice is to allow Israel to participate with God in the intimate acts of building community and restoring relationship as recognized in their cultural tradition.

In addition to serving as a way to restore relations with God, sacrifice served another crucial purpose. Individual instances of sin or trespass against the law need to be remedied, not because the individual is in danger of divine punishment or has offended God's honor, but because sin—via its social consequences—is contagious. According to William Robertson Smith, if it is not cleansed, the "offence is dangerous not merely to [the individual] but to the whole community."[28] Sin, as anything that fractures personal and social relationships, can quickly spiral out of control, engulfing entire communities.[29] As noted by Mary Douglas in her study of the critical role of ideas of purity, pollution, and contagion in ancient religion, "the social consequences of some offenses ripple out in all directions and can never be reversed."[30] Remember that not too long ago, when Moses was speaking with God in the mount, the people had experienced such a contagious episode. The golden calf incident had introduced a contagion of idolatry that had contaminated the entire populace, putting them at risk of upending the systems that God was trying to institute in liberating them and regressing back to Egyptian systems of inequality.

The sacrificial rites, then, identified any instances of sin and scrubbed them out of the community before they had a chance to spread and infect the populace. In a sense, sin is viewed as an extension of the bodily conditions and diseases that compromise the health and well-being of individu-

---

27. Marcus J. Borg and John Dominic Crossan, *The Last Week: A Day-by-Day Account of Jesus's Final Week in Jerusalem*, 37; emphasis in original.
28. William Robertson Smith, *Lectures on the Religion of the Semites*, 44.
29. René Girard, *Violence and the Sacred*, ch. 2.
30. Mary Douglas, *Purity and Danger: An Analysis of the Concepts of Pollution and Taboo*, 137; see also Johnston, *Religions of the Ancient World*, 496–513.

als.[31] As disease is contagious and is thought to compromise purity, so sin is contagious and requires eradication from the community. Individual instances of sin, then, are openings for contagion, threats to the purity of the community (as manifest in the social and economic relationships), rather than stains on individuals in need of forgiveness to restore personal worthiness before God.

Nowhere is this idea of the importance of communal cleansing more apparent than in the ritual of the scapegoat. This rite takes place yearly, on *Yom Kippur*, or the Day of Atonement. A goat is designated by casting lots, and the officiating priest

> shall lay both his hands on the head of the live goat, and confess over it all the iniquities of the people of Israel, and all their transgressions, all their sins, putting them on the head of the goat, and sending it away into the wilderness. . . . The goat shall bear on itself all their iniquities to a barren region; and the goat shall be set free in the wilderness. (Lev. 16:21–22)

This ceremony takes place once a year and is a sort of failsafe for any sins, transgressions, or impurities that may have been missed or "improperly dealt with" in the other sacrificial events of the year.[32] These must be expelled for the good of the community, and they are symbolically carried away by the scapegoat.[33] So we see that in addition to providing opportunities to affirm and reaffirm their commitment and gratitude for God's freely given salvation, another purpose of sacrifice is to keep the community clean and to reaffirm the commitment to living in community, not to provide forgiveness and cleansing for individuals.[34]

---

31. Although we need to acknowledge the compounded marginalization of women that resulted from Israelite patriarchal culture combined with the purity codes.

32. Greenberg, *A New Look at Atonement in Leviticus*, 135.

33. It is critical to note that in this ritual most closely tied to atonement in ancient Israel, the goat that bears the sins of the community is *not* killed. This should give us pause when we try to directly metaphorize the killing of other sacrifices to Jesus's death on the cross.

34. Greenberg, *A New Look at Atonement in Leviticus*, concludes that the overall purpose of the sacrificial rites was to provide opportunities and means for Israel to repair a broken relationship with Yahweh. We will explore this idea and its relation to atonement further in chapter 5. For now, we can note that given the explicit social and economic focus of the commandments and code of conduct given to Israel, it seems clear that the status of relationship with Yahweh is reflected in the character of the social relationships in the community.

Prophets and a New Reality

The period of Israel's history that saw the rise of kings and kingdoms also saw the coming of many prophets. We know many of their stories of miracles, such as Elijah raising the widow of Zeraphath's son from the dead (1 Kgs. 17), his confrontation with the priests of Baal (1 Kgs. 18), or more infamously, the bears attacking the youth for taunting Elisha (2 Kgs. 2). It would be useful, however, to examine the prophetic movement in general during this time. Can we discern a throughline in the twists and turns of the narrative? What are these prophets, and by extension, God, so concerned about during the reign of Israel's kings?

In his book *The Prophetic Imagination*, Walter Brueggemann discusses the purpose and method of the prophetic movement in ancient Israel.[35] He suggests that the vocation of a prophet is not simply to warn the people of future devastation if they do not change their current ways and behavior. Instead, Brueggemann suggests:

> The task of prophetic ministry is to nurture, nourish, and evoke a consciousness and perception alternative to the consciousness and perception of the dominant culture around us. . . . [I]t attempts to . . . engage in a rejection and delegitimizing of the present ordering of things. On the other hand, that alternative consciousness to be nurtured serves to energize persons and communities by its promise of another time and situation toward which the community of faith may move. . . . [T]o live in fervent anticipation of the newness that God has promised and will surely give.[36]

The radical liberation of the Hebrews from Egyptian bondage illustrates this prophetic agenda. Through Moses, God was not only liberating Israel from physical bondage to the Egyptians, God was also attempting to help them envision a new possibility for existence. This would be for them a new reality—a new society that did not depend on systems of oppression and domination, a society and community where all were taken care of, and where justice and compassion reigned rather than power and greed.

In God's acts of deliverance, God showed the Israelites that the social and political systems of the Egyptians could not deliver on their promises. These systems of empire had been in place for centuries and must have seemed like they would be in place forever. What's more, the religion of the Egyptians reinforced this notion. The very fact that Egypt was so prosperous and the empire so vast and powerful was seen as evidence that the

---

35. Walter Brueggemann, *The Prophetic Imagination*.
36. Brueggemann, 3.

gods were approving of the whole imperial project. How could anyone expect to win against the power of these gods? Pharaoh himself was considered a god, blessing and prospering his own empire in a twisted tautology.

The god of Israel, however, was dynamic and unpredictable. Rather than take a backseat to the machinations of the powerful, this god acted in history for the benefit of the poor and oppressed. It's not easy for us, with our long history of Christianity and monotheism, to appreciate just how radical this revelation of God was. Israel lived in a time of many gods.[37] Before their bondage in Egypt they worshipped a number of them,[38] and their sojourn in Egypt introduced them to many others. Because of the reach of Egypt's empire, the gods of Egypt must have seemed all-powerful in the eyes of Israel. Thus, the contest between this cocky new god of the Israelites and these gods of empire promised to be quite a show, and the outcome of liberation was in no way assured in the minds of Israel.

The plague narratives, then, can symbolize not just the physical confrontation over liberation between Moses and Pharoah, but the psychological tug-of-war in the minds of Israel over their current view of reality and the one announced by Moses.[39] As noted by Brueggemann, the first two plagues were "matched by Egyptian 'research and development' people. Two plagues into the scene nothing is changed and the power of Egypt is not challenged."[40] But then they could not match the third, and the fourth, and the fifth, and so on until Israel stood dumbfounded on the shores of the Red Sea, having witnessed the utter annihilation of the Egyptian army. Something profound had shifted.

When Israel was liberated, the gods of Egypt were shown to be a lie. The empire was shown for what it was, a human system of domination and oppression. The gods who sanctioned and blessed this system were rendered powerless before the god of Israel. And when the gods were shown to be powerless, the system they supported was stripped of its power in the mind of the Hebrews as well. The whole social and political order based on these gods crumbled. God's temporal salvation proved it possible to

---

37. Snell, *Religions of the Ancient Near East*; Johnston, *Religions of the Ancient World*; Holland, *Gods in the Desert*.

38. Most traces of this polytheism were erased from the biblical record by the reforms of the Deuteronomists under king Josiah in the seventh century BCE (2 Kgs. 23).

39. We can see a similar struggle in the later narrative of Elijah's contest with the priests of Baal (1 Kgs. 18).

40. Brueggemann, *The Prophetic Imagination*, 10.

build a new reality together, with the mercy, justice, and compassion of God as its linchpin.

Idolatry and Oppression

Israel's conquest of the land of Canaan following their lengthy sojourn was never fully completed and is framed as an act of disobedience to the Lord's order of genocide.[41] Between first occupying the land and later establishing kings, Israel had no centralized government; issues of law were instead decided by judges. This was also a time of many threats from outside military campaigns against Israel. These threats, as noted by Bruce Birch, "allowed for the raising up of charismatic military leaders to bring deliverance from the threat, but this office did not become institutionalized beyond the crisis, and never involved all of Israel's tribal groups."[42]

The biblical narrative does not depict Israel as purely innocent victims in these conflicts. Instead, many times throughout the narrative, Israel is portrayed as doing "evil in the sight of the Lord, forgetting the Lord their God, and worshipping the Baals and the Asherahs" (Judg. 3:7). This idolatry is offered as reason enough for their enemies to attack, and in many cases for God to give victory to their enemies. So the narrative cycle goes: Israel does evil in the sight of God, they are given over, or "sold into the hand" of rival nations, they cry to God for deliverance, recognizing their unfaithfulness, and God delivers them through a rotating cast of champions.

Reading this, one is struck by the repetitive nature of the narrative. The accusation of idolatry is constant, followed by the bondage of Israel and their deliverance. It is made very clear that idolatry will not be permitted, but very little is explained regarding this, even in the initial giving of the law. Later, after the rise of the kings, the narrative spends much of its time detailing Israel's descent into idolatry, decrying their turning away from God to idols. We are left with the impression that this is the single greatest factor in the demise of Israel. Why is idolatry so evil in the sight of God?

---

41. As noted above, this extermination order from God seems unlikely. It is possible that when reassessing their history from their Babylonian exile, the writers attributed their ultimate defeats to the influence of the Canaanites. The extermination order may have been a way of retroactively providing a strategy to avoid their failure to keep the law and lapse into idolatry and unfaithfulness, which ultimately led to the downfall of their nation.

42. Birch, *Old Testament*, 216.

In the first of the Ten Commandments, Israel is explicitly commanded to have no other gods before Yahweh:

> I am the Lord your God, who brought you out of the land of Egypt, out of the house of slavery; you shall have no other gods before (besides) me. You shall not make for yourself an idol, whether in the form of anything that is in heaven above, or that is on the earth beneath, or that is in the water under the earth. You shall not bow down to them or worship them; for I the Lord your God am a jealous God. (Ex. 20:2–5; Deut. 5:6–9)

This commandment makes it sound like the sole reason for the prohibition of idolatry is because God will be offended if Israel does not worship God, and God alone. But this cannot be the whole story. The Ten Commandments were given as a prologue to the full law. They established the initial terms of relationship between God and Israel, and between the members of the community. The prohibitions dictated ways to safeguard the social and economic well-being of the community. If the central purpose of the law was to provide a way for Israel to maintain the effects of God's liberation in their community, then we can assume that the prohibition of idolatry at the top of the list serves an especially important purpose in maintaining that liberation.

We can begin to understand this relationship further by remembering that idols do not stand alone. What I mean by this is that idols are not something that is worshipped outside of a social and cultural context.[43] The idols and gods of Egypt were worshipped in the service of a system, both political and religious, that supported them. This system blessed without question the oppressive actions of Pharaoh and other members of the ruling class. The idols were not incidental to this system; they were a function of and perpetuated that system. When God liberated Israel, this showed the powerlessness of the gods symbolized by these idols to save the people, which might be thought as reason enough to abandon them. If they have no power, what's the point in worshipping them? Jon Sobrino cuts to the heart of the matter:

> But the lifelessness of the other gods—on which theology lays so much stress when speaking of idols—is not the only or the most important aspect of the "other" gods of the first commandment. The prophets drew from this [first] commandment a completely new conclusion when they applied it to the divinization of earthly instruments of power. Then, though lifeless with regard to saving, these gods forged and adored by men cease to be lifeless

---

43. Jon Sobrino, *Jesus the Liberator: A Historical Theological Reading of Jesus of Nazareth*, 180–89.

and become very active. According to the prophets, then it is useless to put one's trust in idols, actualized in foreign powers and wealth, but furthermore—and this is the decisive point—these idols produce victims: orphans, widows, refugees, the poor, the weak, the miserable. . . . These victims are the evidence of the evil of the idols, not just their inability to save their adherents. And this is the objective reason for not adoring other gods: because their reality is essentially the contrary to the reality of the Lord. If the Lord produces life, the others produce death.[44]

Herein we can see the real motivation behind the prohibition of idolatry. What is so damaging about idols is not the golden image but the fact that idolatry symbolizes both an ideology of domination and oppression and the institutions that support and sustain such ideologies. This leads to the establishment and perpetuation of systems of exploitation, where wealth, property, and accumulation are prioritized over the lives and livelihood of people. The choice between God and idols is no less stark than a choice between life and death for the poor and marginalized.

The prohibition on idolatry is therefore a prohibition to revert back to social and economic systems of oppression, rather than continue in the justice and equity for which God had liberated Israel, the very relationship that was the foundation of God's covenant with them. During the time of the judges, idol worship leads to Israel becoming the victim of oppression at the hands of a number of competing powers. But the narrative takes great pains to stress that when they are righteous and faithful, things go well for them. We see Joshua as the dispenser of justice and equity, distributing land and other resources among the male heads of houses of the various tribes (Josh. 14–21). Nowhere do we get the sense that Israel deals unjustly with their own, regardless of the violence they visit on others in the land. This will all change under the reigns of the kings.

Kings and Kingdoms

Both internal and external pressures drove Israel to eventually adopt a centralized government in the form of a monarchy.[45] The growth of population, success in military campaigns, and the incorporation of other peoples and groups within their communities led to increased prosperity and wealth, which would have become more and more difficult to protect

---

44. Sobrino, 188.
45. Walter Brueggemann, *Theology of the Old Testament: Testimony, Dispute, Advocacy*, 1199–1201.

and manage. In terms of external pressures, while Israel's early years were dominated by brief skirmishes with a number of adversaries, the rise of the Philistines as a dominant military power threatened them with an ongoing military campaign that required more coordinated military effort than could be marshaled by a coalition of tribes.[46]

Samuel, called as a prophet in his youth in response to the blasphemous activity of the sons of the priest Eli, reluctantly appointed Saul as a king for Israel. This appointment, however, came with this warning:

> These will be the ways of the king who will reign over you: he will take your sons and appoint them to his chariots and to be his horsemen, and to run before his chariots, and he will appoint for himself commanders of thousands, and commanders of fifties, and some to plow his ground and reap his harvest, and to make his implements of war and the equipment of his chariots. He will take your daughters to be perfumers and cooks and bakers. He will take the best of your fields and vineyards and olive orchards and give them to his courtiers. He will take one tenth of your grain and of your vineyards and give to his officers and courtiers. He will take your male and female slaves, and the best of your cattle and donkeys, and put them to his work. He will take one tenth of your flocks, and you will be his slaves. And in that day you will cry out because of your king, whom you have chosen for yourselves; but the Lord will not answer you in that day. (1 Sam. 8:11–18)

Following the reign of David, who established a stable kingdom for Israel, Solomon began to fulfill this prophecy. While he is much lionized for his wisdom, judgment, and magnificent temple, what our usual surface reading of his reign conceals is that it was primarily one of empire building.[47] Solomon initiated his reign by eliminating all his rivals to consolidate power (1 Kgs. 2) and marrying the daughter of Pharaoh to make an alliance with Egypt (1 Kgs. 3). He then proceeded to expand his kingdom.[48]

First Kings goes into great detail regarding Solomon's retainers, wealth, and empire. We are told that "Judah and Israel were as numerous as the

---

46. Birch, *Old Testament*, 216–18; Horsley, *Covenant Economics*, 202–3.

47. For Israel, God's covenant was to be fulfilled by establishing them as a nation which would expand and fill the earth. The reigns of David and especially Solomon established a stable (although comparatively small) empire for Israel, hence the writers' portrayal of these kings as righteous and faithful notwithstanding scriptural evidence to the contrary. Their imperialism was viewed as evidence of God's favor and blessing.

48. See Norman K. Gottwald, *The Hebrew Bible: A Socio-Literary Introduction*, 934–39, for a detailed discussion of Solomon's kingdom building and the rise of the Israelite monarchy.

sand by the sea; they ate and drank and were happy. Solomon was sovereign over all the kingdoms from the Euphrates to the land of the Philistines, even to the border of Egypt" (4:20–21). Despite this rosy outlook, the vast majority of Solomon's subjects did not enjoy the extravagant excess of his court. While the long lists of officials and officers can be a challenge to wade through, what underlies this restructuring of the kingdom under Solomon is a systematic dismantling of the statutes and protections of the law of Moses in favor of a political and economic system designed to support the lifestyles of him and his court. As explained by Bruce Birch,

> The concern for equitable distribution of economic resources reflected in the covenant codes is displaced with an economics of privilege that begins to create sharp class divisions of wealthy and poor within Israel. The redivison of tribal territories signals the beginning of forced shifts in land tenure and inheritance that move the land out of the realm of continuous family inheritance and initiate the accumulation of land by royal retainers and wealthy elite classes associated with royal power structures.[49]

With peace being established in his kingdom—a goal that his father David was never able to accomplish—Solomon set to work building the temple. For this, he conscripts forced labor "out of all Israel; the levy numbered thirty thousand men" (1 Kgs. 5:13), as well as tens of thousands more laborers and stonecutters. In an explicit violation of God's edict against the oppression of resident non-Israelites (Lev. 19), Solomon took a census and conscripted over 150,000 Canaanites into forced labor (2 Chr. 2:17–18).

Taking seven years to build, Solomon's Temple is described in magnificent detail but pales in comparison to the royal palace, which took thirteen years to build. The palace included a "House of the Forest of the Lebanon," a "Hall of Pillars," a "Hall of the Throne," and several other buildings, including an extravagant house for his wife (1 Kgs. 7). Aside from conscripting his own people and a portion of the resident Canaanites for forced labor (as well as levying tribute on all non-Israelites), his huge and ongoing building projects—including a fleet of ships, "storage cities, the cities for his chariots, the cities for his calvary and whatever Solomon desired to build, in Jerusalem, in Lebanon, and in all the land of his dominion" (9:19)—required forced labor on a massive scale. For this, he enslaved all the Canaanites who were left in the land.

Although initially favored of the Lord and promised a perpetual dynasty, Solomon fell from grace. He "loved many foreign women along with the

---

49. Birch, *Old Testament*, 248.

daughter of Pharaoh; Moabite, Ammonite, Edomite, Sidonian, and Hittite women" (1 Kgs. 11:1). His harem included seven hundred princesses and three hundred concubines. This was in direct violation of the prohibition that God had given Israel of marrying foreign wives. The narrative says that at the urging of his wives, Solomon began to follow many foreign gods and goddesses, building "high places" for them where their followers could perform their sacrificial rituals and thus spread imperial ideology throughout Israel. However, given Solomon's wholesale adoption of the ideologies and practices of Empire, it seems the biblical authors largely scapegoated Solomon's wives who were themselves evidence of his political and imperial ambition and exploitation. Though his wives no doubt fed his imperialism by exposing him to foreign ideas and methods of rule which he then adopted, Solomon's rearrangement of the affairs of the kingdom to support and increase the wealth and power of himself and his retainers indicates that his idolatry was foundational to his kingdom building and reign. The familiar terse but ominous descriptor enters the narrative again, where it will stay and be repeated until the destruction and captivity of Israel, "So Solomon did what was evil in the sight of the Lord" (v. 6).

As a result of this explicit idolatry (to say nothing of the oppression which resulted from his administrative policies), God became angry with Solomon and vowed to take the kingdom from him. After his death, the tribal leaders of Israel begged Solomon's son, Rehoboam, to "lighten the hard service of your father and his heavy yoke that he placed on us" (1 Kgs. 12:4). Rather than agree to lighten Israel's load, he vowed to increase it and ratchets up the brutality: "my father disciplined you with whips, but I will discipline you with scorpions" (v. 14). Incensed, the ten tribes of Israel secede, making Jereboam, one of Solomon's officers, their king, leaving only Judah (with Benjamin) for Rehoboam to rule over. Jereboam, however, was also quick to turn to idolatry. Afraid that the people would turn on him and return to Rehoboam if they continued to focus their worship in Jerusalem, he made two golden calves and declared their sanctuaries the new resting place of God in the northern kingdom (as opposed to the temple in Jerusalem), placing them in the cities of Bethel and Dan and initiating an annual pilgrimage festival. He then consecrated priests for the high places of "any who wanted to be priests" (13:33).

From this point on, the narrative includes more and more prophets. In contrast to their traditional role of counsel and criticism, prophets during the reigns of the kings took an almost uniformly antagonistic stance. This underscores the extent of the idolatry in which Israel and Judah became immersed. In addition to the constant threat and effects of idolatry, the kingdoms of Israel and Judah found themselves in a precarious position due to their repeated conflicts with neighboring kingdoms and empires. In addition to periodic civil wars that never had a clear victor, both Israel and Judah found themselves harassed constantly by a number of enemies. Conflicts with Egypt, Syria (referred to also as Aram), Moab, and Assyria severely weakened both kingdoms and led to their eventual destruction.[50] Israel was conquered first by the Assyrians, with Judah being destroyed later by the Babylonians. This state of uncertainty and constant threat of military campaigns, both to expand their territory and defend it, would have taken a huge toll on the Israelites—especially those whose existence was most tenuous. In addition to taxes and tithes collected by their own political and religious rulers, taxes and tributes to the rulers of foreign kingdoms and empires would have added to the economic burden felt by the poor. Conscripted service in military conflicts meant the ever-present threat of battle and death, with possible ruin and starvation for those left behind. Occupation and destruction of villages, towns, and cities by invading forces meant terror, death, enslavement, rape, and trauma on a large scale. Thus, the systemic injustice and oppression of the policies in the divided kingdoms were compounded and amplified by the political and military threats to their national sovereignty throughout this period.

Though the narrative focuses predominantly on the spiritual aspects of idolatry and does not spend much time on the effects of the oppression and exploitation that became institutionalized under Solomon, nestled in the larger conflict between Ahab and Elijah is a story that details the fact that God is very aware of the injustice and inequity that accompany the monarchy. Ahab wanted to take possession of the vineyard of Naboth: "Give me your vineyard, so that I may have it for a vegetable garden, because it is near my house" (1 Kgs. 21:2). Naboth, however, refused Ahab's offer to purchase the property: "The Lord forbid that I should give you my ancestral inheritance" (v. 3). After learning of Naboth's refusal, Ahab's wife, the Phoenecian princess Jezebel, conspired with the nobles and elders of Naboth's village to falsely accuse him of blasphemy and treason and have him stoned to death. Jezebel then delivered the vineyard to Ahab.

God's judgment was swift. Elijah accosted Ahab in Naboth's vineyard: "Have you killed, and also taken possession? Thus says the Lord: In the place where dogs licked up the blood of Naboth, dogs will also lick

---

50. Birch, *Old Testament*, ch. 10.

up your blood" (1 Kgs. 21:19). He then prophesied that Ahab would be killed, with disaster falling on his house. This dire pronouncement coming directly on the heels of Ahab's possession of Naboth's vineyard through conspiracy and murder underscores the seriousness with which God views the abuse of the poor and vulnerable. The Mosaic law explicitly forbids just such conduct, and violations of these protections constituted a violation of Israel's covenant. Furthermore, we can be certain that this was not an isolated practice; it was systemic in the political systems of the day.[51]

The systemic nature of injustice is made clearly evident in the later account of Nehemiah, a priest and governor who oversaw the reconstruction of Jerusalem and other Jewish settlements during the return from exile in the Persian period. Summarizing what must have been myriad pleas for justice, the account reports:

> Now there was a great outcry of the people and of their wives against their Jewish kin. For there were those who said, "With our sons and our daughters, we are many; we must get grain, so that we may eat and stay alive." There were also those who said, "We are having to pledge our fields, our vineyards, and our houses in order to get grain during the famine." And there were those who said, "We are having to borrow money on our fields and vineyards to pay the king's tax. Now our flesh is the same as that of our kindred; our children are the same as their children; and yet we are forcing our sons and daughters to be slaves, and some of our daughters have been ravished; we are powerless, and our fields and vineyards now belong to others." (Neh. 5:1–5)

Nehemiah was furious at the suffering and misery visited upon the poor by this return to unjust practices, and he called the officials and nobles to account and instituted reforms in order to return society to a just and equitable community: "Let us stop this taking of interest. Restore to them, this very day, their fields, their vineyards, their olive orchards, and their houses, and the interest on money, grain, wine, and oil that you have been exacting from them" (Neh. 5:10–11). After instituting these reforms, Nehemiah also "called the priests, and made them take an oath to do as they had promised" (v. 12). This explicit inclusion of priests in the oath is indicative of how far Israel had fallen from the justice and equity of the covenant tradition. Corruption had seeped into all aspects of social, political, and even religious life. This pervasive corruption foreshadows the social and religious situation that would play a major role in the prophetic ministry of Jesus.

---

51. The destitution of the widows during the prophetic ministries of both Elijah and Elisha (1 Kgs. 17; 2 Kgs. 4) is further evidence of the rampant injustice and casting aside of the covenant system of economics during the divided kingdom.

Pleas of the Victims

The political and economic policies of Israel's kings would have produced widescale oppression, exploitation, suffering, and misery; however, due to the way the Bible has been compiled and edited (and the resulting way we tend to read it), the voices of these victims are far removed from and abstracted from the stories to which they belong. The period of the divided kingdom is detailed in the books of Kings and Chronicles, but it is in the book of Psalms that we can recover the voices of the victims during this period. The timing of this book, thought to have been written sometime between the ninth and sixth centuries BCE and compiled later, places it squarely during the period of the divided kingdom.[52] While the narratives of the divided kingdom focus predominantly on the interactions of the kings and prophets, the psalms are written from the perspective of the victims, giving us singular insight into the damage to relationships and trauma wreaked in a society in which oppression is rampant.[53] Indeed, as noted by James Williams, this book "contains the first sustained outcries in world literature of the single victim who is persecuted by enemies."[54]

Pleas for deliverance from enemies run constantly throughout the book. While there are plenty of calls on behalf of Israel for God to fight her battles and grant her victory over the enemies that threaten her national sovereignty, there are many pleas of a more personal nature. These seem to describe individuals who stand with their backs against the wall and with nowhere left to turn to avoid the evil that threatens to overcome them:

> Their mouths are filled with cursing and deceit and oppression;
> under their tongues are mischief and iniquity.
> They sit in ambush in the villages;
> in hiding places they murder the innocent.
>
> Their eyes stealthily watch for the helpless;
> they lurk in secret like a lion in its covert;
> they lurk that they may seize the poor;
> they seize the poor and drag them off in their net.
> (Ps. 10:7–9)

This is the reality of countless poor, oppressed, and marginalized people at the mercy of those who would destroy them in the name of personal gain. Of all the statutes in the Mosaic law, the prohibition against appropria-

---

52. Adele Berlin and Marc Zvi Brettler, eds., *The Jewish Study Bible*, 1266–67.
53. S. Mark Heim, *Saved from Sacrifice: A Theology of the Cross*, 82–84.
54. René Girard, *I See Satan Fall Like Lightning*, xviii.

tion of land inheritances played a crucial role in maintaining equity among Israelites. The people farmed and worked their lands for the subsistence of their families. Surplus was rare, and survival or destitution was often a matter of a good or poor harvest. Under the system of taxation set up by Solomon to support the lavish lifestyle of him and his courtiers, in which tribal lands were divided into arbitrary districts and plundered by nobles, many peasant families struggled to survive. In times of drought and famine, such as that described in 1 Kings 17, the taxation did not cease, forcing many to secure loans that were offered with interest, which violated the covenant obligation under the Law. When people defaulted on their loans, their farms and fields were taken, reducing them to "tenant farmers, debt servants, or landless wage laborers."[55] Parents sold their children as slaves,[56] people were forced into prostitution (which would still earn them the scorn of the community, notwithstanding their desperation), and others desperately turned to anything they could to survive. Many people simply starved.

The story of Elijah and the widow of Zarephath in First Kings exemplifies this plight. While discussion of this narrative usually focuses on the miracle of the flour and cruse of oil and the raising from the dead of her son by Elijah, its horrifying description of absolute financial ruin and utter dejection caused by the economic policies of the state should be just as impactful. In this account, there should be little wonder that upon the death of the widow's son, Elijah—who had asked so much of this woman, to which she has responded in incredible faith—is appalled and "cried out to the Lord, 'Oh Lord, have you brought calamity upon the widow with whom I am staying, by killing her son?'" (1 Kgs. 17:20).[57] God's response, the miracle of restoring life to the dead son, can be viewed as an explicit rejection of the oppression and exploitation that snuffed out this innocent life and many others far too early, an emphatic affirmation of the right to live in the face of human systems which produce dehumanization and death.[58]

---

55. Gottwald, *The Hebrew Bible*, 324.

56. This would have been particularly tragic and devastating for women, as male slaves were to be released every seven years, while women were held as slaves in perpetuity, likely as concubines, as long as they "pleased" their masters (Ex. 21:7).

57. See Nobuyoshi Kiuchi, "Elijah's Self-Offering: 1 Kings 17,21," for a fascinating discussion of Elijah's solidarity with the widow and the symbolic meaning of Elijah's method in the raising of the dead boy to life.

58. This explicit repudiation of systems of death and affirmation of the right to life will reach a spectacular culmination in the later resurrection of Jesus.

In situations of such extremity, the delicate social fabric which holds communities together would be shredded. Unable to provide for the needs of their families, people would become desperate. Petty slights or misunderstandings may blow up into unforgivable feuds. Friends may turn on one another. With corruption and bribery the norm in the legal system, there is little to deter one from displacing a member of the community and taking their land. Accusations of violations of the law, particularly against women (such as an accusation of prostitution or adultery), would likely end catastrophically given the heightened tension and desperation. The people are forced into a zero-sum game, where everyone is out for themselves and where one's own survival and the survival of their family is necessarily at the expense of another's. This cutthroat reality is made clear in these pleas (e.g., Ps. 35). The absolute desperation and feelings of hopelessness are rendered with imagery of sinking, struggling to find a grip on something before slipping under:

> Save me, O God,
> for the waters have come up to my neck.
> I sink in deep mire, where there is no foothold;
> I have come into deep waters,
> and the flood sweeps over me.
> I am weary with my crying;
> my throat is parched.
> My eyes grow dim with waiting for my God. . . .
> Do not let the flood sweep over me,
> or the deep swallow me up,
> or the pit close its mouth over me.
> (Ps. 69:1–3, 15)

The starvation, heavy labor, and unsanitary conditions that many poor lived under led to a continual presence of disease and sickness. Not only is a sick person unable to work, greatly increasing the burden on the family, in the ancient world their unexplained or congenital or chronic illness could be taken as a sign of divine disfavor or personal or familial sin. This commonly led to shunning or worse. In times of extremity, communities were prone to turn on such individuals, expelling them from the community or killing them in a last-ditch effort to rid themselves of their perceived sin or contamination and restore divine favor.[59] The desperation is palpable.

---

59. Girard, *Violence and the Sacred*, chs. 1–3; Heim, *Saved from Sacrifice*, ch. 2; James G. Williams, *The Bible, Violence, and the Sacred*, 6–14; Raymund Schwager, *Must There Be Scapegoats: Violence and Redemption in the Bible*, ch. 1.

Divine Response

God's response to these cries of the poor, contained in the biblical books known as "the Prophets," constitutes a forceful and explicit condemnation of the exploitation and oppression that occurred during this time period.[60] For example, Isaiah delivers God's explicit critique of the hypocrisy of religious ritual in the face of injustice in scathing terms:

> What to me is the multitude of your sacrifices?
> says the Lord?;
> I have had enough of burnt offerings of rams
> and the fat of fed beasts;
> I do not delight in the blood of bulls,
>   or of lambs, or of goats. . . .
> incense is an abomination to me. . . .
> I cannot endure solemn assemblies with iniquity.
> Your new moons and your appointed festivals
>   my soul hates;
> they have become a burden to me. . . .
> your hands are full of blood. . . .
> cease to do evil, learn to do good;
> seek justice,
> rescue the oppressed,
> defend the orphan,
> plead for the widow.
> (Isa. 1:11–17; see also Amos 5:21)

Here God makes clear how the sacrificial practice had become corrupted. It was meant to solemnize God's salvation for Israel and to continuously deepen and restore their relationship with Yahweh. According to Isaiah, to share a sacrificial meal with God while your own sisters and brothers are starving and destitute is a violation of the very covenant pledged to and remembered in those sacrifices. It is a complete disregard for the justice enabled and protected by this covenant relationship and community. In a word, it is blasphemy.

Isaiah goes on to itemize the many ways Israel's ruling class have ruined the poor by abandoning their covenant obligations. He denounces those who accumulate seemingly endless wealth ("Their land is filled with silver and gold, and there is no end to their treasures, their land is filled with horses, and there is no end to their chariots" [Isa. 2:7]), those who seek to accumulate property ("Ah, you who join house to house, who add field to

---

60. Horsley, *Covenant Economics*, ch. 5.

field, until there is room for no one but you, and you are left to live alone in the midst of the land" [5:8]), and those who bring lawsuits under false pretenses ("No one brings suit justly, no one goes to law honestly; they rely on empty pleas, they speak lies, conceiving mischief and begetting iniquity . . . they rush to shed innocent blood . . . the way of peace they do not know, and there is no justice in their paths" [59:4, 7]). Isaiah further makes explicit the ruin of the poor by the rich: "It is you who have devoured the vineyard; the spoil of the poor is in your houses. What do you mean by crushing my people, by grinding the face of the poor?" (2:14–15).

God's response to the pleadings of the poor continues throughout the prophetic books, illustrating the many ways Israel's rulers had violated the economic stipulations of the covenant community. Jeremiah castigates those who have become "great and rich . . . sleek and fat" and do not "judge with justice the cause of the orphan" or "defend the rights of the needy" (Jer. 5:27–28). Micah calls out those in power "who devise wickedness and evil deeds on their beds! When the morning dawns, they perform it, because it is in their power. They covet fields, and seize them; houses, and take them away; they oppress householder and house, people and their inheritance" (Micah 2:1–2). Later, he uses grotesque and graphic imagery to indict the heads of state for their oppression of the people:

> Listen, you heads of Jacob
>   and rulers of the house of Israel!
> Should you not know justice?
> you who hate the good and love the evil,
> who tear the skin off my people,
> and the flesh off their bones;
> who eat the flesh of my people,
> flay their skin off them,
> break their bones in pieces,
> and chop them up like meat in a kettle,
> like flesh in a caldron.
> (3:1–3)

Amos, while focusing much of his prophetic ire on those in Israel who "sell the righteous for silver, and the needy for a pair of sandals—they who trample the head of the poor into the dust of the earth" (Amos 2:7), makes it clear that injustice against the vulnerable is just as abhorrent in the kingdoms of Israel's enemies "because they have threshed Gilead with threshing sledges of iron, . . . because they carried into exile entire communities, . . . [and] because they have ripped open pregnant women in Gilead in order to enlarge their territory" (1:3, 6, 13).[61] As if anticipating Israel's exoneration of its own sins and abuse of its people by comparison to the war crimes of its neighbors, Amos puts any question of relative guilt to rest: "Are you better than these kingdoms?" (6:2). The answer is emphatically in the negative; the scope of God's abhorrence for social injustice and violations of human rights crosses political and national boundaries, and God identifies with the vulnerable and oppressed regardless of their nationality or covenant status.

Salvation History and Hope

Internal societal collapse combined with external political and military pressures eventually led to the destruction, exile, and scattering of the kingdoms of both Israel and Judah. This is framed, by the writers, as being due to Israel's failure to heed the warnings of the prophets to abandon their idolatry. It is difficult to imagine how devastating and disorienting this time was for Israel. Time and again in their history, God had delivered them from enemies. For Israel, God's covenant was the promise of a perpetual inheritance in the land—a political dynasty where they would rule with God, breaking in pieces all rival kingdoms and powers. The destruction of both Israel and Judah, in particular the razing of Jerusalem and the temple by Babylon, must have constituted a tremendous blow to their covenant hopes. While the pleas in the psalms are punctuated with gratitude and praise for God's deliverance, those who are brutalized and left stunned by the sack of Jerusalem can claim no such solace. The severity of their crisis is captured in the poetry of the book of Lamentations, thought to have been "composed in or near the ruins of the city" by a group who remained behind.[62] The book is a heartbreaking cacophony of suffering voices mourning the utter ruin of the people and their society. As is always the case, it is the poor and vulnerable who suffer the most for the sins of the rulers. Some scenes depicted in the abandoned city are almost too horrific to recount, the suffering of the innocent so extreme:

> My eyes are spent with weeping; . . .
> because of the destruction of my people,
> because infants and babies faint
> in the streets of the city.

---

61. R. Kessler, "The Crimes of the Nations in Amos 1–2," 209–14.

62. David Janzen, *Trauma and the Failure of History: Kings, Lamentations, and the Destruction of Jerusalem*, 90; John Barton, *A History of the Bible : The Story of the World's Most Influential Book*, 30.

> They cry to their mothers,
> "Where is bread and wine?". . .
> as their life is poured out
> on their mother's bosom. . . .
>
> Happier were those pierced by the sword
> than those pierced by hunger,
> whose life drains away. . . .
>
> The hands of compassionate women
> have boiled their own children;
> they became their food
> in the destruction of my people.
> (Lam. 2:11–12; 4:9–10)

Throughout this grieving, Israel moves from dumbfounded horror at God's unreasonable anger and indiscriminate destruction, to blaming herself for what has befallen her, to simply begging God to acknowledge her suffering.[63] The many voices and whiplashing perspectives indicate that there is no simple narrative that can make sense of the massive trauma this crisis has inflicted. A sense of profound loss and abandonment permeates these utterances. Israel is without hope. They have gone too far. There can be no return. The litany of suffering flows in an unbroken flood, as if perhaps giving an explicit and exhaustive account of their pain will force God to acknowledge them and their plight. They plead and hope against hope for God to remember them: "Why have you forgotten us completely? Why have you forsaken us these many days? Restore us to yourself, O Lord, that we may be restored; . . . unless you have utterly rejected us, and are angry with us beyond measure" (Lam. 5:21–22).

And yet, the memory of God's salvation in their history cannot be snuffed out completely. As if willing themselves to believe again, in the face of all evidence to the contrary, that God can be good, merciful, just, and loving, they dare to hope for a way back from their exile: "The steadfast love of the Lord never ceases [Lord, we are not cut off], his mercies never come to an end; . . . 'therefore I will hope in him'" (Lam. 3:22, 24). Even in Israel's suffering, desperation, and destitution, the memory of God's salvation is bright. The hope, even if it is a hope against hope, cannot be dimmed by the passage of time. The relationship that God had entered into with Israel had become their lifeblood. God's great act

---

63. See Janzen, *Trauma and the Failure of History*, chapter 5, "Lamentations and the Failure of Collective Trauma" for an in depth and fascinating examination of the narrative voices and themes of each chapter of Lamentations.

of liberation in delivering them from Egyptian bondage remains in their memory, solemnized and reinforced down the centuries through the repetition of "perpetual ordinances" such as the celebration of Passover and the annual Festival of Unleavened Bread, commemorating the "very day I [Yahweh] brought your companies out of the land of Egypt" (Ex. 12:17). God had sustained them throughout their history, and their faith in God's continual love and providence could not be relinquished, no matter how dire their circumstances seemed or how undeserving they felt.

God responds to this acute crisis of Israel's faith through an oracle attributed to the prophet Isaiah,[64] written in the wake of the destruction and exile:

> But Zion said, "The Lord has forsaken me,
> my Lord has forgotten me."
> Can a woman forget her nursing child,
> or show no compassion for the child of her womb?
> Even these may forget, yet I will not forget you. . . .
> Surely your waste and your desolate places
> and your devastated land—
> surely now you will be too crowded for your inhabitants,
> and those who swallowed you up will be far away.
> The children born in the time of your bereavement
> will yet say in your hearing:
> "The place is too crowded for me;
> make room for me to settle."
> (Isa. 49:14–15, 19–20)

To a people stripped of home, nation, and community, God promises cities teeming with life and promises safety from all who wish to do them harm. God further promises a renewal of the lands, crops, and homes that have been trampled, burned, and destroyed. Walter Brueggemann explains the significance of this promise:

> The ultimate image of judgment and ruin is that the city should be uninhabited, so that it becomes either a place for thorns and briars or a place of wild, unclean animals. It is the language of desolation that characterizes Jerusalem while the exiles are absent. . . . Now, says the poet, Israel will be dazzled by its multiplication. It will be bewildered and not understand how barrenness has turned to generativity. The forsaken has become the blessed precisely

---

64. Janzen, *Trauma and the Failure of History*, 89, indicates that the writers of second Isaiah, from which this oracle comes, likely had direct access to the pleas of Lamentations, positioning Isaiah 49 as a direct response to this suffering.

because Yahweh has comforted and had compassion, because Yahweh has not—ever—forgotten and forsaken.[65]

In short, God has not abandoned Israel. God's response shows that God knows the specific character and nature of their suffering, going so far as to assure them that their infant children will not only survive but will flourish. As Patricia Willey puts it, "even though the bitter conditions may have led some women even to forget their own young, . . . YHWH bridges the chasm of disaster by continuing to remember Jerusalem."[66]

This is the essence of God's covenant. God's revelation in history is as a god who is moved by, willingly enters into, experiences, and liberates Israel from their suffering. As Jon Sobrino writes,

> Israel knew God above all in relation to the real historical life of its people. . . . So Israel thought of God in connection with life and the living—particularly with social relationships among the living—and its religion consisted precisely in bearing witness to this God.[67]

God's covenant is a promise to remain in relationship with Israel until the bitter end, and to turn each new seeming end into salvation and renewal. As a result, their pleas for salvation are not of an existential sort. They are anchored in the sweat and hunger of mortality and grounded in "a faith that has been drenched by tears and reddened by blood."[68] The torrent of pleadings and dogged hope in the face of bleak and overwhelming odds are a moving and timeless testament to the reality of a God who has revealed, assured, and effected salvation on these terms.

---

65. Walter Brueggemann, *Isaiah 40–66*, 117.

66. Patricia Tull Willey, *Remember the Former Things: The Recollection of Previous Texts in Second Isaiah*, 200.

67. Jon Sobrino, *Christ the Liberator: A View from the Victims*, 37. Sobrino notes that Israel did not develop an extensive theology of the afterlife despite being surrounded by cultures which had firm beliefs in this regard. He suggests that this was directly due to the explicitly historical, temporal revelation of God they experienced.

68. Gustavo Gutiérrez, *On Job: God-Talk and the Suffering of the Innocent*, 83.

Chapter 2

Jesus and the Reign of God: Salvation as Covenant Community

For Jesus, oppression and injustice were not limited to a specific historical situation; their causes go deeper and cannot be truly eliminated without going to the very roots of the problem: the disintegration of fellowship and communion.
— Gustavo Gutiérrez

Returning from his time of fasting and prayer in the wilderness, Jesus must have been shocked to hear of the arrest of his cousin John (the Baptist). He had been feeling for some time that he had been called to something, and his time in the wilderness was a formative experience in terms of shaping his growing understanding of his work and mission. John's arrest seems to have been the catalyst that pushed him into formal ministry, with the Gospels reporting that "after John was arrested, Jesus came to Galilee, proclaiming the good news of God, and saying 'The time is fulfilled, and the kingdom of God has come near; repent and believe in the good news'" (Mark 1:14–15).

What was the good news that Jesus was urging the people to believe? What was the nature of the kingdom of God that he said was "coming near" or "at hand"? How did he understand his own calling and the function of his ministry? The people in his hometown were first to hear:

> When he came to Nazareth, where he had been brought up, he went to the synagogue on the sabbath day, as was his custom. He stood up to read, and the scroll of the prophet Isaiah was given to him. He unrolled the scroll and found the place where it was written:
>
> > "The Spirit of the Lord is upon me
> > because he has anointed me
> > to bring good news to the poor.
> > He has send me to proclaim release to the captives
> > and recovery of sight to the blind,
> > to let the oppressed go free,
> > to proclaim the year of the Lord's favor."

And he rolled up the scroll, gave it back to the attendant, and sat down. The eyes of all in the synagogue were fixed on him. Then he began to say to them, "Today this scripture has been fulfilled in your hearing." (Luke 4:16–20)

Bringing good news to the poor, releasing the captives, letting the oppressed go free. This is how Jesus chose to frame his ministry.

Years earlier, Mary had already had a profound insight into the purpose and focus of Jesus's ministry in the short but beautiful song of praise that she offers following the annunciation of the impending birth of her son. This song, called the Magnificat, is presented by Luke in the first chapter of his Gospel:

And Mary said,

> My soul magnifies the Lord,
> and my spirit rejoices in God my Savior
> for he has looked with favor on the
> lowliness of his servant.
> Surely, from now on all generations will call
> me blessed;
> for the Mighty One has done great things
> for me,
> and holy is his name.
> His mercy is for those who fear him
> from generation to generation.
> He has shown strength with his arm;
> he has scattered the proud in the thoughts
> of their hearts.
> He has brought down the powerful from
> their thrones,
> and lifted up the lowly;
> he has filled the hungry with good things,
> and sent the rich away empty.
> He has helped his servant Israel,
> in remembrance of his mercy,
> according to the promise he made to our ancestors,
> to Abraham and his descendents forever.
> (Luke 1:46–55)

This brief but powerful pronouncement by Mary situates Jesus's ministry squarely in a liberative framework. It echoes the sayings in many of the psalms and by many prophets who had castigated Israel's rulers for their oppression of the poor. The language of scattering the proud, bringing down the powerful, lifting up and feeding the lowly and hungry, and sending the rich away empty are images that could have been uttered by any of the Old Testament prophets.[1] In addition, as pointed out by Amanda Witmer, "it is telling that Mary's song does not describe personal salvation from individual sin in relation to the promised son, but rather social and political deliverance from oppression at the national level."[2] We are still firmly in the realm of temporal salvation.

This interpretation of the focus of Jesus's ministry may be surprising to those of us who have grown up with the understanding that the function of his life and death was to pay the price for our sins so that we could be forgiven and experience salvation in the next life. But as demonstrated in the last chapter, God's salvation was experienced and hoped for as a liberation from bondage and oppression, from illness and disease. Those in Nazareth to whom Jesus quoted Isaiah were not looking for someone to come save them from their sins. They were looking for someone to liberate them from Roman oppression and from the burden of taxes that were levied by the state and temple administration. They were looking for a way to pay their debts, which they had accrued as the only way to plant crops in their fields. They were wondering how to provide for their families now that their homes and fields had been taken away in foreclosure. These were the problems of the people Jesus pronounced "good news" to. These were those for whom the kingdom of God was at hand.

These are not the "religious" problems we usually think of when we think of the meaning and purpose of Jesus's life. They are the real problems of history. Whatever he came to understand about the impact of his ministry on humanity generally, we can be sure that Jesus was deadly serious about addressing the problems faced in the everyday lives of his people (the fact that he was killed by crucifixion, a method reserved for political criminals, indicates his strategy for doing so was overtly political and viewed as a threat by the authorities). Why else would he have chosen to announce his mission and ministry in his hometown? These were his friends, his neighbors. He wanted desperately to help them, and he felt called by God to do so. In order to understand the lived reality of these people and the injustice he saw and sought to change through his ministry, we have to place Jesus in his proper context. To truly understand the salvation that was hoped for and that he offered to those Galilean peasants, we have to enter the world of the so-called "historical Jesus."

---

1. See also Zechariah's prophecy regarding Jesus; Luke 1:65–79.
2. Amanda Witmer, *Jesus, the Galilean Exorcist: His Exorcisms in Social and Political Context*, 41.

Uncovering the Historical Jesus

How do we understand the historical Jesus? Is it as easy as going back to the Bible and closely reading the Gospel accounts? This presents a conundrum because much, if not all, of what has been written about Jesus was written after his life by adherents to a developing religious tradition that came to assign a very specific identity to him and a specific purpose to his life and death. Because of this bias, it is very difficult to separate the life of Jesus the man from the image of Jesus the son of God and savior of the world, a timeless divine being dropped into, but not really a part of, the specific historical context in which he lived. As Johannes Metz puts it, we tend to think of Jesus as a god who "dip[ped] into our existence, wave[d] the magic wand of divine life over us, and then hurriedly retreat[ed] to his eternal home."[3] To counter this perception and to understand the significance of his mortal ministry for his day and ours, we must search out the historical Jesus.

The search for the historical Jesus has been ongoing since the late 1700s.[4] It was initiated by scholars who recognized the importance and, at the same time, the extreme difficulty of accurately reconstructing the life of Jesus from the records and writings that have been produced.[5] While any search for the historical Jesus will necessarily be biased by those conducting it, any who wish to learn more must understand the sources of some of this bias. As noted by William Herzog, there are three "gaps" that we must consider in any attempt to come to understand the historical Jesus.[6]

First is the fact that we are living in a day and age two thousand years removed from when Jesus lived. This means that we cannot superimpose our social, cultural, economic, religious, and political context onto that in which Jesus lived, because this will give us a biased and inaccurate interpretation of the reasons the people in his time did what they did and the way they would have understood the meaning of his teaching and ministry. Thus, we need to do all we can to understand the world in which they lived. This is the purview of archeologists, historians, anthropologists, and

---

3. Johannes Baptist Metz, *Poverty of Spirit*, 17.

4. See Albert Schweitzer, *The Quest of the Historical Jesus*, for a summary of the development and initial findings of this quest.

5. For a summary and discussion of some of the major themes in this debate, see Richard A. Horsley, *The Prophet Jesus and the Renewal of Israel*, chs. 1–5, and William R. Herzog II, *Jesus, Justice, and the Reign of God*, ch. 1.

6. Herzog, *Jesus, Justice*, 34–36; see also John Dominic Crossan, *Jesus: A Revolutionary Biography*, ix–xiv.

social scientists, and we can learn much from the work they have done and continue to do on uncovering the world of first-century Palestine.

In this regard, particular care should be taken to understand the religious context into which Jesus was born and the religious understanding with which he grew up. Christianity, as we know it, with its doctrines and practices, did not exist in the time of Jesus. Neither did Judaism. Jesus taught and lived in a community with a rich, tragic, and powerful history and understanding of God's action in the world and of Israel's place within that unfolding history. He inherited a prophetic tradition that served to remind and recall people back to the ways of covenantal justice established by God via the Mosaic Law. This would have been the lens through which Jesus and those he ministered to understood his life and mission. If we are to have any chance of understanding the teaching and ministry of Jesus, they must be interpreted in the context of this inescapable fact.

Second, the accounts written in the Gospels are not firsthand accounts. They were written after Jesus died by writers who were not concerned with creating an accurate, unbiased account of Jesus. Mark was likely written first, and his Gospel was used by Matthew and Luke (with a possible third source, "Q," short for the German *quelle*, which is theorized to have contained only sayings of Jesus) to write their accounts; John's unique Gospel followed later. Because of this, it can be important to try to identify what is likely an original saying or account, and what has been embellished or added by the Gospel writers. This becomes particularly important in understanding the meanings behind some of Jesus's sayings and parables. Only by being able to "sift the layers of tradition"[7] that have obscured the original account or saying will we be able to recover what Jesus actually did or said and better interpret its significance for his day and ours.

The third gap to always remember is that, try as we might, we will never be able to perfectly and in an unbiased manner recreate the image of the historical Jesus. Different methods will produce different results, and different agendas will lead to different interpretations. This is not so much a problem if those who are doing the studies are aware of this fact, and recognize that in the end each analysis will likely contain some truth and some overreach. By combining together different methods and perspectives, we can hopefully get closer to understanding the lived reality and significance of Jesus of Nazareth.[8]

---

7. Herzog, *Jesus, Justice*, 36.

8. For an indispensable introduction to the historical Jesus for a Latter-day Saint audience, see James W. McConkie and Judith E. McConkie, *Whom Say Ye*

The Social, Political, and Religious World of the Gospels

Jesus lived in what is known as the Second Temple period, which followed the return from Babylonian exile that was permitted under the Persian empire. Israel (now called Jews) were allowed to rebuild their temple and establish again their economic and religious activity. They were never, however, able to return to the full independence and influence they had achieved under their prior nation state. Judea, while largely left alone by a series of changing empires, was eventually brought under Roman rule in 63 BCE when Jerusalem was conquered by Pompey. The Romans deposed the current rulers of Judea and Galilee and in their stead set up Herod (known as Herod the Great) as a client king friendly to the emperor who would be left alone as long as their rule did not impede Roman interests. Herod's son (Herod Antipus) was given a similar client kingship of Perea and Galilee,[9] while Judea was eventually brought and maintained under a prefecture of Rome.[10] In Jesus's day, the prefect was Pontius Pilate.

The historical and political context in which Jesus lived can be considered an advanced agrarian society under the rule of a traditional aristocratic empire.[11] This society was set up with the top 1 to 2 percent of the population as the ruling class. Their main goals were to amass wealth and to maintain power. To achieve this, they bargained with and set up local cadres of nobility and established bureaucracies that allowed for the successful control of the military (who kept the peace) and the economic exploitation of the peasant population (from whom they extracted tribute and taxes).

That I Am: Lessons from the Jesus of Nazareth.

9. John Dominic Crossan, *God and Empire: Jesus Against Rome, Then and Now*, suggests that the prophetic movements of both John the Baptist and Jesus of Nazareth were in response to the economic crisis in the peasant fishing villages surrounding the Sea of Galilee which resulted from Herod's building of Tiberias (named after the new Roman emperor) as his new capital city. This project saw extensive urbanization and a move by Herod to commercialize fishing in order to increase his tax base and secure Roman approval to expand his kingdom (p. 102–3). See also Richard A. Horsley, *Jesus and Empire: The Kingdom of God and the New World Disorder*, 33, for discussion of the economic strain placed on Galilee by Herod's reign and building projects.

10. Margaret Froelich, *Jesus and the Empire of God: Royal Language and Imperial Ideology in the Gospel of Mark*, 127–28.

11. Gerhard E. Lenski, *Power and Privilege: A Theory of Social Stratification*; John H. Kautsky, *The Politics of Aristocratic Empires*. This section is indebted to the work of William Herzog, *Jesus, Justice, and the Reign of God*.

Within the villages, market towns, and cities were an assortment of retainers appointed by the ruling groups. These retainers served two functions. First, by comprising about 5 percent of the population, they combined with the ruling 2 percent to greatly increase the manageability of controlling the remaining 93 percent (peasants who worked the fields, merchants, and artisans). By being spread out over the towns and villages, they were able to enforce the "predatory policies of the elites."[12] Second, in standing between the peasants and the ruling class, they also took the brunt of the animosity from the peasants, thereby insulating the ruling class from any direct threat or hostility. At all levels of the bureaucracy and ruling class, individuals sought any way possible to increase their own wealth and solidify their own positions and institutionalize their political and economic gains, putting them in constant tension with one another and leading to even more exploitation of the peasants. Thus, ruling classes in agrarian societies were "locked in permanent struggles with one another for the increasing wealth needed to fuel their constant struggle for power and prestige."[13]

The temple, while in theory still representing the center of Jewish religious life, had been corrupted into a tool of the ruling class by a number of factors.[14] First, the authoritative line of high priests had been broken. Herod the Great was unable to maintain the office of high priest, as had the Hasmonean dynasty before him, because he was not from a legitimate priestly family line. Recognizing the potential threat the high priests posed to his power and in an effort to consolidate his rule and influence, "Herod imported priestly families from the Diaspora and arrogated to himself the power to depose and appoint high priests."[15] This unstable position of the high priests meant that their allegiance was to Herod rather than to the people who they were supposed to serve. The high priests, along with the elders who supported them, controlled the temple and its institutions, and they sought ways to maintain their own power and influence rather than ensuring the purity of the temple practice. In addition, in an explicit corruption of the Mosaic law, wealth amassed by the temple from

---

12. Herzog, *Jesus, Justice*, 96.
13. Herzog, 92.
14. We must note here, that while we readily differentiate between "political" and "religious" concerns and activity in our day, this distinction did not exist in ancient Palestine. The choice between the god of Rome (Caesar) and the god of Israel (Yahweh) was an explicitly political choice, with real-life consequences that extended far beyond any "religious" realm.
15. Herzog, *Jesus, Justice*, 91.

the taxes required of the people to maintain the sacrificial practices was used by the aristocrats as loans to peasants for the purposes of eventually foreclosing on their land and fields when they defaulted. Records of these debts were kept by scribes and stored in the temple. Thus, the temple itself became a means to destroy the lives of peasants. According to Herzog, "as the temple amassed wealth, the people of the land were getting poorer and poorer."[16] This led to increasing tension and hostility between the peasants and the temple state.

The temple was also the center for copying the Torah and writing and promulgating interpretation of it for the rest of the population through readings by scribes and Pharisees in local gatherings (synagogues). This became increasingly important as a way to maintain religious orthodoxy in the scattered villages and hamlets which surrounded the urban centers. These interpretations of law and scripture, however, became increasingly strained, functioning as propaganda to perpetuate the class differences between peasants and the ruling class, further fostering distrust between the people and the temple. Add to all of this the fact that the temple itself, as the symbol of the Jewish refusal to assimilate to the ways of Roman rule, placed the high priests in a position of tension between the people they were meant to serve and the Roman rulers who made their continued existence and livelihood possible. This meant that high priests both represented the interests of the Jews to the Romans but also brokered Roman policy in ways that could either favor the people or favor the priests and the temple administrators. As Lester Grabbe explains, the Romans "looked to the high priest as the main representative of the Jewish people. Whether officially or unofficially the high priest appears to have been the *de facto* head of the native administration."[17] Unfortunately, the high priestly families tended to side with the Romans over the Jews in political matters, which ensured their continued wealth and prosperity but increased the hostility between the people and the temple. The temple administration had also declared any peasants who could not pay their temple dues—a great many, due to the tax and tribute required of the state—unclean and therefore cut off from the cleansing temple rituals in perpetuity.

Decades of this type of tension made Judea and Galilee volatile places where protest and the possibility of revolt were ever-present.[18] The ruling class monitored the peasants for any sign of rebellion or coalescing around

---

16. Herzog, 142.
17. Lester L. Grabbe, *An Introduction to Second Temple Judaism*, 46.
18. Horsley, *Jesus and Empire*, ch. 2.

a political or religious figure who could gain a following large enough to present problems or increase the chance of armed revolt, and any protests or revolts were brutally suppressed. As William Herzog notes,

> All of these factors left the province of Judea in a precarious position. It was a powder keg waiting to explode. Above all, it meant that any prophet, like Jesus, who criticized the temple could expect to receive prompt attention and a hostile response from a ruling class already stretched to the limit.[19]

It was into this "powder keg" that Jesus was born and in which he moved about and conducted his work. Having set the stage, we now turn to specific events and features of his ministry.

The Temptations

We do not have much information about Jesus's early years. Instead, all four Gospels situate his ministry within the prophetic pronouncement of John the Baptist. There, Jesus comes to John to be baptized, receives heavenly approval, and then retires into the wilderness, where he is tempted by the devil. Though depicted as a singular encounter between Jesus and the devil, it seems likely that the account represents an ongoing internal struggle that Jesus had as to what kind of ministry his would be. He would have been clearly aware of the messianic hopes and prophecies that comprised the religious milieu in which he lived. He grew up in poverty, among people who felt the full weight of the Roman occupation and the political and religious oppression of corrupt Jewish authorities. He likely spent time with fringe political groups. He also clearly felt called to some divine vocation, as evidenced by his desire to "be about his father's business" from an early age.

Whatever the specifics of his early years, we can be sure that Jesus began to feel strongly that his was to be a ministry among the people. This would have been confirmed by his encounter with John at his baptism. God had called him to do something. The question he must have been grappling with was, what was it? The specifics of the way he pursued his ministry could have far-reaching political effects. He must have considered, even in these early stages, how such reverberations might affect his family, friends, and himself. As noted by C. S. Song,

> What Jesus has to deal with is the history of a people. What is at stake is the destiny of a nation. . . . Jesus must have had to face such questions during his

---

19. Herzog, *Jesus, Justice*, 105.

ministry. The story of the temptation in the Gospels of Matthew and Luke gives us some idea of how Jesus wrestled with them. Obviously, that story does not only mark the beginning of his ministry. It is in fact the story of his life—a story that gives us some idea of how seriously Jesus had to deal with the political implications of his ministry.[20]

The temptations can therefore be understood as the real struggle that Jesus had with how to solve the problems of the people he encountered during his ministry. As noted by Song, this would not have been a one-off at the beginning of his ministry as portrayed in the Gospel accounts. These would have been ever present temptations. It is clear that to succumb to them would have been Jesus misusing his power and warping his vocation, so what do they represent?

Jesus is first tempted to "command these stones to become loaves of bread" (Matt. 4:3). This must have represented a particularly difficult aspect of his ministry. Jesus moved and worked among the poor, the most marginalized in Galilee. He must have encountered many starving people. The desire to feed them must have been great. Is this not what this opportunity would mean? Food for the starving, life for the dying? Why then, would Jesus reject this?

Jesus's response that "one does not live by bread alone, but by every word that comes from the mouth of God" (Matt. 4:4) does not indicate that he is unconcerned with those who suffer from hunger; rather, it indicates that he views his mandate from God, his ministry, to involve a more sweeping and permanent change than would be achieved by acts of "magic" used to feed a few people.[21] He could probably have easily changed stones to bread. He could have done so wherever he went, feeding people and alleviating misery. But this fix would have been temporary. After all, the starvation in Jesus's day was not due to a shortage of food; it was due directly to the exploitative and oppressive policies of the state that bilked the peasants out of their subsistence in support of endless city-building, military campaigns, and lavish lifestyles for the ruling class and high-priestly families in charge of the temple. Providing bread magically would do nothing to change the foundational rot of this society. It would not change the material conditions that led to perpetual starvation. The only thing that would change these conditions would be a sweeping and far-reaching change in the hearts of the people. This is the change that Jesus sought to bring about.

---

20. C. S. Song, *Jesus, the Crucified People*, 166–67.
21. Song, 168–75.

The scene of the next temptation is the parapet of the temple. Jesus is tempted to throw himself down and wait for God to command angels to catch him. This act seems harmless enough, but what it signifies is Jesus again turning his ministry into a magic show. Only this time, rather than feeding a few people magically, the consequences would prove the undoing of history itself.

The context of Jerusalem for this temptation indicates the backdrop of the history of Israel as a nation. The temple in Jerusalem signified the promise of future fulfilment of the covenant God had made with Abraham. As far as Israel was concerned at the time of Jesus, this covenant was still in need of fulfilment. They looked for a political messiah, and Jesus could have been that person. But in diverting his ministry from one of struggle and solidarity with people to one of performative miracles, even ones that led to the liberation of Israel, he would have been betraying the people he meant to save.

"Emmanuel," a messianic title that Christians use for Jesus, means "God with us," indicating a God who stands by and struggles with the people (Matt. 1:23; Isa. 7:14). This God is made manifest in the struggles for liberation *and* in the liberation, but liberation without struggle would not be liberation. Freedom from bondage and oppression would not be so if there were no bondage and oppression. It is the struggle for liberation that defines it as such. It is the arc of history, defined by humanity's struggle for liberation from systems of oppression and exploitation, that comprises the course of God's justice. By throwing himself from the parapet, Jesus would have minimized the struggles for liberation that comprised the history of Israel.[22] By voiding the meaning of that history, Jesus would have also erased God from Israel's history. He would have placed himself over against God, who was manifest in Israel's long struggle for liberation. He would have been usurping the position of the God he was trying to manifest in his ministry.

In the final temptation, Jesus is shown "all the kingdoms of the world and their splendor" (Matt. 4:8). He is offered all this on the condition that he fall down and worship Satan. Again this appears to be Jesus struggling against a particular interpretation of what his ministry could involve. This time, it involves kingship. Whereas the temptation of the stones and the temple involved using his power to perform miracles, the final temptation involved using his power and influence to secure worldly power. But

---

22. Song, 178–80.

would this be so bad? Surely Jesus would be a king in the lineage and form of David, who was lionized for the way he did the will of God. He could use his kingship and power to free his people and to establish a just reign all over the world.

But what of the caveat? That little bit about worshipping Satan. While it may seem that this would just be a performative gesture, a bit of a trick Jesus could use to secure power with which to do good, in actuality it voids the possibility of using power in this way. In the larger temptation narrative, Satan can be thought to represent a number of different aspects. In the first two, he represents the pull to use God's power for performative purposes in ways that wow and amaze but do not leave lasting impressions or produce systemic change and instead cheapen humanity's suffering and struggle. In this third temptation, Satan represents the political and military means used to establish and maintain empire, the deaths of millions of innocents, the oppression that results from the pursuit of accumulation of wealth and solidifying of power, and the corrupting effect of having absolute power over people.

As shown in the empire of Egypt, the divided kingdoms of Israel's own history, Rome, and the imperial regimes of our own day, worldly kingdoms and power are not the instruments God uses to bring to pass divine purposes. God liberates people from these systems and institutions in order to fulfill these purposes. Even those who rely on power with good intentions inevitably use violence and repression to establish their power, and then almost invariably that power corrupts them (D&C 121:39). The good intentions of justice for all turn into vendettas against political enemies. The equity promised the people turns into oppression for the purpose of enriching the powerful and wealthy, and the quest for ever-expanding wealth and power spreads far and wide into nation after nation, corrupting governments, fomenting conflict and war, and oppressing and killing scores of innocent women, men, and children. In the end, worldly power in the form of kings and kingdoms depends on, and reproduces, Satanic systems and structures.[23] It is, as we saw in the previous chapter, the face of idolatry, and it is antithetical to the reign of God that Jesus preached and for which he worked. This connection to idolatry and the fundamental incompatibility of pursuit of worldly power with the work of God is made clear in Jesus's response to this temptation: "Away with you

---

23. The dramatization of the Garden of Eden story in our own temple endowment makes clear that wealth and power are used to create and maintain Satanic systems and structures of oppression, destruction, and death.

Satan! For it is written, Worship the Lord your God, and serve only him" (Matt. 4:10). Here, Jesus prefigures his later statement "you cannot serve God and wealth [mammon]" (6:24).

The Miracles

When the people heard that Jesus was back in Capernaum, so many gathered to hear him that there was no room for them in the house. In an extraordinary scene, four of them go up on the roof and dig a hole through in order to let down a paralytic man on a mat. "When Jesus saw their faith, he said to the paralytic, 'Son, your sins are forgiven'" (Mark 2:5). This leads to a confrontation with some scribes, who accuse Jesus of blasphemy: "Who can forgive sins but God alone?" (v. 7). Jesus, perceiving their accusation, responds with a miracle: "I say to you, stand up, take your mat and go to your home. And he stood up, and immediately took the mat and went out before all of them; so that they were all amazed and glorified God, saying, We have never seen anything like this!" (vv. 11–12).

We have just concluded above that Jesus rejected a ministry of magic. He looked to change the hearts of the people so that they themselves could bring about meaningful and lasting systemic change. So what do we make of this miracle and others like it? We often interpret this instance as further proof of the divinity of Jesus. After all, who but a divine being could perform miracles in this way? Or we use this story as a way to focus on faith. The people who brought the paralyzed man had so much faith that they figured out a way to get him before Jesus. If we have faith, we can come up with unique and interesting solutions to our problems. No doubt many have been nourished and uplifted by these interpretations. But if we consider the historical context in which Jesus is working and the way in which he viewed his own ministry, another interpretation seems clear.

Jesus, as we have said, was working firmly in the prophetic tradition of Israel. This tradition was focused on the covenant community. While many prophets directly challenged kings and prophesied destruction in order to wake up the rulers to the nature of their violation of their covenant obligations, Jesus seems to have taken a different approach. In the desert confrontation with the devil, he had already explicitly rejected a role as a messianic king in the lineage of David, a political savior for Israel. His focus, instead, was on proclaiming and bringing to pass the reign (or kingdom) of God. And for Jesus, the kingdom of God is not some future afterlife. He was not urging people to repent so they could be worthy to participate in such a kingdom. He was urging them to believe that the kingdom is already near. In fact, when asked when the kingdom of God was coming, Jesus answered, "The kingdom of God is not coming with things that can be observed; nor will they say, 'Look, here it is!' or 'There it is!' For, in fact, the kingdom of God is among you" (Luke 17:20–21). The Greek term for kingdom in this case is *basileia*, which denotes not a spatial or geographical location for the kingdom of God but a base or foundation upon which it is built.[24]

This pronouncement gets to the heart of Jesus's liberative approach to his ministry. As discussed in Chapter 1, a prophet's vocation is not only to tell the people what God would have them do. A prophet's job is to wake the people up to the possibility of a new reality and to call their attention to the true nature of things in their world. Prophets allow people to see things for what they really are and to envision ways to change things to encourage justice and help their communities flourish. By shifting the focus of the kingdom of God from some future point in time, Jesus is pulling such a prophetic move here. By saying that "the kingdom of God is among you," he is also hearkening back to God's covenant community with Israel—only now, he is reconstituting this community among the people. He is asking them to believe that the kingdom of God is not a place that they will inherit someday when they defeat their enemies. The kingdom of God is achieved anywhere that people live in present justice and equity.

If Jesus's goal for his ministry is to renew and reconstitute Israel as a covenant community then it will be crucial for him to help them recognize and remove any barriers that stand in the way of such a community. The healing of the paralytic is one of many such attempts to do this. Notice that first Jesus pronounces the man's sins forgiven. This action is what brings the ire of the scribes on him. The reason for this is that in Jesus's day, forgiveness of sins had been turned into a business. As discussed earlier, the original purpose of the sacrificial practices had been to solemnize the covenant and to keep the community clean from sin, but the temple in Jerusalem was now a center of economic activity. The people were required to pay a temple tax to maintain the sacrificial practice (and to sustain the lifestyle of the high priestly families). If they could not pay the tax or afford the time or money to travel to Jerusalem, they could not procure their sin offerings. If their sin offerings were not made,

---

24. This word can also be translated as "reign." Usage of this term rather than "kingdom" further clarifies this concept as referring to a type or quality of living in community rather than a location which is ruled by God.

they remained unclean. In the case of the perpetually unclean such as the paralytic, they would not even be offered the chance to participate in such ritual cleansing. Thus, due to poverty, illness, or disease, many people did not have access to the rituals that formalized the covenant community and bestowed divine favor. They were left on the outside, with no way in. When the people brought the paralyzed man to Jesus, they were setting up a clash with profound implications for the way the community understood their options for divine access and covenant belonging.

By pronouncing the man forgiven, Jesus assumed the role of the temple priest. He had no right to do this. He was not of priestly lineage; there has been no exchange of money, no sacrifice, but the man's sins were forgiven. The scribes rightly realized that the entire temple system hung in the balance. If Jesus could offer a way to forgiveness and divine favor that did not involve the temple, this would undermine everything. William Herzog elaborates, "When Jesus declares God's forgiveness of the paralytics sins (debts), he steps into the role of a reliable broker of God's forgiveness, and by simply assuming this role, challenges the brokerage house in Jerusalem called the temple."[25]

The scribes, realizing the seriousness of the situation, challenged Jesus and accused him of blaspheming in his pronouncement of God's forgiveness. In an act of defiance, Jesus asked the scribes, "Which is easier, to say to the paralytic, 'your sins are forgiven you,' or to say, 'stand up and take your mat and walk?'" (Mark 2:9). He then doubled down on his authority to pronounce God's forgiveness and healed the man.

The profound implications of Jesus's actions here cannot be overstated. This double move, of first forgiving and then healing, effectively unblocks all access to God. By bypassing the temple system of forgiveness, he opened up the way to receive and renew divine favor without the onerous tax and burden required for temple patronage. But moreover, by healing the man of his infirmity, Jesus placed him once again on the inside of the covenant community. The scribes were left without a leg to stand on. All the ways that the system they uphold sought to block access to God have been obliterated. In this miraculous act of healing, Jesus firmly announced his intention to remove boundaries and expand access to God's covenant community, effectively undermining the entirety of the institutional religious system. This radical agenda set him on a collision course with the ruling powers that inevitably led to his death.

---

25. Herzog, *Jesus, Justice*, 128.

So we can see here that Jesus's healings throughout the Gospels have as their goal the expanding of the covenant community by breaking down the barriers that the institutional religious system had placed between the poor and access to God. Those that had been placed on the outside through sickness or disease were reclaimed. Nowhere is this breaking of boundaries and expanding of the covenant community made more clear than in the healing of the woman with the issue of blood:

> And a large crowd followed him and pressed in on him. Now there was a woman who had been suffering from hemorrhages for twelve years. She had endured much under many physicians, and had spent all that she had; and she was no better, but rather grew worse. She had heard about Jesus, and came up behind him in the crowd and touched his cloak, for she said, "If I but touch his clothes, I will be made well." Immediately her hemorrhage stopped; and she felt in her body that she was healed of her disease. Immediately aware that power had gone forth from him, Jesus turned about in the crowd and said, "Who touched my clothes?" And the disciples said to him, "You see the crowd pressing in on you; how can you say 'Who touched me?'" He looked all around to see who had done it. But the woman, knowing what had happened to her, came in fear and trembling, fell down before him, and told him the whole truth. He said to her, "Daughter, your faith has made you well; go in peace, and be healed of your disease." (Mark 5:24–34)

In this remarkable account, usually referenced as a way to commend the faith of this woman, we have another example of Jesus utterly and completely rejecting the societal and religious customs and regulations that placed boundaries between the people, God, and the covenant community. No doubt the faith of the woman was incredible, but the symbolic import of this encounter goes far beyond a mere example of great faith. Indeed, this healing is exemplary of Jesus's whole attitude towards the prevailing societal and religious boundaries and purity culture which excluded so many from the covenant community.

The woman had been hemorrhaging for twelve years. Twelve years! She had spent all her money, had ruined herself financially in a fruitless pursuit of healing by physicians. In all this time, she would have been considered ritually unclean (Lev. 15:25), unable to participate in any temple ritual sacrifices, unable to receive forgiveness or purification from sin, and unable to participate in the community. She was shut out. There was no covenant community for her. She was considered barely human.

In touching Jesus, she again violated the purity prohibition, this time of bleeding women touching men. How dare she! Who did she think she was? And a man such as Jesus. A holy man. By touching him, she made him unclean. When he began scanning the crowd, surely she must have thought some punishment was in store for her. A scolding at least, but with a crowd such as this, accusations could easily turn into violence. Who would speak for her on her behalf?

In his brief but tender reply, Jesus upended the entire system of purity boundaries. He obliterated the boundaries placed on this woman: for being poor, for being a woman, and for bleeding as only a woman can bleed. He refused to undergo ritual purification, refused to shame and punish her, and refused to demand that she abide by the purity codes. By acknowledging her, searching for her in the crowd and publicly admitting and blessing the healing that had taken place at her initiative, he affirmed her social status, legitimated her audacious claim to her denied but rightful place in the covenant community, and reestablished her humanity in the eyes of the crowd.

This encounter is typical of Jesus's ministry of liberation. The blind, the lame, the deaf, the leprous, and even the dead were healed and reclaimed through his ministry of mercy. The eyes of the community were opened to the worth, long denied, of those on the outside, marginalized through circumstances beyond their control.

Jesus's ministry was about breaking through boundaries, reaching across lines of exclusion to include all in the covenant community. His own creation of an inclusive community via his table fellowship illustrates this. He shared meals with many throughout his ministry who were considered impure and unclean: tax collectors, prostitutes,[26] women, and sinners. Like much of his activity, this simple practice took on a profoundly combative aspect for the Pharisees, who rigidly enforced boundaries and purity codes at all times but especially at meals. "Jesus reclined with the impure and unclean, without apology or hesitation. He turned the meal into a different kind of community, but it had an edge."[27] Herzog further explains:

> When he does recline at table Jesus is acting out a different vision for Israel. He rejects the priestly model for purity and the table at the temple as the paradigms for the table at the village. He also rejects the barriers of purity and stigmas of impurity that would render his table companions unclean, indebted, or outside the fellowship of the true Israel.[28]

---

26. This term was a common insult and the "standard description for any women outside of the bounds of normal social convention or normal male control." Crossan, *Jesus: A Revolutionary Biography*, 111.

27. Herzog, *Jesus, Justice*, 153.

28. Herzog, 153–54; See also Crossan, *Jesus: A Revolutionary Biography*, 66–70.

Thus, in his table fellowship, Jesus was indicating that the covenant community is not an exclusive club; rather, it is a fellowship of any who desire to live together in love and harmony. His healing further demonstrated that there were no boundaries to inclusion in his community, the kingdom of God.

A large part of Jesus's healing work was the casting out of demons. This seems strange and foreign to us in our day. People possessed by evil spirits is not something that we commonly experience. So is it the case that more people suffered from possession in Jesus's day, or is there another way we can understand these occurrences?

One way to understand possession in Jesus's day that has much scholarly support is as mental or psychosomatic illness. The people at the time did not understand disease in terms of modern conceptualizations of the brain or of psychological and mental phenomena. Everything in life had a spiritual cause. This is why disease was taken as indicative of some type of sin on the part of the afflicted person, and the disease was evidence of God's punishment. (This is clearly evident in the account of Jesus healing the blind man in John 9:1–3.) Likewise, people who were afflicted with mental or neurological illness that caused them to behave in bizarre, unpredictable, self-injurious, or disruptive ways were taken to have an "unclean spirit." This is clearly the case in the healing of the boy with epilepsy, who is described as being "convulsed," "mauled," and "dashed to the ground" by a demon (Luke 9:40–44; Matt. 17:14–16). Thus, in one sense, Jesus's healing of "demoniacs" in the Gospels can be thought of as an extension of his general healing of physical ailments. The theme of liberation in these instances, in opposition to the possession of an individual by a malicious spirit with ill intent, is made stark and clear.

A closer examination of the accounts of exorcism when viewed through the lens of mental illness, however, can help us understand both the scope of the trauma inflicted by the oppression of the poor in Galilee and the community healing Jesus catalyzed through his exorcisms. In the Gospels, Jesus's exorcisms are mentioned more than any other type of specific healing activity, five times in total,[29] and Jesus explicitly ties his casting out of demons with his bringing in of the reign of God (Luke 11:20). It is clear that this activity threatens the religious establishment, as evidenced by the hostile response of the scribes who accused him of either exorcising by the

---

29. Paul W. Hollenbach, "Jesus, Demoniacs, and Public Authorities: A Socio-Historical Study," 567–88.

power of the devil or being possessed by a devil himself (Mark 3). What can be going on here?

Spirit possession is a universal cultural phenomenon, but it occurs reliably in certain social and political contexts. These contexts have been identified as those that are characterized by oppression and exploitation, scarcity of resources, uncertainty and violence, and high levels of tension between a wealthy ruling class and the poor.[30] As previously discussed, these are the conditions of the Galilean poor among whom Jesus ministered. While the specific psychological nature of spirit possession is unclear, it has been suggested to result from extreme stress produced by oppressive conditions. Historical sources indicate that Galilee and Judea at the time of Jesus were simmering with unreleased tension that boiled over into protests (and some revolts) at times of particularly egregious injustice. These protests were put down brutally, with thousands killed. The peoples under Roman military rule were intentionally exposed to campaigns designed to instill fear and submission. Richard Horsley explains

> In the countryside . . . Roman military conquests were intentionally and systematically brutal. The Roman legions purposely terrorized subject peoples in the "shock and awe" devastation of villages and their land, slaughter and enslavement of the people, and public crucifixion of any who dared lead resistance.[31]

Being exposed to this type of brutality and the constant threat of violence, and having no way to retaliate or appropriately process or alleviate the stress and trauma that accompanies it, are the conditions under which severely debilitating mental conditions (such as post-traumatic stress disorder (PTSD) and dissociative states) routinely manifest themselves. PTSD can manifest in a number of ways, including nightmares, flashbacks, increased reactivity to triggering events, depersonalization, dissociative states, risky or destructive behavior, aggression,[32] and a variety of somatic symptoms such as headaches, trouble breathing, and inability to regulate arousal.[33] Taking a step back from the clinical diagnostic framework and considering the circumstances and behavior of those in the Gospels who were viewed as being possessed by demons, the correspondence between the modern clinical conditions caused by trauma and

---

30. Witmer, *Jesus, the Galilean Exorcist*, 95–96; Hollenbach, "Jesus," 573–77.

31. Horsley, *The Prophet Jesus*, 80; see also Horsley, *Jesus and Empire*, 26–31.

32. American Psychiatric Association, *Diagnostic and Statistical Manual of Mental Disorders, Version 5*.

33. Linda Joelsson, "Exorcisms as Liberation: Trauma, Differentiation, and Social Systems in Luke."

chronic stress and the spirit possession described in the Gospels is striking. Indeed, as noted by Paul Hollenbach, "the most important criterion [for determining demonic possession] in first-century Palestine seems to be the radically divided self."[34]

The story of the healing of the man from the country near Gerasa (the Gerasene demoniac) serves as a dramatic and explicit example of the way that personal and collective trauma born of oppression and violence can combine to fracture and warp community and social relationships.[35] The account appears in Mark, Matthew, and Luke:

> They came to the other side of the sea, to the country of the Gerasenes. And when he had stepped out of the boat, immediately a man out of the tombs with an unclean spirit met him. He lived among the tombs; and no one could restrain him any more, even with a chain; for he had often been restrained with shackles and chains, but the chains he wrenched apart, and the shackles he broke in pieces; and no one had the strength to subdue him. Night and day among the tombs and on the mountains he was always howling and bruising himself with stones. When he saw Jesus from a distance, he ran and bowed down before him; and he shouted at the top of his voice, "What have you to do with me, Jesus, Son of the Most High God? I adjure you by God, do not torment me." For he had said to him, "Come out of the man, you unclean spirit!" Then Jesus asked him, "What is your name?" He replied "My name is Legion; for we are many." (Mark 5:1–9)

This account is chilling for the ways it describes the complete and total dehumanization of this man. If we stop our inquiry at demons, we need go no further. But if we inquire into the political history of this town of Gerasa, we uncover much more violence and can begin to see the kind of trauma that could drive someone to such extremes of existence. There are demons here, but, as is usually the case, they have a very human face.

The name this man gives, Legion, is telling. As noted earlier, Roman legions wreaked horrific damage and slaughter on the civilians in the countryside in their military campaigns. This town of Gerasa and the surrounding villages would be wiped out during the Jewish War several decades later. The Roman-Jewish historian Josephus records that the Roman general Vespasian

> sent Lucius Annius to Gerasa; and delivered to him a body of horsemen, and a considerable number of footmen. So when he had taken the city, which

---

34. Hollenbach, "Jesus," 570.

35. See Brian D. McLaren, *Do I Stay Christian? A Guide for the Doubters, the Disappointed, and the Disillusioned*, 115–19, for similar discussion.

he did at the first onset, he slew a thousand of those young men, who had not prevented him by flying away. But he took their families captive; and permitted his soldiers to plunder them of their effects. After which he set fire to their houses, and went away to the adjoining villages. While the men of power fled away, and the weaker part were destroyed; and what was remaining was all burnt down.[36]

Given the severity of this treatment, it seems that Gerasa was a hotbed of revolutionary sentiment. The area itself had been at the receiving end of military repression from a number of successive powers. As Walter Wink notes,

fiercely jealous of their right to mint their own coin and levy their own taxes, [they] had watched their freedoms be stifled, first by the Ptolemies, then by the Seleucids, then by the Jews, then by Herod. Their attitude towards Rome was ambivalent in the extreme.[37]

With many of the towns and villages opening their gates to the Romans in their march to Jerusalem, Gerasa kept theirs closed, forcing an assault on the town. Galilee was known for its anti-Roman sentiment and had a history of rebellions and banditry.[38] This social history of the area indicates that the region was peppered with revolt and repression, thus making it highly likely that residents were exposed to violence and suffered trauma.

What of the man possessed by a legion of demons? We do not know his particular history, but Leslie Weatherhead, in an imaginative reading of this passage, gives an indication of what could have transpired:

In the First World War a man was found in no-man's land, wandering about between our trenches and those of the enemy, and the only word he could say was "Arras." This was the town in which he had been tortured to make him impart information, and the torture had driven him mad. . . . Here in St. Mark's story, we have a man muttering the word "Legion," and it is not fanciful to suppose that he had suffered some shock at the hands of the Roman legion. We know from the story of the massacre of the innocents the kind of thing the Roman legion could do, and, indeed, it is possible that this patient had witnessed this dreadful affair. If he had seen tiny children slaughtered, and had rushed in from the sunny street terrified of the approaching soldiers whose swords were dripping red with blood, and had cried, "Mummy,

---

36. Flavius Josephus, *The Jewish War; or, the History of the Destruction of Jerusalem* 4.9.1.

37. Walter Wink, *Unmasking the Powers: The Invisible Forces that Determine Human Existence*, 44–45.

38. Richard A. Horsley, *Galilee*, chs. 1, 12.

Mummy, legion!" . . . then it would be no flight of imagination that the childhood's shock . . . would be quite sufficient to drive him into psychosis. And now the community had exiled the patient right out of the security of their own fellowship into a wild graveyard in a foreign land, where he is left to live amongst the pigs, terrified by spasms of fear which leap up from his repressed memories into consciousness, and express themselves in maniacal frenzies and in loud cries.[39]

While clearly embellished, this account imagines a plausible scenario of a childhood atrocity that, when combined with a life of poverty, exploitation, and oppression, finally pushes this man over the edge into a chronic mental health crisis.

While the name "Legion" could very well refer to a childhood trauma, it can also be viewed symbolically as an indication of the severity of oppression that was experienced by the Galileans under the Romans and their client kings. This existence constitutes a "death by a thousand cuts." According to Frantz Fanon, it is difficult to "appreciate the scope and depth of the wounds inflicted on the colonized during a single day under a colonial regime."[40] The societal order strips people of their identity. The Jews were already relocated from their Babylonian exile. Their tribal lands were no longer theirs. Any land they had was subject to exploitation or expropriation at the whim of the rulers. Their families were forced into wage labor, or slavery, or prostitution. It is easy to see how a childhood trauma, combined with a life repeatedly stripped of humanity, could lead someone to such a state. Thus, Legion is symbolic of the crushing weight of Empire, the oppression that dehumanizes, kills, and strips people of their humanity. The man has internalized the oppression visited upon him and countless other women, men, and children who have been swallowed by the Roman imperial machine. He has become a living manifestation of the long and ongoing history of his own personal and community trauma.

The community, unable to keep the man from lashing out in violence, banishes him to the tombs. Perhaps they were unwilling to face up to the trauma or the oppression that the man, and no doubt many of them, had lived through or faced on a daily basis. Wink suggests further that in the man, the community found a scapegoat for their own seething hatred of Roman and Herodian oppression, and they found in the paroxysms of the demoniac an outlet for their own repressed desires for violence, retalia-

---

39. Lesley D. Weatherhead, *Psychology, Religion, and Healing*, 65–66.
40. Frantz Fanon, *The Wretched of the Earth*, 182.

tion, and freedom.⁴¹ In this bizarre symbiosis, the community had found a way to periodically release the tension that was sure to boil over if not given some release valve—a boiling over that would have brought violent retaliation from the state if allowed to take its natural course.

When Jesus first commands the spirit to come out of the man, he is not successful. He then asks him for his name. In the ancient world, names possess power. To know the name of someone is to have power over that person or entity, or to enter into a relationship of trust with someone where both parties may be benefited but are also vulnerable. In situations of extreme oppression, such as the Roman colonization experienced by the Galilean peasants, Fanon further clarifies, "Because it is a systematized negation of the other, a frenzied determination to deny the other any attribute of humanity, . . . [this situation] forces the colonized to constantly ask the question: 'Who am I in reality?'"⁴² By asking him his name, Jesus entered into a genuine dialogue with the man. He did not try to restrain him or do him violence, as had his community all these years. He simply asked the man who he is, and by so doing, allowed the man to begin examining his own history of trauma and to reflect on what he had been made to become.

The demons begged Jesus not to "send them out of the country." The Romans, as symbolized here, had no desire to leave. They wanted only to continue their expansion and exploitation. In a move loaded with symbolic meaning, Jesus allowed the spirits to take possession of a nearby herd of pigs. These two thousand pigs, the real-life symbol of Roman excess and wealth, stampede off the cliff and drown in the waters below. This move can be seen as both Jesus's utter repudiation of the Roman colonial empire and a prophetic act of justice on behalf of the oppressed Galileans—an act that serves to inspire hope in a future freedom from oppression.

When the people came and found the man "clothed and sitting in his right mind, the very man who had had the legion; they were afraid" (Mark 5:15). They had heard about the pigs, an enormous economic loss for the Roman rulers. No doubt the retribution would be swift. More violence. More trauma. But the healed man also meant that the uneasy balance had been broken; the people now had to deal directly with their own trauma and repressed violent impulses. The reality of a history of trauma and oppression had to be faced, and Jesus provided the opening for healing to occur in the community, but, recognizing the emotional toll and effort it would take, the villagers were afraid and would rather go back to the

---

41. Wink, *Unmasking the Powers*, 45–46.
42. Fanone, *The Wretched*, 182.

way things were. They begged Jesus to leave, unwilling to face up to the task ahead. With their personal and community trauma brought to the surface, the real work of healing and reconciliation must begin. When the healed man begged to follow Jesus, Jesus refused him: "Go home to your friends, and tell them how much the Lord has done for you, and what mercy he has shown you" (v. 19). The man returned, a crucial role to play in the healing of his community in their journey to wholeness. "And he went away and began to proclaim in the Decapolis how much Jesus had done for him; and everyone was amazed" (v. 20).

Considering the healing of those possessed by demons in this light makes it clear why Jesus considered this work to be a critical part of his bringing in the reign of God. It also clarifies why the authorities were so concerned with his exorcising activities. Someone who is declared mad or demon-possessed faced no consequences or retaliation for vocally expressing their hatred of an occupying regime.[43] They were not a threat to the powers that be. This was important to the ruling class, including their retainers, among whom were the scribes and Pharisees, who held onto a tenuous agreement for power with the Romans which depended on maintaining law and order. They were allowed to remain in power as long as things didn't get out of control. This is likely why Jesus explicitly connected his exorcisms and healings with Herod's desire to kill him (Luke 13:31–32). Herod had heard of these healings and exorcisms, and of the public following they produced, and he recognized them as a threat.[44]

Furthermore, someone who reveals corruption or injustice could be labeled mad or demon-possessed by the authorities in order to delegitimize their criticisms and "shut them up." It is clear that this strategy was used by the ruling powers to control the poor and prevent dissent during Jesus's time.[45] By healing the demon-possessed in full view of massive crowds, in addition to bringing them once again into the covenant community, Jesus again pulled a double move with potentially disastrous consequences for the ruling powers. Those now loudly decrying the injustices of the state (including the temple state) could bring devastating retaliation on their communities by the authorities and could jeopardize

---

43. Hollenbach, "Jesus." See also Cheryl Pero, *Liberation from Empire: Demonic Possession and Exorcism in the Gospel of Mark*; Richard A. Horsley, *Jesus and the Politics of Roman Palestine*, ch. 4, for discussion of the social and political context of demonic possessions and exorcism in ancient Palestine.

44. Witmer, *Jesus, the Galilean Exorcist*, 30; Hollenbach, "Jesus," 569, 583–84.

45. Witmer, *Jesus, the Galilean Exorcist*, 27–31; Hollenbach, "Jesus," 577–79.

the power of the temple and high priestly rulers. Furthermore, given the highly public nature of these exorcisms, the once demon-possessed could not be demonized by the authorities to shut them up. A powerful method of social control was lost to them. No wonder that Jesus was accused of being himself possessed by demons or using the power of the devil in his own healings. His brazen flouting of the authorities could not stand unchallenged. His ministry of healing and reconciliation was pushing the fragile systems of domination to their breaking point. The reign of God was breaking through, and the people were beginning to see it.

The Parables

While Jesus's healing activity was meant to break down barriers and expand access to the covenant community, much of his teaching explicitly acknowledged the economic conditions of his followers and the strain these placed on their lives. The Lord's prayer has often been taken merely as a pattern for how to pray, but if we consider the lives of those who would have heard and offered this prayer, it is much more than a template for individualized adaptation. Indeed, it is, much like the psalms discussed above, a pleading for God's salvation, with nothing less than survival hanging in the balance.

> Our father in heaven,
> hallowed be your name.
> Your kingdom come,
> Your will be done,
> > on earth as it is in heaven.
> Give us this day our daily bread.
> And forgive us our debts,
> as we have also forgiven our debtors.
> (Matt 6:9–13)

The term that Jesus uses for God, *Abba*, is a term of trust and relationship that a child would use for a father. It could be thought of as similar to "Daddy" in English. This was an innovation specific to Jesus; it was not the way Galileans referred to God and has no precedent in Israel's history. As noted by Joachim Jeremias, "It would have seemed disrespectful, indeed unthinkable, to the sensibilities of Jesus's contemporaries to address God with this familiar word."[46] His usage of this referent indicates that Jesus experienced God not as some impersonal deity who looked on

---

46. Joachim Jeremias, *New Testament Theology: The Proclamation of Jesus*, 67.

creation with disdain and punished infractions harshly. Rather, God for Jesus is a God of relation. God is to be trusted and loved, not feared. Boundaries placed between God and humans were not instituted by God to keep divine honor or maintain divine purity; they were enforced by humans who failed to grasp the inclusive nature of God's kingdom. Thus, this way of referring to God seems to be less a teaching by Jesus about the specific character or attributes of God—that God is male and our literal father—than a reflection of his personal experience of intimate relationship with God.

In his prayer, Jesus addressed the very specific problems of hunger and debt that haunted the days and ruined the lives of his followers. Moreover, he tied the resolution of these problems to the advent of the kingdom of God. This hearkens back to his opening pronouncement where he proclaimed that he was bringing the "acceptable year of the Lord." This is a reference to the year of Jubilee (Lev. 25), a covenant stipulation where all land would be returned to its tribal families every fifty years to prevent inequality from becoming entrenched. In Jesus's day, these and other economic covenant obligations were either explicitly ignored or skirted via legal means. Here as well as in the Beatitudes, Jesus explicitly linked his ministry with a liberative purpose, a temporal renewal. Richard Horsley explains: "The petitions for sufficient food and (mutual) cancellation of debts in the prayer for the coming of the kingdom of God indicate just how concretely economic the renewal is understood to be."[47] His vision is a return to the covenant community where the hungry are fed, the debtor's debts forgiven, and their foreclosed fields and farms returned. Jesus's teachings thus often explicitly identify aspects of his follower's social situation that prevent them from realizing this community, and gives them instruction as to how to establish it. Horsley notes:

> To poor, hungry, mourning people who are "at each other's throats" in resentment over unrepaid loans, with insults and accusations, Jesus demands that they recommit themselves collectively to the covenantal principles and commandments of mutual cooperation and support in the village community.[48]

It is in this context that we can now begin to explore the meaning and purpose of the parables.

---

47. Horsley, *The Prophet Jesus*, 106.
48. Horsley, *The Prophet Jesus*, 127. See also Richard A. Horsley, *Covenant Economics: A Biblical Vision of Justice for All*, chs. 7–8.

In our church meetings and personal study, we often view the parables as stories told by Jesus to illustrate what the kingdom of God will be like. They are read as uncontroversial statements of ethics, little stories that turned traditional moral positions on their heads to show how God viewed the situation. The person in the privileged position (the lord, master, or king) is usually taken to be a representation of God, while those of lower status (the laborers and servants) are stand-ins for various groups of humans.

This framework makes the parables easy to approach, but it often renders the meanings obscure. There is an undercurrent of injustice to many of these parables that is often explained away by appealing to the difference between our moral standards and those of God. In this view, the obscurity is intentional, so that not everyone would understand. (I was taught that the reason why not everyone could understand is because if you were able to understand, you were accountable before God for a violation of the ethics described in the parable.) The parables from this perspective serve as coded ethical statements that reveal a higher moral standard for those able or enlightened enough to be able to see and grasp that standard.

This view of parables is convenient, if a little opaque, when we tend to extract them from their historical setting and view them through our modern lenses. We are helped in this reading by the fact that the Gospel writers often frame the parables in terms of their being an illustration of the kingdom of God. But many scholars agree, based on a number of different types of historical and textual analyses, that this framing is likely not authentic to the original parable.[49] Thus, we are left with a conundrum. On the one hand, the parables as written and interpreted seem to say one thing, but the reality of the nature and focus of Jesus's ministry seems to beg for another interpretation.

If we really believe Jesus's ministry was to liberate the Galilean peasants from oppression and exploitation, what good would be accomplished from an existential reading of the parables as an illustration of some abstract "kingdom of God" to come at some point in the future? Jesus was deeply concerned about the lives of the poor, oppressed, and exploited he ministered to. What role did parables play for these people? How did they relate to the "good news" of the gospel as hoped for? Most importantly for the present study, can we see how Jesus worked through the parables towards liberation and salvation for these people?

---

49. William R. Herzog II, *Parables as Subversive Speech: Jesus as Pedagogue of the Oppressed*, ch. 3.

Viewed through Jesus's overall ministry of liberation, the parables served a crucial purpose: *revealing the reality of the world of oppression the people lived in.* In ancient societies, as today, it wasn't easy for a small minority of the population to maintain rule and control over a large majority. This required propaganda on a large scale, and religious organizations played this role by casting the rulers as divinely appointed and maintained. Recall the function of the religious authorities in Egypt. Kings and pharaohs were divinely appointed to their roles, as were the poor and slaves. This view was propagated in all facets of life. Teaching and training by religious and public leaders, court rulings, and interpretations of laws all served to institutionalize the message that society was divinely ordered this way.

Most insidiously, peasants were taught to blame themselves for their lot in life and their misery. The rich were rulers because of their superior intellect or moral fiber; the poor were poor because of their inferior morality and lack of drive. Paired with a belief in purity codes that cast the very conditions to which poverty gives rise as sin, and what you get is "internalized oppression"—a situation in which the reality of oppression and exploitation is not seen for what it is. As James Cone writes, "Often the poor internalize the values of their victimizers, thereby closing their consciousness to the events of freedom in their history."[50] In this situation, as noted by André LaCocque, "Liberation implies . . . a clear vision of what, for the time being, is obscure, an opening, on what is, momentarily, closed off."[51] This clarity was sorely needed by the Galilean poor whom Jesus hoped to awaken to the reality of their situation. His parables "codify systems of oppression in order to unveil them and make them visible to those victimized by them."[52]

Jesus's strategy in his parables is nuanced and varied, and we cannot detail all of them here (those interested in more detailed analyses should see the masterful treatment in William Herzog's *Parables as Subversive Speech*).[53] What we can say is that the parables often present little "slices of life" in the day of a member of Galilean society. These vignettes often juxtapose those of different social classes in economic situations. What may not be obvious to those of us unfamiliar with the workings of society in his day is that Jesus's parables place members of the ruling class opposite those they are exploiting in scenarios that would never happen, as presented, in

---

50. James H. Cone, *God of the Oppressed*, loc. 1926 of 5313.
51. André Lacocque, *The Book of Daniel*, 44.
52. Herzog, *Parables*, 87; see also Paulo Freire, *Pedagogy of the Oppressed*.
53. What follows in this section draws heavily from Herzog's work.

real life. This unrealistic juxtaposition serves to explicitly illustrate both the identity of the oppressor, and the nature of the oppression of those in the peasants' situation.

We can get a good idea of how viewing parables through a liberative lens shifts the meaning by considering two of the most well-known examples: the laborers in the vineyard and the wicked tenants. The parable of the laborers in the vineyard has usually been interpreted as an illustration of the generous economy of God. All who labor in the kingdom will receive a generous reward, regardless of when they join in the work. This interpretation is based off assuming that the owner of the vineyard represents God. If this is the case, the other major players fall right into place. But as mentioned above, we must resist the temptation to cast God in the role of the wealthy landowner and consider the fact that Jesus would have been very familiar with the social positions and roles of those he cast in the parable. If we take the parable as a snapshot in the daily life of one of Jesus's followers, it takes on a much different character.

We can start by understanding the key actors. First is the "landowner." In Jesus's day, "the owners of great estates increased their holdings through foreclosures on loans, leading to hostile takeovers of peasant farms."[54] Those peasants who still owned small parcels of land worked it for their subsistence and that of their families. A vineyard was an altogether different undertaking in this economy. Herzog explains,

> vineyards were most likely owned by elites because they produce a crop that can be converted into a luxury item (wine), monetized, and exported. A vineyard also represents a major capital investment during the initial four years of its existence when it is not bearing fruit but requires constant tending.[55]

To the peasants in Jesus's day, a vineyard was an immediate symbol of an illegitimate landgrab and profit accumulation at the expense of subsistence of the poor. Thus, even before the story begins, Jesus already situates the landowner in a familiar position as a member of the wealthy ruling class who makes his living by exploiting peasants.

Next are the laborers. These are those whose farms had been foreclosed and whose families had been broken up in an effort to simply find a way to survive. In a society where land ownership and control was the primary means of generating income, the vast majority (around 70 percent) of individuals subsisted by working and cultivating the land. Given

---

54. Herzog, *Parables*, 85.
55. Herzog, 85.

that the rulers already controlled the product of the land, those who were reduced further to the status of tenant farmers or wage laborers were in a particularly precarious position. Under normal conditions, they were barely able to produce enough to survive, given the demanding taxes and tributes that the ruling elites extracted. If their means of working for subsistence were taken in foreclosure, they "were left with nothing left to sell but their bodies or their animal energies" or reduced to the level of "expendables."[56] These were the children of people who could no longer survive on the meager living provided by the household. Fathers and mothers were "forced to send their children into the streets as itinerant day laborers who might work during harvest or planting season but had to beg the rest of the year."[57] Herzog further explains,

> The presence of expendables was the inevitable outcome of a system driven by unbridled greed. As the elites squeezed the dwindling resources of their peasant base, they forced households to exile their children into the most degrading and lethal form of poverty. For the expendables, life was brutal and brief; characteristically, they lasted no more than five to seven years after entering this class.[58]

The laborers in this parable are desperate people who have no other means of subsistence. They are reduced to competing with one another for the same jobs. Little wonder that they are standing around all day, hoping against hope to find some work.

In a symbolic rhetorical move, Jesus has the wealthy landowner himself go to the square to recruit laborers. This serves the function of revealing the true face of the economic exploitation in the parable. Normally, elites would send their retainers or stewards to hire laborers; going themselves was beneath them. This must have been a purposeful move by Jesus, which served to pull the veil back on the bureaucratic shield that normally concealed the wealthy elite's participation in the systems of oppression and exploitation.

The landowner "agrees" with the laborers for a usual daily wage. It should be obvious from the description of the desperation of the position of the itinerant laborers that these individuals possess no bargaining power. The wealthy set the wage, which was constantly being depressed because of the masses of people being forced into looking for work, and the laborers had to choose to take whatever was offered to them or starve.

---

56. Herzog, 65.
57. Herzog, 65.
58. Herzog, 66.

Jesus and the Reign of God: Salvation as Covenant Community

The landowner returns to the square several times to hire more laborers, always promising them that he will pay them "whatever is right."

At the end of the day all the laborers receive the same wage.[59] This is a kick in the teeth to those who have been working the longest in the hot sun: "These last worked only one hour, and you have made them equal to us who have borne the burden of the day and the scorching heat" (Matt. 20:12). The landowner asserts his superiority in his reply: "Friend, I am doing you no wrong; did you not agree with me for the usual daily wage?" (v. 13). As Herzog explains, the term translated as "friend" here does not denote true friendship or an equal relationship of respect. Instead, "it is condescending and subtly reinforces their different social stations, yet feigns courtesy."[60] "Take what belongs to you and go," the laborer is told. The threat implied here is clear. "The spokesperson has been banned, shunned, blackballed, or blacklisted; he will not likely find work in that neighborhood again. This is no casual 'go in peace' as some would have it, but a final fatal dismissal."[61]

Further humiliating the laborers, the landowner says, "Am I not allowed to do what I choose with what belongs to me? Or are you envious because I am generous (is your eye evil because I am good)?" (Matt. 20:15). In this situation, in which peasants may very likely have been forced to work on a vineyard that was created from their own foreclosed fields and farms, the landowner has subtly yet firmly affirmed his superior status and the fact that the laborers have no other options. Theirs is not the relationship of bargaining between employer and employee. The landowner holds all the cards and calls all the shots. They can do nothing but work for him for a poverty wage. He knows it, and they know it. His "generosity" amounts to little more than the ability to exploit without consequence.

With this type of relationship and animosity between tenants, laborers, and landowners, is it any wonder then that the parable of the "wicked" tenants unfolds as it does? Without belaboring the point, here we have "the takeover of peasant land and its subsequent conversion into a vineyard."[62] Right away, given what we know about how society is structured, we can be sure that the conditions of tenancy favor the landowner in the extreme.

---

59. Although the exact amount of the wage, a *denarius*, is hard to specify, it likely was little more than a subsistence wage for an individual, let alone a family.
60. Herzog, *Parables*, 92.
61. Herzog, 93.
62. Herzog, 104.

When the landowner sends his servant to extract the profit from the vineyard, the tenants "beat him, and send him away empty-handed" (Luke 20:10). This goes on with the tenants refusing to pay a series of servants—"some they beat, and others they killed"—until finally the landowner sends his son. The tenants recognize the son as the heir, and they kill him in an effort to secure the vineyard for their own inheritance—a clearly futile pursuit, but one no doubt driven by desperation. The ominous "What then will the owner of the vineyard do?" (v. 15) ends the parable on a note of destruction and death for the tenants. Such brutal repression was the foregone conclusion of any such revolts.

Setting aside the traditional interpretation of this parable as a history of Israel culminating in the death of Jesus (there is ample reason to suspect this as a theological move by the writers of the Gospels), what is illustrated here is a "spiral of violence" that is a natural outcome of a social situation where one class is exploited to the point of no other alternatives. Herzog elaborates

> The eruption of violence reinforces the reading of the opening scene of the parable.... If peasants resorted to violence only when their subsistence was threatened, then the conversion of land from farmland to a vineyard would be an event that would trigger just such a response.... Having been forced beyond the narrow parameters required for their survival, they had no choice but to rebel. It is one such small rebellion that is codified in this parable.[63]

This way of reading these parables is jarring at the least, and it might seem heretical or even blasphemous given how used we are to identifying the landowner with God. But if we think about the tone and tenor of Jesus's ministry, suddenly it begins to make sense. This was not a way for Jesus to describe what awaited his followers in their next life or to sketch an abstract history of Israel. This was Jesus, concerned as always with the material and temporal conditions of those he ministered to, trying to help them see past their internalized oppression and make clear the true nature of the oppressive system they lived under. Jesus is pulling a prophetic move of showing them the true nature of reality in an effort to allow them to envision a new reality and work towards it. "He who has ears to hear, let him hear."

When we can begin to see through this lens, like falling dominos the parables start to open themselves up as coded illustrations of the domination and oppression systems of Jesus's day. The parable of the sower (Matt. 13) becomes a scathing indictment of those who "eat up, scorch, and choke" the peasant's seeds and means of subsistence, countered by

---

63. Herzog, 107–8.

the vision of the abundance with which God has blessed the land if God's statutes and economic policy is followed. The parable of the talents (Matt. 25) becomes a story of trickle-down exploitation. Given the only means to generate wealth was to exploit those on whom its extraction depended, the usual villain of the story who buries his talent becomes the only servant who refuses to exploit his fellow peasants. The parable of the unjust servant (Luke 16) illustrates both the cutthroat reality of the situations the people were forced into and the degeneration of the societal and communal bonds that results.[64]

Given the extremity the people were forced into, it's no wonder that many chose violence. But the parable of the wicked tenants decisively illustrates the futility of violent revolt as a means to produce lasting change. All that results is a downward spiral into more violence. The kingdom of God will not come in this way. It must come via the establishment of covenant communities. Even in their extremity, the people must pledge themselves to the way of communal living and debt forgiveness, establishing a safe haven for one another. Jesus's way is not one of violent revolt, but one of nonviolent resistance in the form of an ever-expanding covenant community of love that eventually envelops even the oppressors and exploiters.

The Cross and the Empty Tomb

Jesus's Galilean ministry was problematic for the religious authorities, and they kept a close eye on his movement among the people. But when his political activity reached its pinnacle in his protest at the temple, they knew they had to act. Judea was already under direct Roman rule, and their temple privileges were hanging on by a thread. If their religious beliefs and practices constituted a political threat to Rome, they feared the worst. Jesus had already publicly undermined the institutional religious hegemony by his healings and exorcisms, his table fellowship with the refuse of society voided the purity codes, and his forgiveness pronounced on adulterers and the ritually unclean rendered the temple sacrifices unnecessary.

But the public assault on the temple constituted an attack of a different order. This represented the culmination of his prophetic movement. Up until this point, Jesus had unveiled the true nature of the oppression facing his followers, but now he was close to pulling the most dangerous move of all—one that would once and for all reveal the corruption and greed of what the temple system had become. There would be no going

---

64. Herzog, *Jesus, Justice*, 158; Herzog, *Parables*, chs. 8–9.

back from this if Jesus pulled it off. If he equated the corruption and oppression of the people directly with the temple, the high priests, and temple administrators, the tenuous hold the rulers had over the people would be severed. The divine sanction for the status quo would be undermined beyond recovery.

We don't really know what pushed Jesus into a physical confrontation at the temple. Perhaps it was seeing in person the corrupt machine that the temple had become. The incident of the widow's mite (Mark 12; Luke 21), which occurs directly before the temple cleansing, has often been interpreted as indicative of the widow's faith, but it also signifies the way the temple had been turned into a propaganda machine that was used to exploit and bilk the poor out of their subsistence and livelihood. While usually interpreted as a commendation of the widow's faith, Jesus's response can also be read as disgusted disbelief at the corruption of a religious system that would take a widow's last means of subsistence in the name of piety. Whatever the cause, Jesus explicitly invokes the prophecy of Jeremiah as the reasoning for his attack on the temple, making it clear that it is the high priests who are to blame for the corruption which has made a mockery of the covenant and ruined the poor: "It is written, 'My house shall be called a house of prayer'; but you are making it a den of robbers" (Matt. 21:13). Jeremiah had castigated the people for holding up the piety of their temple sacrifices and worship while abandoning the poor to ruin.

> Thus says the Lord of hosts the God of Israel: Amend your ways and your doings and let me dwell with you in this place. Do not trust in these deceptive words: "This is the temple of the Lord, the temple of the Lord, the temple of the Lord." For if you truly amend your ways and your doings, if you truly act justly with one another, if you do not oppress the alien, the orphan, and the widow, or shed innocent blood in this place, and if you do not go after other gods to your own hurt, then I will dwell with you in this place, in the land that I gave of old to your ancestors forever and ever. (Jer. 7:3–7)

Jeremiah was not the only prophet to call Israel out for prioritizing worship over justice. Isaiah, Hosea, and Amos had all forcefully conveyed that God was more concerned with justice than formal worship: "What to me is the multitude of your sacrifices" (Isa. 1:11), "I hate, I despise your festivals" (Amos 5:21), "I desire steadfast love and not sacrifice" (Hosea 6:6). The word of these prophets makes it unequivocally clear, according to Marcus Borg and John Crossan, that "God insisted not just on justice *and* worship, but on justice *over* worship. God had repeatedly said, 'I reject your worship because of your lack of justice,' but never, ever, ever, 'I reject your justice because of your lack of worship.'"⁶⁵ Through Jeremiah, God had threatened to destroy the temple because it had become "a den of robbers" (Jer. 7:11), calling the people to remember the destruction of the seat of the ark of the covenant by the Philistines:

> Go now to my place that was in Shiloh, where I made my name dwell at first, and see what I did to it for the wickedness of my people Israel. And now, because you have done all these things, says the Lord, and when I spoke to you persistently, you did not listen, and when I called you, you did not answer, therefore I will do to the house that is called by my name, in which you trust, and to the place that I gave to you and to your ancestors, just what I did to Shiloh. (Jer. 7:12–14)

To the people who would have been very familiar with the history of Israel and the disastrous consequences of its idolatry, Jesus invoking this specific line of prophecy would have clearly been seen as a repudiation of what the temple had become.⁶⁶ In this context, his action in the temple and his own pronouncement of its destruction can be considered "a prophetic sign of God's judgment on it."⁶⁷ It would have been considered a legitimate political threat by the ruling powers. They knew how popular he was and how much of a following he had. If he whipped his followers into a frenzy, it might prove disastrous. The entire system hung in the balance. If the people revolted against the temple, thus destabilizing the Jewish kingdom, Roman retribution would come down like a hammer.

So he had to die. It was better to "have one man die for the people than to have the whole nation destroyed" (John 11:50). The chief priests and temple administrators were, of course, more concerned with their own lives and lavish lifestyles than with the nation as a whole. The temple was their means of prosperity, and if the Romans clamped down on it due to revolt or political threat, their lives of luxury and power would be over. In the final analysis, setting aside all the theological import and implications his death has been accorded over the centuries, from the perspective of the ruling authorities, killing Jesus was an easy political calculation.

So what was the significance of this death? In many ways, Jesus was no different than others who had dared to question or fight against the ruling

---

65. Marcus J. Borg and John Dominic Crossan, *The Last Week: A Day-by-Day Account of Jesus's Final Week in Jerusalem*, 44.

66. This interpretation is in contrast to the common reading of Jesus's anger at the money changers as being due to them "doing business" in the temple, thereby desecrating the sanctity of the house of God.

67. Herzog, *Jesus, Justice*, 143.

powers. Certainly that's how the religious authorities viewed him: a threat to their power. His death to them was putting out a fire, stamping out an annoyance before it grew into something unmanageable.

But what of Jesus's followers? How did they view his death? The biblical record does not give much information on this count. We must read between the lines to feel the humanity of the situation. We can only imagine the devastation that they felt watching what transpired in Jerusalem. The crucifixion was attended by a large crowd, as was customary at public executions. The apostles were not present, no doubt in hiding somewhere.

> There were also women looking on from a distance; among them were Mary Magdalene, and Mary the mother of James the younger and Joses, and Salome. These used to follow him and provide for him when he was in Galilee; and there were many other women who had come up with him to Jerusalem. (Mark 15:40–41)

Many of these women had been healed at Jesus's hands. Many of them would have been included in his table fellowship and had shared meals with him. Given the low status of women in ancient Palestine, his inclusion of them in his daily life and ministry would have been nothing short of life changing. After having been taught and treated as lesser their whole lives, here was a man who treated them as an equal and who cared nothing for the religious and social customs that denied them their basic humanity. In his eyes, they had value. Jon Sobrino notes: "Jesus has not only given new value to their existence in a patriarchal society but has called them to be disciples."[68] Furthermore, according to Amanda Witmer, "Their restoration to health and wholeness implied a change to their social status. By taking the women into his group, Jesus provided an alternative community for them and perhaps also began the process of defining a new type of community."[69]

---

68. Jon Sobrino, *Christ the Liberator: A View from the Victims*, 62.

69. Witmer, *Jesus, the Galilean Exorcist*, 141. Elizabeth Schüssler Fiorenza, *In Memory of Her: A Feminist Theological Reconstruction of Christian Origins*, argues that one of the reasons why early Christianity was so appealing to women was because it called believers into a fellowship of equals, where both women and men officiated at church, performed baptism and eucharist, and prophesied and served as apostolic witnesses of the divinity of Jesus Christ. It was this equality that contributed to the persecution of the church due to its unwillingness to submit to the patriarchal mode of the family and society. This tension led to the eventual subordination of women in the church, and the familiar "house

Aside from those who had followed him and shared in his daily life and ministry, many had looked to him as a promised Messiah—a political savior who would deliver them from Roman occupation. His death must have been a crushing blow to their hopes. Some small measure of the depth of loss is captured in the brief statement of those walking on the road to Emmaus: "But we had hoped that he was the one to redeem Israel (*to set Israel free*)" (Luke 24:21).

If, as discussed above, Jesus viewed his own ministry through the lens of the prophetic Israelite tradition of liberation, how did he view his death? What significance did he attach to it? As his ministry led to more and more confrontation with the religious authorities, he must have sensed that the conflict would eventually lead to his death. He must have known that the powers that be would not stand for an all-out assault on them without retaliation. He already knew what had happened to John the Baptist. As Jesus systematically dismantled the boundaries erected by the temple state in his ever-expanding covenant community, he must have felt the darkness closing in. Towards the end, he speaks more and more frequently of his impending death. We can be certain that it was ever on his mind.

Jesus's words at the Last Supper give us some indication of the way he viewed the significance of his life and death. There, he gathered his disciples together for one last meal, where he washed their feet and offered them bread as a symbol of his broken body and wine as a symbol of his "blood of the covenant, which is poured out for many" (Matt. 26:28). If we consider these words in relation to the content of Jesus's life and ministry, what can we conclude that Jesus thought about his own death? Jon Sobrino offers some thoughts, no less profound for their apparent simplicity:

> According to this whole [Gospel] tradition, at the supper Jesus interprets his own death as service, the continuation and culmination of his life. His death is not, therefore, absurd and useless, either for him or for others. Jesus directly offers to all people the meaning of a life of service, and this is what he proposes to his disciples.[70]

In the days and weeks following Jesus's death, many of his followers experienced resurrection events. They experienced powerful and personal manifestations of the risen Christ. In a profound symbolic move, Jesus returns to Galilee following his resurrection to teach and spend time with

---

codes" in the New Testament, where women are commanded to submit to their husbands, silenced in church, and stripped of their authority.

70. Jon Sobrino, *Jesus the Liberator: A Historical Theological Reading of Jesus of Nazareth*, 203.

his followers. This was where it all began, but now their old worldview had been shattered and a new reality had taken hold. No longer did they look for the kingdom of God as a political upheaval; they understood that lasting change, both personal and political, could come as communities worked together to care for one another. No longer content to wait for deliverance from a distant or future God, they realized that their real salvation lay in the new worldview that Jesus had gifted them: the good news of the gospel.

Jesus's resurrection vindicated his life and mission. He had worn out and, in the end, given his life in the service of the poor, the marginalized, the rejected, the unclean, and those outside of the boundaries of the covenant community. His ministry was to bring them into the fold of that community. By resurrecting Jesus, God puts a final, incredible stamp of approval on his entire life and ministry. It confirms that Jesus's way is God's way. It confirms God as a god for the poor and oppressed, and by so doing affirms explicitly the full humanity and right to life of those whom Jesus championed.

Jesus's resurrection also serves as an explicit repudiation by God of the temple state and the Roman authorities who conspired to kill Jesus. He had rejected their purity codes and oppressive practices during his life, claiming authority from God to do so. By resurrecting Jesus, God once and for all laid to rest any claims of the divinity of the temple authorities or Roman imperial rulers. Jon Sobrino captures this meaning: "Resurrection, therefore, means first and foremost doing justice to a victim, not merely giving new life to a corpse. . . . It refers not simply to a death, but to a cross; not simply to dead people, but to victims; not simply to a power, but to a justice."[71]

The Crucified People of the World

In the final analysis, what more can be said about Jesus's death and resurrection? Millions of words, thousands of pages have been spent in trying to parse out its meaning. For many in the world today, the cross of Jesus is not merely symbolic but experienced as a daily reality. They desperately need saving. For them Jesus's life, death, and resurrection provide hope for salvation in their own lives. He becomes, according to C. S. Song,

> Christ who is born, lives, heals, comforts, saves, dies, and rises again, not only once, not only ten times, not only a thousand times, but as many times as there are people who have to be healed of their ailments, who long to be

---

71. Jon Sobrino, *No Salvation Outside the Poor: Prophetic-Utopian Essays*, 102.

Jesus and the Reign of God: Salvation as Covenant Community   81

saved from their misery, who need to be given power to live in the midst of suffering, and who seek the assurance of life in the face of death.[72]

Throughout history as in the time of Jesus, there have been and will always be the poor, the oppressed, the marginalized. As one of these, Jesus resisted the powers that would destroy the lives and livelihood of those outside the circle of influence, those not privileged with wealth and power. Jesus took on these powers head-on, and he was killed by them on a cross reserved specifically for the public torture, execution, and humiliation of political criminals. There could be no mistaking the symbolism here. The state mobilized its forces to crush a political threat to its power and domination.

The similarities between the life and death of Jesus and those billions throughout history and in the world today who suffer poverty, starvation, oppression, torture, and murder at the hands of the powerful are stark and sobering. Jon Sobrino, whose colleagues and collaborators were executed by the Salvadoran military, compares these suffering people to none other than Jesus himself. Through a profound and moving reflection on human suffering and Paul's metaphor of the body of Christ, he asserts that the "crucified peoples" of history are literally the crucified body of Christ in the world:

> The crucified peoples are those who fill up in their flesh what is lacking in Christ's passion, as Paul says about himself. They are the actual presence of the crucified Christ in history, as Archbishop Romero [one of the Salvadoran martyrs] said to some terrorized peasants who had survived a massacre: "You are the image of the pierced savior." These words . . . mean that in this crucified people Christ acquires a body in history and that the crucified people embody Christ in history as crucified.[73]

This interpretation flips the traditional logic of salvation on its head and deepens our understanding. Rather than viewing Jesus's death as a means to bring about individual salvation, we can see his torture and death reflected in the lives of those who suffer needlessly in the world at the hands of the rich and powerful. Those poor who Jesus served and blessed in his life have become the living symbol of his suffering and death. Again from Sobrino: "the crosses of history are a mediation of the cross of Jesus. And, importantly, through being real, they lead to its reality."[74] His salvation then becomes not just a once for all time event, but an ongoing historical

---

72. Song, *Jesus, the Crucified People*, 218.
73. Sobrino, *Jesus the Liberator*, 255. See also Oscar Romero, *Voice of the Voiceless: The Four Pastoral Letters and Other Statements*, 182.
74. Sobrino, *Christ the Liberator*, 228.

reality. His broken body, symbolized in the bread he tore and offered to the disciples at the last supper and which we partake in our own sacrament, becomes incarnated in the broken, starving, and suffering poor in the world. Our promise to "always remember him" takes on a different meaning when the broken and "dis-membered" body of Christ has a physical face and requires a literal "re-membering" or being put back together in its brokenness. Though taken as a metaphor in its usual reading, this interpretation casts Jesus's words regarding the righteous in a stark new light:

> for I was hungry and you gave me food, I was thirsty and you gave me something to drink, I was a stranger and you welcomed me, I was naked and you gave me clothing, I was sick and you took care of me, I was in prison and you visited me. Then the righteous will answer him, "Lord, when was it that we saw you hungry and gave you food, or thirsty and gave you something to drink? And when was it that we saw you a stranger and welcomed you, or naked and gave you clothing? And when was it that we saw you sick or in prison and visited you?" And the king will answer them, "Truly I tell you, just as you did it to one of the least of these my brethren, you did it to me." (Matt. 25:35–40)

When all is said and done, Jesus gave his life in the service of humanity, however we choose to interpret the specifics. By so doing, he showed us all how to be truly human. To love one another, to champion the poor, the oppressed, and the marginalized. To show mercy. To give voice to the voiceless. To struggle against the powers of the world that would deny any their humanity or erect boundaries which compromise the full and inclusive community of love that comprises the kingdom of God. His life of service reaches out across the centuries as the perfect example of how to manifest God's love in the world. He is the crucified millions who suffer and the resurrected hope of liberation. This love and liberation is both the promise and the responsibility of the salvation he offers. He invites us to "Go and do thou likewise" (Luke 10:37).

> This Jesus who concentrated his life on proclaiming and building the Kingdom of God for the poor, who showed ultimate mercy to them, who for defending the victims of this world faced up to his executioners and ended up as a victim himself, who through all this placed himself face to face with God and placed God before us—this Jesus is liberation and good news for the poor and for all those who seek to be human in this world.[75]

---

75. Sobrino, *Jesus the Liberator*, 272.

Chapter 3

Christian History: Salvation Turns Personal

[The church] did not look first at the creature's suffering, but at his guilt.
— Johannes Baptist Metz

To the ancient Israelites, God had demonstrated salvation in liberation—from bondage in Egypt, from other kingdoms and powers during the formative years of the nation of Israel, and from their enemies during the reigns of the kings. This salvation was an honoring of the covenant God had made with Abraham. God had chosen to enter into a special relationship with Israel, and the history of the Old Testament shows that even through the twists and turns of wars, idolatry, suffering, and trauma, God is ever willing to honor this commitment to this relationship.

Jesus showed again the temporal character of God's salvation. His ministry was focused on helping the people envision and bring to pass the reign of God. This involved setting out clearly the political, economic, and religious systems and conditions that were keeping them from flourishing and living in full relationship with God. He gave them eyes to see a better way of living in mercy and justice one with another. His death had revealed the corruption and true face of the political powers of the nation and temple state, and his resurrection vindicated his ministry and vision of the reign of God, giving his followers a sure foundation upon which to build their early communities. His gospel was to extend the boundaries of the covenant community to those who had been denied membership by social, political, or religious custom.

How did the understanding of salvation in these expansive, liberative terms come to be interpreted as Jesus being offered to God as a sacrifice to pay the price for our individual sins, thereby taking our just-deserved divine punishment, and reserving an individual spot for us in heaven? The history and evolution of ideas about Jesus, sin, atonement, and salvation is complex and beyond the scope of this book. For much of the early period of Christianity, there was no uniform doctrine of salvation.[1] In

---

1. Justin S. Holcomb, ed., *Christian Theologies of Salvation: A Comparative Introduction*.

general, theologians were predominantly engaged in specifying the nature of God and especially of Jesus.[2] Theological inquiry was occupied with questions as follows: was Jesus divine, was he human, was he both human and divine, how was this possible, and what did it say about who and what God was? Theologians and church officials were more concerned with hammering out the shape of divine orthodoxy and with rebutting, refuting, and punishing views they found heretical than in exploring the specific character of salvation.[3] Thus, during these formative centuries,

---

2. The first few decades after Jesus's crucifixion and resurrection saw a move away from considering him as the fulfilment of the Jewish hope for a prophet, high priest, king, or political figure who acted as the mediator of God's salvation for the nation of Israel. This understanding and hope had been signified by the terms *Messiah* and *Son of Man* throughout the Old Testament. Early Christians began to adopt the position, influenced by Greek religious and philosophical thought, of Jesus as an eternal divine being who was able to effect salvation apart from God and ought to be worshipped and revered in his own right. This shift saw the increased usage of the terms *Son of God* and *Lord* (along with increased acceptance of Jesus as the personification of the *logos*, an idea which bridged Judaic and Hellenic understandings and tradition) within Christian communities and the reinterpretation of the prophetic tradition of Israel to conform to the developing Christian interpretation of Jesus's life and mission. This shift also corresponded with and was hastened by the confusion and disappointment of the failure of the *parousia* (second coming) to occur in the years shortly following Jesus's ascension. The hope for salvation was shifted from a present-day kingdom to the end of times, when Jesus would return as king and judge to destroy the wicked and enact justice for the righteous. We must also note that the Christian understanding of the supersession of Hebrew scripture and tradition by the life and ministry of Jesus (implied most clearly in John 1:17) must not be seen as a total abolishment or subsuming of Old Testament scripture or prophetic tradition ("the law" as opposed to "the word" or "the truth" in Jesus), as has been suggested by some Christian interpretations and twisted to antisemitic ends. Rather, the supersession should be viewed as a rejection of nationalistic and retributive ideas and narratives of God in the Old Testament (and in *any* other scripture or interpretation) in favor of the God of love revealed in Jesus. See Jon Sobrino, *Christ the Liberator: A View from the Victims*, chapters 8–14, for discussion of the evolution and meaning of the titles applied to Jesus.

3. This focus on the nature of Christ during the early centuries of Christianity came at the expense of a concern for what Jesus had been most concerned about during his ministry: the ushering in of the kingdom of God and the uncovering of political and religious ideologies that prevented its realization. This shift paved the way for the church to be more concerned with orthodoxy, or what the church

"God's salvation for humanity was less important than the God who was the ground of that salvation."[4]

Most importantly for our present discussion, this theological focus led to a change in the way salvation was viewed. Because the end goal of theological activity during this time was to determine the universal attributes of God, the view of God as one who acted within history to save specific groups of people was replaced with a universal, transcendent God whose saving activity was indiscriminate and no longer exercised within history according to a preferential affinity for the poor and oppressed. Jon Sobrino explains:

> revelation of God (and hence "definition" of God) comes about through historical actions, definite of necessity but also partial, the fruit of God's unassailable freedom. "The king who comes down to set his people free," "the God who comes to us in a kingdom for the poor," "the God who raises the victim Jesus" is a definite God but also a partial and even dialectical God, on the side of some and against others. But, *later*, God was to become—with no distinctions—a God of all. . . . The result was that, in place of a God who acts concretely and historically, a God who acts universally and transcendentally, the creator, survived; in place of a God who exercises lordship over historical processes, a God who is universal lord survived; in place of a God who saves the oppressed, the poor, and the marginalized, we were left with a God who saves anyone and everyone.[5]

Thus, the absolutizing and universalizing of God in the councils and creeds of the institutional church during these centuries effectively removed God's salvation from history.[6] Salvation was a theoretical and theological, not a historical, problem. Salvation came to be understood as a solution to

---

believed, than orthopraxis, what the church *did* to relieve the suffering of the poor and to better the world. This shift in focus became particularly pronounced once the aims of the state and church became more opposed and harder to reconcile after Christianity became the state religion of the Roman Empire. See Sobrino, *Christ the Liberator*, ch. 15, for discussion.

4. Holcomb, *Christian Theologies of Salvation*, 13.

5. Sobrino, *Christ the Liberator*, 264, italics in original.

6. The same can be said of the theology and creeds about Jesus during this time. The words of Krister Stendahl, ironically in relation to the differences between the Sermon on the Mount and the teaching of the resurrected Christ in 3 Nephi, are applicable in describing the effect of these theological changes: "It is the very absorbing of Jesus into the image of a Redeemer and lifting him out of history into a more timeless space." Krister Stendahl, "The Sermon on the Mount and Third Nephi," 139–54.

the sin of humanity (broadly defined) rather than being concerned with specific and discrete historical events of temporal liberation. The church, Johannes Metz explains, "did not look first at the creature's suffering, but at his guilt."[7] Sin, and therefore salvation, was still the business of humanity as a whole rather than having particular relevance for individuals—though this was to change in coming centuries. The change was gradual and involved a number of theological, institutional, and historical developments, making general statements of causality difficult. If we make an attempt, however, to parse the history of Christianity (a massive undertaking in itself)[8] with an eye for how salvation turned personal, we can trace the evolution to three main figures: Paul, Augustine, and Martin Luther.

Paul and Justification

The apostle Paul has had an arguably greater impact on the Christian understanding of salvation than Jesus himself. If that sounds odd, consider how much our talk of salvation and atonement refers astonishingly little to the words of Jesus, and more to concepts like sacrifice, justification, works, faith, law, sin, redemption, and grace. These concepts were first mentioned by Paul as metaphors in his epistles, which blended images and symbols from both Jewish and Gentile religious tradition and culture. Later interpretations of them were codified by various church authorities as doctrine, which was then retrojected back onto an understanding and interpretation of the literal meaning of Jesus's life, and especially of his death.[9] According to Stephen Finlan,

> [Paul's] metaphors are more than just vehicles for a message, they provide content for the message as well. . . . The end result is that Christians have accepted that the death of Christ *was* a ritual [sacrificial] event, *was* a costly payment; and it was not just *like* these things.[10]

Thus, interpretations of Paul's metaphors have been declared as authoritative statements about the nature of sin, faith, atonement, salvation, and the character and purpose of Jesus's life and ministry. But, as we shall

---

7. Johannes Baptist Metz, quoted in Jon Sobrino, *No Salvation Outside the Poor: Prophetic-Utopian Essays*, 116.

8. For a comprehensive study, see Diarmaid MacCulloch, *A History of Christianity: The First Three Thousand Years*.

9. Stephen Finlan, *Problems with Atonement: The Origins of, and Controversy About, the Atonement Doctrine*.

10. Finlan, *Problems with Atonement*, 31; italics in original.

see, these interpretations have led to a misunderstanding about both the nature of Paul's apostolic calling and message and what God was trying to reveal about the nature of salvation through Paul's work.

The apostles, afire with their witness and calling from the resurrected Jesus, range about, performing healings and other "signs and wonders," adding "great numbers of both men and women" (Acts 5:14) to the community of believers. These early communities were established along explicit economic lines:

> Now the whole group of those who believed were of one heart and one soul, and no one claimed private ownership of any possessions, but everything they owned was held in common. With great power the apostles gave their testimony to the resurrection of the Lord Jesus, and great grace was upon them all. There was not a needy person among them, for as many as owned lands or houses sold them and brought the proceeds of what was sold. They laid it at the apostles' feet, and it was distributed to each as any had need. (Acts 4:32–35)

The seriousness with which God holds this commitment to communal ownership and equity is illustrated in the story of Ananias and Sapphira, whose dishonesty and unwillingness to impart the whole of their substance to the livelihood and support of the community they had claimed to embrace ended tragically in their own deaths (Acts 5). However we interpret God's part in this story, it clearly shows that Jesus's early disciples understood that the justice and equity of God's kingdom, made possible and preserved by explicit economic arrangements, is of deep import.

It is in this context of the rapid growth of believers that we meet a young man named Saul. We know little of his history, only that those who stoned the disciple Stephen laid their coats at Saul's feet, "and Saul approved of their killing him" (Acts 8:1). In the midst of the miracles and preaching that leads to the conversion of so many, Saul was single-minded in his persecution of the believers, "ravaging the church by entering house after house; dragging off both men and women, he committed them to prison" (v. 3), and he was in league with the religious rulers who had a vested interest in quashing this nascent "Jesus movement":

> Meanwhile Saul, still breathing threats and murder against the disciples of the Lord, went to the high priest and asked him for letters to the synagogues at Damascus, so that if he found any who belonged to the Way, men or women, he might bring them bound to Jerusalem. (Acts 9:1–2)

Saul then pursued his course towards Damascus. While on his way, he was struck blind by a strange light from heaven, and all who were traveling with him heard a loud voice proclaiming Jesus as the one whom Saul was persecuting. Saul was then brought to Damascus, where he spent three days blind and eating nothing before being healed and subsequently joining the ranks of the disciples.

Following Saul's experience on the road to Damascus, we are not told much of his activities over the next year or so. We do know that he went with Barnabas to Antioch, where they stayed a year teaching the believers, who were called "Christians" for the first time there (Acts 11). He and Barnabas also were put in charge of collecting donations for relief of hunger for believers living in Judea during a famine.[11] While in Antioch, Saul and Barnabas were set apart and began their formal ministry. From this point on, Saul was addressed as Paul.

Paul understood that he was called to bring the good news of the gospel to the Gentiles. Up until his call, the apostles and disciples had predominantly focused their efforts on Jews; their strategy had been to convince them, using scripture and miraculous healings, that Jesus was the promised Messiah. Many believed. Peter had had a vision showing him the importance of proclaiming the gospel to the Gentiles (Acts 10:9–16), which he did with some success in Caesarea. But Paul understood his mission as having special relevance to the Gentiles. This comes about due to rejection by the Jews in Antioch, to which Paul and Barnabas replied:

> It was necessary that the word of God should be spoken first to you. Since you reject it and judge yourselves to be unworthy of eternal life, we are now turning to the Gentiles. For so the Lord has commanded us, saying, "I have set you to be a light for the Gentiles, so that you may bring salvation to the ends of the earth." (Acts 13:46–47)

From this point on, Paul and Barnabas traveled widely, preaching and convincing the people of the divinity of Jesus and performing many "signs and wonders." Many Jews believed, as did many Gentiles. This caused no small degree of tension in the church due to clashes of social and religious custom. In fact, the bulk of Paul's exhortation in his letters had to do

---

11. Joseph Spencer suggests that this collection of monetary aid from the Gentiles for the Jews at Jerusalem was a critical aspect of the early Christian mission, and a fulfilling of prophecy in the Hebrew Bible. He argues that this collection and redistribution of Gentile wealth to Jews was a critical component of Paul's apostolic strategy to convince them of the hope provided by the Gospel of Jesus Christ for a fulfillment of the Abrahamic Covenant. See Joseph M. Spencer, *For Zion: A Mormon Theology of Hope*, 4–5.

with his attempts to resolve the discord in the churches that came about because of the extension of the gospel to the Gentiles.

Paul's letters to the churches range widely over a number of topics, use beautiful and powerful language, and employ and blend "metaphors from the cultic, economic, and political realms"[12] (part of the reason they are often difficult to understand) to convey the joy and hope he had found in the gospel of Jesus Christ. A recurring theme is that of justification. Summarizing a great many arguments, predominantly made in his letter to the Roman believers, Paul's general thesis in regard to justification was that obedience to the works of the law (the Ten Commandments and the Torah, interpreted in our day to extend to all commandments and prohibitions) cannot justify a person before God. A person is justified only through faith on Christ, which imparts God's grace to the person in order to sanctify them and give them strength to live as God would have them live. Paul further argued that "there is no one who is righteous"; by virtue of Adam's sin, man by nature is fallen, and only through Christ's act of righteousness can mankind be made righteous or have Christ's grace imputed to them. This was spoken of by Paul in terms of symbolically dying and being raised with Christ into new life, which is catalyzed by baptism. He used the metaphor of the old sinful self being "crucified with Christ," therefore being "dead to sin," and the new person living anew "in Christ."[13] What is clear through all of Paul's teaching is that he did not believe that obedience to the law dictated how righteous or justified one is before God. Only Christ's life and sacrifice are deemed righteous by God, and this righteousness can be conferred onto a person if they have faith in Christ. These ideas will play a prominent role in the development of atonement theologies throughout the next two thousand years.

While the discussion of justification and faith has been interpreted in terms of individual salvation, Paul offered just as many statements that indicate his views of salvation were much more communal, swallowing up the individual in the community of believers. For example, Paul's metaphor of believers as constituting the "Body of Christ" is one of the most profound and beautiful explications of the unity of purpose and life that comes from a shared conversion and commitment to the life advocated by Jesus. "For just as one body is one and has many members, and all the

---

12. Finlan, *Problems with Atonement*, 5.

13. See Adam S. Miller, *An Early Resurrection: Life in Christ Before You Die*, for an elegant and insightful contemporary Latter-day Saint interpretation of Paul's theology.

members of the body, though many, are one body, so it is with Christ. For in the one Spirit we were all baptized into one body—Jews or Greeks, slaves or free" (1 Cor. 12:12–13). Thus, believers become one functioning body, notwithstanding their individual members. Paul further explained to the Galatians, "There is no longer Jew or Greek, there is no longer slave or free, there is no longer male and female; for all of you are one in Christ Jesus" (Gal. 3:28). All boundaries and categories of "otherness" that impeded oneness in Christ were rendered obsolete, allowing full fellowship and love to flourish in his covenant community.

The individual letters to the Romans, Galatians, Ephesians, and Corinthians were written to deal with specific problems in the churches located there, and so we don't get many general summations of Paul's views on the character of salvation and the overarching goal that God hopes to accomplish through Christ. But when Paul broke away from specifics into general statements, it is clear that he had in mind a much wider view of salvation than simply the individual. Remember that Paul was thoroughly Jewish, and the idea of salvation for the individual apart from the community did not exist in his time. And so Paul's interpretation of Christ's Atonement took on cosmic significance. Now, instead of being the Messiah only for Israel, with the extension of the covenant to the Gentiles, Paul summarily extended the covenant of salvation to all creation, hoping for the day when "the creation itself will be set free from its bondage to decay" (Rom. 8:21). Thus, for Paul, salvation in Christ consisted of the liberation and renewal of the entire creation.

Augustine and the Guilty Conscience

Augustine, Bishop of Hippo (375–430 CE), has had a greater influence on Western Christianity than anyone except Paul. His figure towers over the beliefs and doctrines that have been codified by the Catholic church, and his theology has bled into core beliefs and tenets of all Christian tradition. While he is most famous for the philosophical ideas explored and theology advanced in his monumental work of *The City of God*, the personal struggle with his own sinfulness and weakness and eventual conversion he documented in his memoirs *Confessions* set the stage for a dramatic shift in the way that Christianity viewed salvation. By using the autobiographical and confessional format, a unique literary device in its day (difficult for us to appreciate in the confessional overexposure of our own era), Augustine foregrounded critical self-reflection and moral guilt in his own conceptualization of salvation, opening the door to a uniquely personal, individualized interpretation.

While written and published for popular reading (it was intended to be read aloud), *Confessions* is deeply personal. The entire work is presented as Augustine's address to and wrestle with God. What is also clearly apparent here is that *Confessions* is the work of a deeply tortured and guilt-ridden mind. Huge portions of the text, particularly the first two books, consist of Augustine lamenting his own depravity and sinfulness. While clearly not able to remember his infancy, he nevertheless indicted himself:

> Who is there to remind me of the sin of my infancy (for sin there was: no one is free from sin in your sight, not even an infant whose span of earthly life is but a single day); who can remind me of it? . . . What then was my sin at that age? Was it perhaps that I cried so greedily for those breasts?[14]

He described himself as being miserable at school as a child, where he was beaten for being "lazy about learning."[15] His first recollection of speaking was in supplication to God in a heartbreaking plea: "By calling upon you I untied the knots of my tongue and begged you, in my little-boy way but with no little earnestness, not to let me be beaten at school."[16] Yet he was quick to assert his own fault even in this: "All the same, we were blameworthy, because we were less assiduous in reading, writing, and concentrating on our studies than was expected of us"[17]—though he clearly sensed the unjustness of him and his schoolmates being punished: "it was simply that we loved to play, and we were punished by adults who nonetheless did the same themselves."[18] Nevertheless, according to him, his boyhood sins were grievous and plentiful, consisting of "countless lies," stealing from his parents "larder and table," seeking to dominate his childhood games by "fraudulent means," and "cheating over nuts and balls and sparrows."[19] "What could have been fouler in your eyes at that time than myself,"[20] he rhetorically asked God.

With adolescence comes sexual awakening, and the opportunity for even greater degrees of self-loathing:

---

14. Augustine, *The Confessions*, Book I, 107.
15. Augustine, Book I, 114.
16. Augustine, Book I, 115.
17. Augustine, Book I, 116.
18. Augustine, Book I, 117.
19. Augustine, Book I, 142.
20. Augustine, Book I, 141.

> From the mud of my fleshly desires and my erupting puberty belched out murky clouds that obscured and darkened my heart until I could not distinguish the calm light of love from the fog of lust. The two swirled about together and dragged me, young and weak as I was, over the cliffs of my desires, and engulfed me in a whirlpool of sins. . . . I was flung hither and thither, I poured myself out, frothed and floundered in the tumultuous sea of my fornications.[21]

His adolescent sins were not restricted to sexual deviance. In an extended passage, he described how he and his friends stole pears from a neighboring vineyard: "We nasty lads went there to shake down the fruit and carry it off in the dead of night. . . . [W]e derived pleasure from the deed simply because it was forbidden."[22] He berated himself and asked God to explain to him how his heart

> was seeking in action which made me bad for no reason, in which there was no motive for my malice except malice. The malice was loathsome, and I loved it. I was in love with my own ruin, in love with decay: not with the thing for which I was falling into decay but with decay itself, for I was depraved in soul, and I leapt down from your strong support into destruction, hungering not for some advantage to be gained by the foul deed, but for the foulness of it.[23]

From this point, the work takes on a more contemplative tone. From his student years in Carthage to his years in Rome and Milan, where he earned an academic appointment, he was inquisitive, pondering many weighty philosophical and theological matters and narrating his encounters with friends and acquaintances and several important life events, including his cohabitation with an unnamed woman for nearly ten years, with whom he had a son, and the death and grieving over of a close personal friend. He sought answers in philosophy, in astrology, in the writings of poets and playwrights, and from his friends. He studied Manichaeism, a religious movement with elements of Zoroastrianism and Gnosticism, with which he struggled for years before finally renouncing it in his conversion to Christianity.

He did stop from time to time to appraise the reader of his sinful state, noting in his heartbreaking narrative of the dissolution of his common-law relationship to make way for an arranged marriage that "meanwhile

---

21. Augustine, Book II, 155.
22. Augustine, Book II, 166.
23. Augustine, Book II, 167.

my sins were multiplying."[24] His conversion was a lengthy process with many twists and turns and phases of exploration, but a crucial juncture occurred with his fresh appraisal of the writings of Paul. He had been struggling for some time over the problem of evil, the age-old paradox which asks how an all-powerful and all-loving God could allow evil to exist. Given how transcendent God is and how clearly evil and sinful humankind is, Augustine was sure that there is no direct way for humans to approach God. He recognized the need for a mediator and found him in "Christ Jesus." Having come to this realization, he threw himself into study of the scriptures, and in so doing "discovered" the writings of Paul:

> It was therefore with intense eagerness that I seized on the hallowed calligraphy of your Spirit, and most especially the writings of the apostle Paul. . . . So I began to read, and discovered that every truth I had read in those other books was taught here also, but now inseparably from your gift of grace.[25]

In Paul, Augustine had found someone who appeared to deal with and had found the answer to the same struggle which he suffered: how to reconcile his desire to do good with his apparent and ongoing inability to do so. In a particularly poignant moment that occured just prior to his conversion, Augustine had been wrestling with these issues and retreated to a garden in utter despondency, weeping uncontrollably over "this deep meditation [that had] dredged all my wretchedness up from the secret profundity of my being and heaped it all together before the eyes of my heart."[26] He heard a voice of a young child, which told him to "pick it up and read."[27] He opened up his bible and read the first verse his eyes found, an injunction from the Apostle Paul: "Not in reveling and drunkenness, not in debauchery and licentiousness, not in quarreling and jealousy. Instead, put on the Lord Jesus Christ, and make no provision for the flesh, to gratify its desires" (Rom. 13:13–14).

This encounter brought him the long-sought-after peace and the needed clarity to finally convert to Christianity and be baptized. He renounced his career, gave his property to the poor, and devoted himself wholly to the service of God and to preaching and pursuing a monastic life. About a decade after his conversion, he was ordained as Bishop of Hippo and worked tirelessly in that capacity until his death.

---

24. Augustine, Book VI, 399.
25. Augustine, Book VII, 467.
26. Augustine, Book VIII, 533.
27. Augustine, Book VIII, 534.

Augustine's influence on Christian thought, for good and ill, cannot be overstated. It is easy to trace a line between the self-loathing and debasement portrayed in *Confessions* and the theological concept of original sin—with its repudiation of the sex act as evil and its depraved view of humanity—that he would later develop more fully. In *Confessions*, Augustine laid the groundwork for these ideas with crystal clarity. Paul's talk of "putting on Christ" provided the perfect metaphor for Augustine to renounce natural human impulses and everything else related to "the flesh" as utterly irredeemable, justifying in his eyes the view of corrupt human morality that was to become one of his most damaging legacies. His *Confessions* was meant to be both a motivator for conversion and an explicit template to follow for prospective converts. The unique blend of self-examination, penance, praise, and sought-after peace documented therein has inspired devotion and hope while instilling a heavy burden of guilt in generations of Christians.

Purgatory, Indulgences, and Individual Penance

Although Augustine's confessional writings began to shift Christian attitudes towards salvation as a personal matter, the official acceptance of this position awaited at least two significant institutional reforms. The first was the codification of the doctrine of Purgatory. This was the belief in an interim location between death and heaven in which the saved underwent punishment (or correction for their sins) before being let into Paradise. The idea for such a place seems to have emerged from formal theological exploration, initially by the Eastern fathers Clement and Origen,[28] but gained steam in the popular consciousness through accounts of the afterlife that were plentiful in the Middle Ages. The vivid account of the mountain of Purgatory, to which Dante Alighieri devoted the entire second book in his *Divine Comedy*, served as a barometer for the understanding and conceptualization of this idea during this time. His depiction of Hell illustrated the specific nature of sin and punishment, whereas his portrayal of Purgatory treated it as an educative process:

> We find not the multifarious crimes by which vice or sin manifests itself in Hell (or on Earth), but simply the seven Capital Vices that lead to sinful acts. Since the souls here are all saved, and eager to act in accordance with divine will, there is no place among them for violence, malice, fraud, rebelliousness, etc. Each vice is treated on a specific ledge (*cornice*) that circles

---

28. MacCulloch, *A History of Christianity*, 148, 477.

the mountain. Souls remain on a given ledge until they feel purged of all slightest subconscious taint of that particular vice, at which point they move up spontaneously.[29]

Although they do not have to suffer the gruesome punishments of the damned in Hell, Purgatory is no cake walk. The proud are required to carry around massive heavy stones on their backs, the envious have their eyes sewn shut, the wrathful are blinded by toxic smoke, the slothful are made to engage in constant activity, the greedy are made to recite psalms lying facedown, the gluttonous are starved in the presence of trees whose fruit they could never reach, and the lustful are made to walk through a huge wall of flame. Thus, although eventually guaranteed Heaven, those in Purgatory are made to suffer as penance for their earthly sins.

The doctrine of Purgatory served an important purpose. It connected the dead with the living and provided hope for progress after this life. The souls of the dead were routinely prayed and fasted for, but a widely accepted theology of the afterlife had not been worked out. Given that death was an ever-present reality in the lives of churchgoers in the Middle Ages, this concept provided some comfort and fed the faith of the believers. Though officially recognized in the thirteenth century, the doctrine of Purgatory became institutionalized in Catholicism as a result of the catastrophic devastation of the Black Death, which decimated Europe in the mid-fourteenth century. Several historic conditions contributed, "Worsening economic conditions had probably made Europe's population growth level out, and people's general resistance to disease was weakened by a steadily less sustaining diet."[30] When the plague was brought from the East, the effects on the already weakened population were devastating. Diarmaid MacCulloch explains:

> Through several years, 1348–53, the effect of the Black Death in Europe was more thoroughgoing than any other recorded disaster: proportionally, it was far more destructive than the First World War, with perhaps as many as one in three of the population dying, and in some places up to two thirds.[31]

The Black Death served as a brutal reminder to Europeans about the reality of death, and they remained "preoccupied by death and what to do about it."[32] The concreteness and specificity of the penance undergone in

---

29. Dante Alighieri, *The Divine Comedy*, The Purgatorio, 795.
30. MacCulloch, *A History of Christianity*, 552.
31. MacCulloch, 552.
32. MacCulloch, 555.

Purgatory was reinforced through the institutionalization of indulgences by the church in the eleventh and twelfth centuries.[33] Indulgences were basically authoritative "get out of jail free" cards, issued by the church to people who did not want to worry about penance for sins after this life on their way to heaven. Indulgences assume that sin demands some type of restitution, or proof of repentance, and that the merits of Christ as well as those of all the saints were available as a repository for helping penitent Christians repent.[34] The pope dipped into this repository and granted these merits through church clergy as indulgences to people as a way of guaranteeing them a shorter time doing penance in Purgatory.

The granting of indulgences required some display of repentance on the part of the sinner, and the usual requirement was the practice of confession (made compulsory by the church during the Middle Ages) coupled with some act of penance, such as recitation of specified prayers, fasting, or the giving of alms. Coupled with the doctrine of Purgatory, indulgences were monetized by some in the church who offered them for both the living and the dead for a price, leading to widespread corruption that church authorities tried unsuccessfully to manage. However, as noted by MacCulloch, this coupling focused pastoral care of congregations

> on the continual need for penance in their everyday lives and on the importance of true contrition and satisfaction when they come to confession; the priest in confession is cast in the role of judge, assessing the sincerity of all this busy work. . . . [This] encouraged an attitude to salvation in which the sinner, lay or clerical, piled up reparations for sin; action was added to action in order to merit years off Purgatory. It was possible to do something about one's salvation.[35]

While there was a long-standing doctrinal assertion that sin required penance, "there was a weak concept of individuality in this society; in early medieval eyes, God would not mind who actually performed the penance demanded, as long as it was done."[36] The institutionalization and monetization of indulgences, more than ever, tied specific acts of penance by specific individuals to specific sins, edging closer to an individualistic interpretation of salvation.

---

33. The origin of indulgences can be traced to the promise made by Pope Urban II that any who died on a Christian crusade in a repentant state would be guaranteed salvation with no penance required. See MacCulloch, *A History of Christianity*, 384.

34. MacCulloch, *A History of Christianity*, 555–56.

35. MacCulloch, 557.

36. MacCulloch, 356.

Atonement Mechanism and Metaphor

This confluence of events and doctrine was also heavily influenced by theological developments regarding the specific mechanism of Christ's Atonement.[37] Up until the Middle Ages, a widely accepted view taught that Jesus's death ransomed the souls of humankind from the devil. Humankind had forfeited their souls to the devil as a consequence of their original disobedience in the Garden, and Christ's Atonement was thought to set free captive humanity. As explained by David Hogg, "humanity was bound under Satan's authority because of our sin and the only way we could be freed was if God paid a price to the devil that would be equal to or greater than the value of all the souls under his authority. Jesus's life was that price."[38]

This view was rejected by Anselm, the Archbishop of Canterbury and a prominent theologian, because of its suggestion that a debt was owed to the devil. He instead proposed the *satisfaction theory* of atonement, which suggests that human sin consists of disobedience, or choosing not to "render to God this honour due to him,"[39] thereby offending God because "there is nothing more intolerable in the universal order than that a creature should take away the honour from the creator."[40] Furthermore, "everyone who sins is under the obligation to repay to God the honour which he has violently taken from him, and this is the satisfaction which every sinner is obliged to give God."[41] Satisfaction demands either restoration of God's honor or punishment.

Christ, through his submissive obedience even unto death, restores God's honor. Moreover, because "his action was not something that was owed, because it was not a matter of indebtedness,"[42] Christ's obedience pays God even more honor than God is owed. Christ therefore accrues a surplus of honor that can be used to pay humanity's debt of honor to God, thereby allowing them to escape punishment for their sins. Anselm's satisfaction theory became a dominant account of atonement during this time.

---

37. See Peter Schmiechen, *Saving Power: Theories of Atonement and Forms of the Church*, for a review of atonement theories.
38. Holcomb, *Christian Theologies of Salvation*, 115.
39. Anselm of Canturbury, *The Major Works*, 283.
40. Anselm, 286.
41. Anselm, 283.
42. Anselm, 351.

This idea of atonement may seem strange to us, but in Anselm's feudal society, this would have made perfect sense. As Stephen Holmes explains,

> Obedience and honour were owed by social inferiors (vassals) to social superiors (lieges): a serf owed obedience to his landlord, a knight to his baron, the baron to the earl, the earl to the king, and so on. . . . If the obedience and honour owed were not given, the offence was considered more and more serious the further up the social scale the liege stood—the magnitude of the crime had far more to do with the status of the person offended against than any absolute justice. . . . Anselm pictures God as the ultimate liege-lord, infinite in honour and majesty, and so deserving of infinite obedience.[43]

These theological ideas greatly influenced the way that clergy thought about atonement, sin, and repentance. These teachings trickled down through congregations and parishes, slowly shifting the way the masses thought about their faith. Together with the institutionalization of confession and increased use of indulgences, they moved the common conceptualization of salvation ever closer to the current orthodoxy of individual salvation in modern Western Christianity. But it wasn't until the landmark shifts in theology and church orthodoxy and practice brought by the Protestant Reformation that individual salvation would become firmly doctrinally and institutionally entrenched.

Luther and the Triumph of Individual Salvation

When Martin Luther tacked his *Ninety-Five Theses* on the door of a church in Wittenberg, Germany, in 1517, thus beginning the Protestant Reformation, he brought to a head objections and feelings that had been simmering for many years. Most importantly for our present discussion, the idea of an individual accounting for one's life at the moment of death had been codified and reinforced over the past several generations in the minds of the church through the institutionalization of indulgences, the very practice Luther condemned in his proclamation. For Luther, indulgences, and later, Purgatory, "with all its attendant structures of intercessory prayer for the dead—chantries, gilds, hospitals—that comforting sense that through divine mercy we humans can busy ourselves doing something to alter and improve our prospects after death,"[44] were an explicit symbol of the way the Catholic Church had corrupted the under-

---

43. Stephen R. Holmes, *The Wondrous Cross: Atonement and Penal Substitution in the Bible and History*, 52–53.
44. MacCulloch, *A History of Christianity*, 608.

standing of salvation. His understanding of the mechanics of salvation relied heavily on his readings of the letters of Paul, particularly his epistles to the Romans and Galatians, and on the interpretation of Paul by "St. Augustine, his most trustworthy interpreter."[45]

Luther's view of salvation can be summarized by one of the five "watchwords of Protestantism," *sola gratia* (grace alone). For Luther, as opposed to the Catholic emphasis on salvation by knowledge of God and the sacraments of the Church, salvation comes exclusively through the grace of God, bestowed on those who have faith in Christ. Taking a cue from Augustine, Luther believed that humankind has been corrupted by the Fall, and this corruption and "total depravity" is so all-encompassing, so complete, that it is impossible for humans to merit anything good or righteous of themselves. His theology contrasts the Law (summarized in the Ten Commandments) with the Gospel (the good news of Christ). Because it is impossible for humans to satisfy the law perfectly, and to do so in a state of perfect love for God, they stand condemned. Because they are unable to perform any righteous works of themselves, the righteousness to do so must be given, or imputed, externally by God. Thus, humankind stands at an impasse, and Christ comes to break it. Those who have faith in Christ are justified before God.[46]

It is in Luther's interpretation of the mechanics of justification that we can clearly see the emphasis on individual salvation. As noted above, ideas about atonement had undergone an evolution over the life of the church, and the predominant view of atonement at the time of Luther was Anselm's satisfaction theory, which was focused on restoring the honor stolen from God by human sin. Sin here is attributed to humankind generally, with less of an emphasis on individual acts of disobedience. The

---

45. Luther, *Heidelberg Disputation*; See Marco Barone, *Luther's Augustinian Theology of the Cross*, for an illuminating treatment of the parallels between Augustine and Luther's thought.

46. Luther's own thinking on salvation and justification were also heavily influenced by the doctrine of *predestination*. This doctrine in its most general form asserts that everything that happens in the world is willed and caused to happen by God. This general doctrine was expanded by later theologians to assert that all humankind were predestined by God to either salvation or damnation, so-called *double predestination*. Luther's understanding of this doctrine heavily informed the development of his own theology of salvation by justification, emphasizing individual predestination and thus the futility of humankind trying to merit anything of themselves. See MacCulloch, *A History of Christianity*, for discussion of the evolution of the doctrine of predestination.

idea of an individual, apart from societal and familial relationships, is yet to emerge in any general way in Europe. With the institutionalization of indulgences, the focus began to shift to individual acts which needed penance on the part of the sinner. This shift to the idea of personal salvation became firmly entrenched with the Reformation as a result of the social concept of "the individual," which "in its modern sense dates from the late sixteenth or early seventeenth centuries."[47] According to Christopher Hill,

> Protestantism popularized the idea of the individual spiritual balance sheet, the profit-and-loss book-keeping of diaries. This presupposes an atomic society of individuals fighting for their own salvation, no longer a community working out its salvation, as it cultivated its fields, in common.[48]

Luther and other Reformation thinkers, particularly John Calvin and Charles Hodge, would add to the gravity of the idea of individual culpability for sin by solidifying a legal interpretation of atonement that codified the relation between individual sins and punishment. This interpretation, known as the *penal-substitution theory*, would utterly transform the way that Western Christianity views salvation. The nearly overwhelming acceptance of this account of atonement was likely due to societal changes during the Middle Ages that constituted "a shift from feudal obligations to criminal law."[49] The idea of individual guilt and criminal culpability was therefore pervasive in society. In addition, the signing of the Magna Carta in 1215 demonstrated that there were some laws that applied even to kings, intimating the possibility that there may be universal laws of justice that apply to and must be enforced by God. Thus, society was primed for the views of atonement developed by the Reformers.

In some respects, penal-substitution theory is similar to satisfaction theory, in that both agree that human sin is an offense to God for which humanity stands condemned. In satisfaction theory, Christ's Atonement, comprising his perfect obedience, restores God's honor, thereby paying our debt. Penal substitution, by contrast, says that sin, constituting a breaking of the law, requires a punishment, and this cannot be foregone by a restoration of God's honor. In this account, Christ receives the punishment that the law requires for sin, thereby allowing us to escape it.

---

47. Christopher Hill, *Reformation to Industrial Revolution: The Making of Modern English Society, Vol. 1 1530–1780*, 26.

48. Hill, *Reformation to Industrial Revolution*, 26.

49. Joel B. Green and Mark D. Baker, *Recovering the Scandal of the Cross: Atonement in New Testament and Contemporary Contexts*, 142.

Being innocent, Christ suffers and is punished for our sins in our place. Luther puts it in these terms:

> But now, if God's wrath is to be taken away from me and I am to obtain grace and forgiveness, some one must merit this; for God cannot be a friend of sin nor gracious to it, nor can he remit the punishment and wrath, unless payment and satisfaction be made. Now, no one, not even an angel of heaven, could make restitution for the infinite and irreparable injury and appease the eternal wrath of God which we had merited by our sins; except that eternal person, the Son of God himself, and he could do it only by taking our place, assuming our sins, and answering for them as though he himself were guilty of them. This our dear Lord and only Savior and Mediator before God, Jesus Christ, did for us by his blood and death, in which he became a sacrifice for us; and with his purity, innocence, and righteousness, which was divine and eternal, he outweighed all sin and wrath he was compelled to bear on our account; yea, he entirely engulfed and swallowed it up, and his merit is so great that God is now satisfied and says, If he wills thereby to save, then there shall be a salvation.[50]

Here the idea of substitution of Christ for our sins is made explicit. The idea of satisfaction is still threaded throughout, however, indicating a blending of substitution and satisfaction theories and the evolution of Luther's own thinking on these ideas. In his later sermons, he stresses even further the individual aspect of Christ's substitution:

> When the merciful Father saw that we were being oppressed through the Law, that we were being held under a curse, and that we could not be liberated from it by anything, he sent his Son into the world, heaped all the sins of all men upon him, and said to him: "Be Peter, the denier; Paul, the persecutor, blasphemer and assaulter; David, the adulterer; the sinner who ate the apple in Paradise; the thief on the cross. In short, be the person of all men, the one who has committed the sins of all men. And see to it that you pay and make satisfaction for them." Now the Law comes and says: "I find him a sinner, who takes upon himself the sins of all men. I do not see any other sins than those in him. Therefore let him die on the Cross." And so it attacks him and kills him.[51]

In Luther's account of atonement, Christ literally took on the sins of all humankind individually as though he had committed them himself, and he is therefore punished by God in our place, effecting salvation

---

50. Martin Luther, *Sermons of Martin Luther. Vol. 2. Sermons on Gospel Texts for Epiphany, Lent & Easter, Vol 2*, 293–94.

51. Martin Luther, *Commentary on the Epistle to the Galatians*, quoted in Kenneth Hagan, "Luther on Atonement Reconfigured," 251–76.

for each of these individuals rather than humanity generally. Later, John Calvin, a French lawyer and theologian, would explicitly tie the legal language of crime and punishment to a formal account of atonement: "Since God is a righteous Judge, he does not allow his law to be broken without punishment, but is equipped to avenge it."[52] Charles Hodge further solidifies this legal perspective:

> Let it be enough to say with the Scriptures, that Christ suffered the penalty of the law in our stead, and that the penalty of the law was that kind and amount of suffering, which from such a person, was a full satisfaction to the Divine justice. . . . This was the penalty of the law; for the wrath of God, however expressed, constitutes that penalty, in its strictest and highest sense.[53]

This legal framework, developed over the next several centuries, is the widely accepted and recognized account of Christ's Atonement. We stand guilty before a righteous and wrathful God-judge, deserving of our punishment, and we are saved by God willfully inflicting that punishment on Christ (whether on the cross or in the garden of Gethsemane)[54] as our sub-

---

52. John Calvin, *Institutes of the Christian Religion, Volume II*, 504.

53. Charles Hodge, *The Orthodox Doctrine Regarding the Extent of the Atonement Vindicated*, 32.

54. See John Hilton III and Joshua P. Barringer, "The Use of Gethsemane by Church Leaders, 1859–2018," for an analysis of the evolution of the reference to Gethsemane by Latter-day Saint leaders in general conference addresses. They show that the early (1850s–1930s) references to Gethsemane were indirect and nonspecific or refer to Jesus feeling sorrow for the sins of humanity generally. They also note that James E. Talmage, in his classic and still officially sanctioned treatment *Jesus The Christ*, first published in 1915, refers to the ordeal in Gethsemane as involving a contest with Satan and the powers of evil and taking on all the sins of humanity (though not in a substitutionary manner). Talmage also asserts that the suffering in Gethsemane eclipsed that of the cross. From the 1940s to the 1970s, the reference to Gethsemane as the location of Jesus suffering vicariously for our sins (as a substitute) becomes more prominent. During this period Gethsemane is increasingly referenced as being a significant location of atonement, with some suggesting the suffering in Gethsemane was more significant to the atonement than that on the cross (Bruce R. McConkie's hugely influential encyclopedic *Mormon Doctrine*, first published in 1958 and in print until 2010 and commonly considered official doctrine despite never being endorsed by Church leadership, takes this position). From the 1980s to the 2010s, there is sustained reference to Gethsemane as the location where Jesus suffered the penalty for our individual sins, but also an increasing emphasis on Jesus suffering and experiencing our pains and infirmities in Gethsemane,

stitute or a sacrifice on our behalf (the sacrificial imagery is particularly appropriated from Hebrew scripture and interpreted as confirming this view). The covenant community that includes all of humanity and creation, and salvation as God's loving liberation from oppression, domination, exploitation, or anything else that inhibits the realization of this covenant, have thus been largely lost in a calculated legal transaction between individuals and God. Although individual theological articulations of this theory are nuanced in their explanations and apologetics,[55] and there remain many useful, moving, and comforting metaphors for the means and effects of Christ's Atonement, this individual transactional aspect of penal substitution looms largest in contemporary Christian understanding.

Paul Revisited

Luther's insight regarding the law, faith, works, and grace came as the answer to his own difficult internal struggle with his own sinful state. For him, Paul's doctrine of justification by faith alone was revelatory. Like Augustine before him, Luther struggled for years,[56] feeling "that [he] was a sinner before God, with an extremely disturbed conscience." He felt that in the demands of the law, by which humanity already "are crushed" due to original sin, God added "pain to pain" by demanding a standard of righteousness that was impossible for humanity to uphold. Through his own dark night of the soul, in which he "raged with a fierce and troubled conscience" and "beat importunately upon Paul" in order to understand his message, he finally came to understand what he would teach as justification by faith alone, the doctrine that formed the basis for all his later theological work and that rocked the foundations of the church in his day and is the foundation of Protestantism and evangelical Christianity.

---

enabling him to comfort and strengthen us. There is also a shift in focus during this time period from Gethsemane *over and above* the cross to Gethsemane *and* the cross jointly as the significant locations of Christ's Atonement.

55. See Holmes, *The Wondrous Cross*. For accounts of this theory that attempt to address contemporary criticisms, see Hans Boersma, *Violence, Hospitality, and the Cross: Reappropriating the Atonement Tradition*, and Simon Gathercole, *Defending Substitution: An Essay on Atonement in Paul*. For contemporary Latter-day Saint perspectives on atonement, see Tad R. Callister, *The Infinite Atonement*; Brad Wilcox, *The Continuous Atonement*; and Fiona Givens and Terryl Givens, *The Christ Who Heals: How God Restored the Truth That Saves Us*.

56. Quotes in this section come from Luther's own account of his conversion, found in *Luther's Works Volume 34, Career of the Reformer IV*, 336–37.

Like Augustine before him, Luther had found in Paul someone who had struggled mightily with the human existential predicament and had found in Christ a personal salvation.

But was this what Paul meant? In an illuminating appraisal of the Reformed interpretation of Paul, Krister Stendahl points out that Luther's view of Paul was situated squarely within the context of his own internal struggles of conscience. Paul's letters to the Gentile congregations were read by Luther as being applicable to the entirety of the human predicament. Stendahl, however, warns against such a leap in interpretation:

> This problem becomes acute when one tries to picture the function and the manifestation of introspection in the life and writings of the Apostle Paul. It is the more acute since it is exactly at this point that Western interpreters have found the common denominator between Paul and the experiences of man, since Paul's statements about "justification by faith" have been hailed as the answer to the problem which faces the ruthlessly honest man in his practice of introspection. Especially in Protestant Christianity—which, however, at this point has its roots in Augustine and in the piety of the Middle Ages—the Pauline awareness of sin has been interpreted in the light of Luther's struggle with his conscience. But it is exactly at that point that we can discern the most drastic difference between Luther and Paul.[57]

Here we run into the same problem discussed above with interpretation of the life of Jesus. That is, we cannot assume that we can retroject the social, political, and religious customs, understandings, and conventions of our day onto the historical life of Jesus (or Paul) and hope to understand their messages and ministry. Where Paul is concerned, it is even more important to consider the context in which his letters are written. Paul is not sharing a general-purpose message about faith and justification that came to him as a result of a personal struggle and conversion. In fact, nowhere does Paul even intimate that he struggled under a similar burden of conscience as Augustine or Luther. He refered to himself several times as "blameless" (Philip. 3:6), and with a "clear conscience before God" (Acts 23:1). Thus, the nature of Paul's teaching cannot be easily thought of as a search for his own internal peace of mind, a quest for his individual salvation.

---

57. Krister Stendahl, "The Apostle Paul and the Introspective Conscience of the West," 200; this reading of Paul was developed by later scholars and is referred to as the "New Perspective on Paul." See James D.G. Dunn, *The New Perspective on Paul*, and Kent L. Yinger, *The New Perspective on Paul: An Introduction*, for review and explanation.

Paul viewed his call and the purpose of his ministry specifically to bring the gospel to the Gentiles. His letters were written to address issues regarding this in the churches. The biggest issue that Paul seems to be struggling with was how to extend the covenant status of the Jews to the Gentiles given the specificity of the covenant practices, or "works of the law," such as circumcision and maintaining the purity of food and table fellowship. Therefore, his letters and the exposition of law, justification, faith, and works need to be considered within this context if we are to make sense of what he was saying.

When Luther struggled mightily with his dark night of the soul, he spoke repeatedly of the difficulty posed by Paul's mention of the "righteousness of God"; Luther "hated the word, 'righteousness of God.'" He had been taught that it meant "the formal or active righteousness according to which God is righteous and punishes sinners and the unjust." He felt that his life as a monk had been "irreproachable," nevertheless he felt like a "sinner before God."[58] For Luther, God's righteousness was an impossible standard of conduct that God required of humans and punished them for failing to reach.

This definition and conceptualization of righteousness is a direct European inheritance from Graeco-Roman thought. In this tradition, James Dunn explains, "'righteousness' and 'justice' were ideal concepts or absolute ethical norms against which particular claims and duties could be measured. . . . [W]e today still echo such a view when we say things like, 'The demands of justice must be satisfied.'"[59] According to this idea, God's righteousness is an inherent ethical quality that God possesses, and which humans strive to attain. It is a way of measuring how good our actions are, and by that perfect standard, we will always fall short.

But for Paul, who was Jewish, the understanding of righteousness within the Hebrew tradition meant something entirely different. Dunn clarifies:

> Righteousness is not something which an individual has on his or her own, independently of anyone else, as could be the case in the Graeco-Roman concept—"righteous" as meeting the standard set by the ideal of "justice." In Hebrew thought, however, righteousness is something one has precisely in one's relationships as a social being. People are righteous when they meet the claims which others have on them by virtue of their relationship. . . . The same is true of God's righteousness. In this case the relationship is the covenant into which God entered with Israel when he chose them to be his

---

58. Luther, *Luther's Works*, 336–37.
59. Dunn, *The New Perspective on Paul*, 206.

people. That is to say, God is righteous not because he satisfies some ideal of justice external to himself. Rather, God is righteous when he fulfils the obligations he took upon himself to be Israel's God.[60]

This understanding of God's righteousness begins the discussion of justification, faith, and works from a completely different angle. Instead of feeling crushed by guilt and wondering how he could avoid eternal punishment and suffering, as were the motivations of Augustine and Luther, this understanding situates Paul's letters within the context of a God who is faithful to the covenant with Israel. The vengeful, retributive God is replaced with a loving, longsuffering God. God has made the covenant in full knowledge of the risk and complexity, and God intends to keep it. Well aware of Israel's shortcomings, God will always provide a way for them to remain in the covenant. This is known as being justified.

Paul's concern was how to extend the covenant relation of the Jews to the Gentiles. How were they to be justified? His call had made clear to him that this was what was required. Indeed, as the apostle to the Gentiles (we might say *for* the Gentiles), Paul at every turn seemed to advocate for the Gentiles already being included in the covenant without having to become Jewish.[61] According to Paul, this inclusion was made clear by Jesus's life and ministry. But for Jews, their membership in the covenant had always been signified by specific obligations to behave in a certain way. This would serve both to maintain the nature of the society for which they had been liberated and to mark Israel off from the other nations and peoples, reminding them of their covenant status. For Paul, Jesus had extended this covenant relationship to the Gentiles. The question was, Did the new believers need to fulfill the outward covenant obligations of circumcision, food purity laws, sabbath observance, and others? These were contentious questions that Paul feared if left unresolved would threaten the church communities in Rome and Galatia.

When we read Paul's letters in this light, we can see that when Paul referred to the "works of the law," or "works" in shorthand, he was clearly referring to the covenant practices which served as boundary markers for Israel, setting them apart from others. Paul definitively rejected the requirement for Gentile believers to follow these practices, in essence, to live like Jews:

---

60. Dunn, 207.
61. Krister Stendahl, *Paul Among Jews and Gentiles and Other Essays*.

> Yet we know that a person is justified not by the works of the law but through faith in Jesus Christ. And we have come to believe in Christ Jesus, so that we might be justified by faith in Christ, and not by doing the works of the law, because no one will be justified by the works of the law. (Gal. 2:16)

For Paul, Jesus had come as the Messiah—not in a political sense, but due to his extension of the covenant status to all. Jesus's ministry had shown Israel that the purity laws and boundaries erected by the temple state, though they had originated as a recognition and perpetual reminder of God's ongoing covenant salvation, had become the means of exclusion from the covenant community for many. God's salvation, reflected in the covenant relationship with Israel, was available to all Jews, even those deemed unworthy by the temple-state elites. Jesus's work was to reveal this reality to the Jews. Paul was now called to bring the good news of the gospel to the Gentiles, a group that had historically been considered impure and enemies of Israel. Paul declared forcefully that the relationship status between Gentiles and God, and by extension between Gentiles and Jews, was revealed to be irrevocably changed with Christ:

> But now in Christ Jesus you who were once far off have been brought near by the blood of Christ. For he is our peace; in his flesh he has made both groups into one and has broken down the dividing wall, that is, the hostility between us. He has abolished the law with its commandments and ordinances, that he might create in himself one new humanity in place of two, thus making peace, and might reconcile both groups to God in one body through the cross, thus putting to death that hostility through it. (Eph. 2:13–16)

We can see that Paul's discussion of works, faith, and justification therefore has little to do with the human existential problem of individual salvation. The personal crisis of conscience, though clearly very important to Augustine and Luther, not to mention millions of other Christians throughout the centuries, seemed to have had little, if anything, to do with Paul's letters to the Romans and Galatians. He seemed to be laser-focused on the problem of covenant relationship.

Paul was not either, as is commonly thought, coming down against some abstract concept of "legalism" or obsession with law or commandments, as represented by Jewish adherence to covenant obligations. It is true that in Paul's day, some Jewish groups viewed their adherence to the Mosaic law, in all its particulars, as a badge of honor that made them more worthy of their covenant status than others. Paul's condemnation of the law in favor of faith in Christ, therefore, indicates that adherence to covenant obligations in the absence of faith does not put the believer in right relation with God. Rather, faith in Christ, as the one who made clear the nature of God's covenant relationship to all of humanity, indeed, all of creation, is a catalyst that changes the way we view ourselves, others, and the world. Living the law of God, those practices and commandments that ensure justice and equity for those around us, particularly the marginalized and downtrodden, is our grateful response to this freely given grace, our best effort to enable God's salvation to flow freely across any man-made boundaries to those in our communities, nations and the world.

Chapter 4

The Calamity Which Should Come: The Restoration in Historical Context

There is a crime here that goes beyond denunciation.
There is a sorrow here that weeping cannot symbolize.
There is a failure here that topples all our successes.
— John Steinbeck

God's salvation has, for the majority of history, been understood and experienced as liberation from oppression into communities of justice and equity. It is only in the past 500 years that salvation has been understood as personal and able to be experienced by individuals outside of community. This individualistic interpretation of salvation has colored the way we view the Restoration. We speak of the meaning behind the Restoration as having to do with priesthood authority, "saving" ordinances performed in temples, God's one "true" church, missionary work, and a privileged understanding of the nature of God and of God's plans for creation.

But the Restoration did not begin by chance at the beginning of the nineteenth century. In a revelation that was to become the first section of the Doctrine and Covenants, the Lord's reasoning for the timing of the Restoration is given:

> Wherefore, I the Lord, knowing the calamity which should come upon the inhabitants of the earth, called upon my servant Joseph Smith, Jun., and spake unto him from heaven, and gave him commandments. (D&C 1:17)

What is being spoken of here? There is an urgency wherein God speaks of "calamity." What kind of calamity? It is easy for us to spiritualize this pronouncement and turn it into God's edict against Christianity in Joseph Smith's day. Authority had been lost, Christianity had fallen into apostasy, and there was now no true church on the earth. Surely this is a calamity. But if we analyze the centuries leading up to the beginning of the Restoration through a liberative lens, taking a long hard look at the social, political, and economic movements that led up to Joseph Smith's day, something else takes shape.¹ Reading between the lines of the history of Western "progress," behind the grand narratives about the Industrial Revolution and the era of prosperity it ushered in, we can begin to clearly see the calamity to which God was referring. Here we see a more sinister reality that needed to be uncovered. Behind the incredible prosperity of a few was the misery and ruin of many. The siren song of idolatry had once again sounded with its ever-present human toll.

Serfs and Peasants

The centuries between the Middle Ages and the Industrial Revolution are known in economic history as the "transition to capitalism." During this time in Europe, the long-standing agricultural framework and practices of the feudal system were transformed, and with them so were the political, economic, and social structures of Europe.² The feudal system developed as the Roman empire dissolved along with its tax system of "agrarian surplus [being] extracted, by force if necessary, from the peasant majority"³ by which it had been sustained. Local elites and nobility came to control the conquered or weakened segments of the empire, acting as landlords to peasants who preferred paying rent to the burdensome state taxes or diverting state taxes to their own municipal advantage.⁴ Former slaves were granted a plot of land by their landlords, which provided a subsistence for them and their families and, more importantly for the

---

1. The explicit reference to a *future* calamity in Doctrine and Covenants 1:17 should give us pause in interpreting the purpose of the Restoration as being to correct a general apostasy that occurred following the death of the apostles. Indeed, this framing suggests the Restoration was meant to counter more recent historical events that would precipitate a global calamity.

2. Karl Polanyi, *The Great Transformation: The Political and Economic Origins of Our Time*; Christopher Hill, *Reformation to Industrial Revolution: The Making of Modern English Society, Vol. 1 1530–1780*.

3. Chris Wickham, *Framing the Early Middle Ages: Europe and the Mediterranean 400–800*, 60.

4. Chris Wickham, "The Other Transition: From the Ancient World to Feudalism," 3–36. Wickham argues that the dissolution of the Roman Empire was a direct result of the breakdown in the ability of the state to generate revenue from taxes due to internal tax evasion, external pressures from the Germanic invasions, and the shift from taxation to landowning as the economic basis for political action and power. See Wickham, *Framing the Early Middle Ages*, ch. 2; Chris Wickham, *Medieval Europe*, 28–30.

landlords, also reduced the constant slave revolts. Landlords also began, Sylvia Federici explains, to "subjugate the free peasants, who . . . turned to the lords for protection, although at the cost of their independence."[5] Thus a considerable number of free peasants and former slaves were brought within the control of the lords as tenants, and the "serf" class was born.[6]

Although it was a much better status than slavery and afforded more security from raids, attacks, and rapacious state authorities than free peasantry, serfdom was nevertheless still an oppressive existence. Serfs were considered property of their landlords, as were all their possessions. The "law of the manor" regulated every aspect of their lives. These "laws" were not standardized or legally codified; they were decided based on custom and differed from manor to manor. Landowners pursued any means of enforcing these arbitrary laws and ensuring the dependence of "their tenants, without whose labour their landed property was valueless."[7]

The most important economic aspect of serfdom was the granting of plots of land. These could be passed down to the children of serfs as an inheritance, and they afforded the serfs a degree of autonomy and independence from the lord. Over time, the serfs began to oppose the regulations and restrictions placed on them by their landlords. From the serf's perspective, the largest burden came from the labor they were required to perform on the lord's land, in addition to the work required to maintain their own plots. The serf response to this requirement was a "massive withdrawal of labor" along with a generally shoddy work ethic and "insubordinate attitude."[8] Resistance of serfs over labor as well as to arbitrary taxes levied by the landlords led to villages being granted increasing concessions in the form of written charters or agreements. These standardized the terms of manorial rule, fixed fines and penalties, abolished arbitrary taxes, and gave the villagers a measure of self-governance.

---

5. Sylvia Federici, *Caliban and the Witch: Women, the Body, and Primitive Accumulation*, 23.

6. We should note that the line between serf and peasant during this time was blurry. Even official records, of which there are few, term the same individuals as serfs or peasants in different accounts. What we can say is that peasants and serfs shared an existence largely comprised of dependence on, and servitude to, the lords of the manor during this time.

7. Rodney Hilton, *Bond Men Made Free: Medieval Peasant Movements and the English Rising of 1381*, 60.

8. Federici, *Caliban*, 26.

Most importantly, the requirement for the serfs and peasants to labor for the lords was subject to commutation by money payments, effectively ending the bondage to the land of serfdom but resulting in disastrous consequences for many.[9] The loss of a stable subsistence and land inheritance stripped the peasants of their autonomy and independence, and many were forced to live as tenants and to work for others as wage laborers to scrape together a meager subsistence for themselves and their families. However, as the peasants defaulted on their loans, failed to make their rents, or were forced off their small plots by landowners seeking to expand their own holdings and convert their lands to pasture, more and more were forced into wage labor.[10] With the change from an agricultural economy (which was based largely in the cultivation and produce of crops from individual manors) to a mercantilist economy (which was based in cities and focused on exportation), rights and exploitation of peasants and workers would be the ground for a constant struggle in the centuries leading up to the Industrial Revolution.

Primitive Accumulation

The transition to capitalism in Europe required a massive amount of surplus wealth.[11] In historical accounts, the horrific and well-documented abuses of women, children, and men that occurred during this time to bring about the Industrial Revolution are mentioned, but they are footnoted in favor of highlighting the great strides made in technology, productivity, and manufacturing. Thus, there is a disconnect between the narratives about the development of Western society and the reality of the suffering and exploitation of the poor whose labor powered the Industrial Revolution.

From a position that attempts to center the story of the poor and oppressed and their struggle for liberation, this account is unacceptable. Our investigation, instead, starts from these people and examines the ways that

---

9. Hilton, *Bond Men Made Free*, 85–86.
10. Hilton, *Bond Men Made Free*.
11. All economic histories agree that this transition relied on accumulated wealth, though they differ in their accounts of how this wealth was accumulated. A common approach is to focus on the development of "the economy," which is an "objective" measure of national income that is abstracted from the means of achieving it, or the "market," which embodies God's providence with its "invisible hand." By focusing on a measure of gross aggregate or market fluctuations, the social and human relationships behind accumulation are blurred, and the cost to human lives and livelihoods is lost.

the transition to capitalism affected them. This approach is known as "history from below," as it focuses on the lives and experiences of the exploited majority rather than the minority of the supposed "great men" of the time: those kings, generals, and philosophers.[12]

The generation of the surplus wealth that financed Europe's transition to capitalism required a steady supply of labor. Workers sold their labor for wages in order to earn a subsistence, and in doing so they were without rights and easily exploited. This exploitation, central to the peasants' plight, has often been minimized, and peasants have been stereotyped as being lazy and bringing difficulty and poverty on themselves. Karl Marx describes the age-old fallacy as follows:

> Long, long ago there were two sorts of people; one, the diligent, intelligent, and above all frugal elite; the other, lazy rascals, spending their substance, and more, in riotous living. . . . Thus it came to pass that the former sort accumulated wealth, and the latter sort finally had nothing to sell except their own skins. And from this original sin dates the poverty of the great majority who, despite all their labour, have up to now nothing to sell but themselves, and the wealth of the few that increases constantly although they have long ceased to work.[13]

The transition from serfdom to "free" workers has been viewed as a gradual movement towards freedom by peasant communities. Once freed from serfdom and "the fetters of the guilds,"[14] men were able to work for themselves and to earn wages for their labor. This idyllic account of the evolution of wealth, however, fails to realize that peasant "freedom" to work was not the result of a struggle to this end by the peasants. Rather, it was the result of forcible seizure of their lands and livelihoods by the wealthy ruling class.[15] This forcible expropriation was a primary source of accumulation of the wealth that gave rise to the capitalist system in Europe. As noted by Chris Wickham, the entire history of development of medieval economic systems "hung on the unequal relationship between lords and peasants, and the surplus which the former managed to extract from the latter."[16] The wealth generated by European colonial projects also played a huge role in underwriting the development of capitalism. Thus,

---

12. This method of historiography was popularized in E.P. Thompson, "History from Below," 275–80.
13. Karl Marx, *Capital: Vol I: A Critique of Political Economy*, 873.
14. Marx, 875.
15. Michael Perelman: *The Invention of Capitalism: Classical Political Economy and the Secret History of Primitive Accumulation.*
16. Wickham, *Medieval Europe*, 112.

rather than the mostly peaceful evolution of wealthy land owners and laborers that depended on their inherent personality strengths and flaws, the rise of capitalism and the primitive accumulation of wealth occurred in much more stark and sinister terms of oppression and exploitation. Our task in this chapter is to examine some of the methods by which a minority of landowners and industrialists came to accumulate and own the vast majority of the wealth in Europe (and plundered from overseas) that was the foundation for the Industrial Revolution and the rise of capitalism. This accumulation required an expropriation of land and resources from the poor and oppressed on a massive, previously unknown scale. As immortalized in the words of Marx, "this history, the history of their expropriation, is written in the annals of mankind in letters of blood and fire."[17]

Enclosure and the Commons

Peasants in the Middle Ages were able to avoid dependence on wages due largely to their use and management of the commons. Commons were uncultivated lands and plentiful in Europe: fields, marshes, streams, lakes, meadows, forests, moors, and bogs. These sustained life and livelihood for commoners, "provided crucial resources for the peasant economy (wood for fuel, timber for building, fishponds, grazing grounds for animals) and fostered community cohesion and cooperation."[18]

Most common lands were privatized by the mid-nineteenth century, a process known as *enclosure*.[19] Though there were enclosure movements throughout Europe, those in England were most vigorous and occurred earlier due in part to greater "industrialization, more rapid population growth, more elastic demand for cash crops, and above all, greater abundance of land in proportion to landowning population."[20] This process began by fits and starts, "reaching one peak during the fifteenth and sixteenth centuries and another during the eighteenth and nineteenth centuries."[21] The end of the eighteenth and beginning of the nineteenth centuries was, according to E. P. Thompson, a time of "wholesale enclosure, in which, in village after village, common rights are lost, and the landless and . . . pau-

---

17. Marx, *Capital*, 875.
18. Federici, *Caliban*, 82.
19. For a comprehensive treatment of enclosure in England, see J. M. Neeson, *Commoners: Common Right, Enclosure, and Social Change in England 1700–1820*.
20. Alek A. Rozental, "The Enclosure Movement in France," 55.
21. Peter Linebaugh, *Stop Thief! The Commons, Enclosure, and Resistance*, 144.

perized labourer is left to support the tenant-farmer, the landowner, and the tithes of the Church."[22] During this time, Parliament passed nearly four thousand enclosure acts, resulting in the closing of over six million acres of commons.[23]

Up until the mid-seventeenth century, common right was firmly established and recognized as crucial to the lives and livelihoods of the commoners. It was also accepted that in most instances, enclosure hurt commoners, producing depopulation and dependence on wage labor. Instead, enclosure enriched one large farmer at the expense of impoverishing twenty small ones. But throughout the seventeenth century, there developed a "public argument in favor of enclosure even when it did cause local distress."[24] Supporters of enclosure argued that though enclosure impoverished the commoners, the poor married earlier and had more children, thus contributing to the labor force and guaranteeing economic growth.[25] Those advocates also slandered the commoners. While they had historically been seen as simple, hardworking, generous, and kind, they were now painted as backward, lazy, wretched, barbarians, violent, and drunk criminals. Their presence on the land devalued it. Common right, recognized for centuries, was now tarred as a crime in and of itself.

But the peasants and poor laborers who cherished their common rights and the independence it granted them did not share the encloser's dreams of progress and improvement. They resisted such efforts, legally and illegally, by "petitioning, spreading false rumors, attacking property, foot dragging, mischief, anonymous threatening poems, grumbling, playing football, breaking the squire's gates, fence breaking, wood stealing, and so forth."[26] These riots and public outcries against enclosure often had a greater effect than official petitions. Petitions were expensive and fell on unsympathetic ears in government after the mid-seventeenth century. Often, "Parliament waived its own rules or made them flexible in order to favour enclosers."[27] While resistance campaigns forestalled enclosure by years or decades, in the end—backed by moneyed interests, the force of the law, and the government—the enclosers won.

---

22. E.P. Thompson, *The Making of the English Working Class*, 198.
23. Linebaugh, *Stop Thief!*, 456.
24. Neeson, *Commoners*, 19.
25. Neeson, 31.
26. Linebaugh, *Stop Thief!*, 151.
27. Neeson, *Commoners*, 273.

Enclosure irrevocably altered social relations. It sharpened the perception of the already-present class differences and led to greater class separation. J. M. Neeson explains:

> Enclosure tore away this mask not only to reveal more clearly than before the different interests of small, middling, and large landowners but also to profit one at the expense of the other. It did so in a remarkably public way. . . . The hostility to enclosure . . . indicates that small owners knew how they lost their lands; how they lost their winter fuel, the grazing for a cow and calf or a few sheep, the feed for pigs and geese. Enclosure had a terrible but instructive visibility.[28]

Stripped of their ability to live a self-sustaining lifestyle and forced into wage labor, the peasants and workers were often forced to leave the country and migrate to the city, where they were at the mercy of manufacturers and industrialists. Their labor and exploitation would form the backbone of the Industrial Revolution. However, in the process something had become lost that could not be regained. The social relations (the covenant relations, if you will) had been shattered, and the resulting divisions, though long present, had been laid bare for all to see.[29] The choice of the wealthy to oppress the poor for profit was made explicit. The dehumanization of the poor was accelerating, and it would reach a fever pitch in the criminal codes and capital punishments of the eighteenth century.[30]

---

28. Neeson, 290–91.

29. The breakdown in social relations that resulted from enclosure contributed directly to the terror of the witch hunts (maps of enclosures and maps of witch hunts even correspond). The women most often accused of witchcraft (older women, widows, unwed young mothers) were those most likely to be hurt by the expropriation of the common means of subsistence, and those most likely to resist. See Federici, *Caliban*; Federici *Witches, Witch-Hunting, and Women*; and Keith Thomas, *Religion and the Decline of Magic: Studies in Popular Beliefs in Sixteenth and Seventeenth Century England*, 660–65. See also Carolyn Merchant, *The Death of Nature: Women, Ecology, and the Scientific Revolution*, chs. 5–7, for discussion of how the time of the witch hunts corresponded with the replacement of midwives with doctors, and how the misogyny that justified violation and torture of women to extract confessions of witchcraft served as a blueprint for Enlightenment thinker's justification for the extraction and plunder of raw materials and other "secrets" from the earth.

30. Though there are many tragic stories of enclosure and eviction during this period, the Highland Clearances in Scotland stand out most for their explicit cruelty. See John Prebble, *The Highland Clearances*; see James Hunter, *Set Adrift Upon the World: The Sutherland Clearances*, for an account of the particularly

Property and the Criminalization of the Poor

As the enclosure movement gained momentum, more poor people were forced out of subsistence lifestyles in the country and into the cities as wage laborers, creating two problems for the ruling elites and wealthy industrialists. First, the amassing of wealth in the form of land had only been possible by expropriating that land from peasants and the poor. Peasants rejected the claims of the land as the private property of the landowners; those that did not go to the cities still frequented the enclosed commons (illegally so and sometimes living there) to collect, fish, and hunt to subsist and feed their families. Landowners were in a difficult position as these infractions were dealt with by the "law of the forest," which varied from forest to forest with no universal statute to deal with poaching or illegal use of the forests and commons.

The second problem was that when the enclosures forced masses of poor into wage dependence, the cities became full of desperate, starving people. (Between the beginnings of the seventeenth and eighteenth centuries, the population of London increased from two hundred thousand to almost one million.) Faced with working long hours for low wages, the poor increasingly turned to other means of survival: theft, robbery, and burglary. Thus, as the means of subsistence for the poor was increasingly privatized, and as they resisted or turned to crime to survive, the negotiation of a new "social contract" had to be undertaken—one that defined and protected the interests of the rich over the needs of the poor. This "negotiation" occurred in the form of a retooling of the criminal codes.[31]

These efforts to rewrite the criminal codes were based around the concept of private property. As ubiquitous an idea as it is today, the notion of private landownership has been a relatively new development in history. Throughout antiquity, land had been considered the property of gods, and stewardship had been granted to various kings or rulers, who in turn

---

brutal Sutherland Clearances. See "The Poetry of the Clearances" for a sample of some of the heartbreaking Gaelic poetry in response to the clearances.

31. The most detailed records available regarding this movement in Europe are from the courts and legislative records in England. London, in particular, was the largest city in Europe and the epicenter of the Industrial Revolution, so provides a useful lens for our purposes. The industrialization and urbanization of the rest of Europe generally occurred later, after the beginning of the Restoration.

granted it to others.³² This resulted, according to Karl Widerquist and Grant McCall, in the "setting up of various forms of complex, flexible, nonspatial, overlapping land-tenure systems with significant collective and communal elements."³³ As late as the beginning of the sixteenth century, only a few societies had set up private property systems. The private property system as we know it was largely the result of the enclosure and colonialist movements, which set up a system of appropriation of land and designation of private property that was rare throughout history and only then being established in Europe itself.³⁴

The justification for this system of expropriation was the political philosophy of men such as John Locke, who argued that private property was the result of a prehistoric "original appropriator." Widerquist and McCall explain, "Locke's original appropriator is the first person (presumed male) who, generations ago, took a piece of unclaimed land and improved it with his labor, thereby gaining the right to permanent, tradable, and heritable ownership of that land."³⁵ Locke's treatise on property is a masterclass in mental gymnastics, in which he moves from admitting that "God . . . has given the earth to the children of men; given it to mankind in common,"³⁶ therefore making it difficult to see "how any one should ever come to have a property in any thing,"³⁷ to asserting that by their labor, men improve the earth and so have the right to appropriate its products and the land itself as their property. Moreover, Locke initially argues that such appropriation is valid only "where there is enough, and as good, left in common for others."³⁸ He not only justifies the appropriation of land as property; he defends doing so without the consent of the commoners by asserting that "he that incloses land, and has a greater plenty of the conveniencies of life from ten acres, than he could have from an hundred left to nature, may truly be said to give ninety acres to mankind."³⁹

Locke and his acolytes eventually satisfied themselves with having proved that private property was a part of society from time immemorial

---

32. Karl Widerquist and Grant S. McCall, *The Prehistory of Private Property: Implications for Modern Political Theory*.
33. Widerquist and McCall, *Prehistory*, 4.
34. Widerquist and McCall, ch. 14.
35. Widerquist and McCall, 33.
36. John Locke, *Two Treatises of Government*, 285.
37. Locke, 285.
38. Locke, 285.
39. Locke, 294.

and that inequality of landownership was an inevitable outcome of any society that valued life, liberty, and property.[40] Furthermore, he argued that the entire function of government was to protect such property.[41] Finally, he anticipated the flood of retributive criminal legislation in his assertion that the definition of political power was the ability to create and enforce the death penalty. These concepts revolutionized social, economic, and criminal justice systems, and they led to the misery, incarceration, and execution of thousands of poor people in the eighteenth century.[42]

Once the concept of private property was enshrined in the political consciousness, the legal system could be used to enforce and justify it. The eighteenth century saw a move within the legal system that developed and brutally enforced penalties for crimes against property. As described by

---

40. Karl Widerquist and Grant S. McCall, *Prehistoric Myths in Modern Political Philosophy*, ch. 4.

41. In modern times, the free-market economist Milton Friedman agreed that this was the purpose of government; see Milton Friedman, *Capitalism and Freedom*; Milton Friedman, "A Friedman Doctrine: The Social Responsibility of Business is to Increase Its Profits," 17. Friedman would later collaborate with the dictator Augusto Pinochet to use the brutally repressed country of Chile as a real-world economic laboratory to test his free-market theories, directly leading to the poverty and immiseration of millions.

42. Given the sharply defined and growing class and wealth distinctions that comprised the centuries leading up to the Industrial Revolution, religious interpretation took on a particularly economic focus for the poor. They rejected tithes and insisted that preachers must labor for their own subsistence. The creeds of many of the "heretical" sects repudiated the expropriation of the lands and livelihoods of the poor by the wealthy merchants and industrialists. Sects such as the Anabaptists rejected private property. The Familists (Family of Love) also held all their property in common. The Levellers, first named for their resistance to enclosure by levelling hedges, later became associated with the term in the sense of levelling the social and economic conditions for rich and poor, citing Christian congregations in the book of Acts who donated all of their property to the church for redistribution. For Gerrard Winstanley, the founder of the Levellers, Jesus Christ is the "head Leveller." See Christopher Hill, *The World Turned Upside Down: Radical Ideas During the English Revolution*; Christopher Hill, *Winstanley: "The Law of Freedom" and Other Writings*. This religious-tinged economic fervor was repeated in the American colonies in the years leading up to and following the American Revolution. See William Hogeland, *Founding Finance: How Debt, Speculation, Foreclosures, Protests, and Crackdowns Made Us a Nation*; Gary B. Nash, *The Urban Crucible: Social Change, Political Consciousness, and the Origins of the American Revolution*.

John Walliss, the so-called "Bloody Code" of this time period made crimes against property a capital offense:

> Between 1688 and 1820 the number of capital crimes in England and Wales increased exponentially from fifty to over 220. . . . Males and females found themselves facing the gallows having being convicted of crimes ranging from murder, through burglary and housebreaking and horse, cattle and sheep theft to theft of goods over twelve pence [a little over £5 ($6) today].[43]

Thus the expansion of the criminal code and enforcement of penalties for property crimes became a critical aspect of judicial proceedings.[44] In an analysis of the lives and trials of those executed in London during the eighteenth century, Peter Linebaugh notes that "most of those hanged had offended against the laws of property, and at the heart of the 'social contract' was respect for private property. It could therefore be argued that . . . each hanging repeated the lesson 'Respect Private Property.'"[45] Hangings were public and occurred on specific "execution days," twice a year, for maximum impact and spectacle.

The specific legislation passed during this period reinforced the use of the legal code as a means of controlling and keeping the poor in check. We consider just a few of these acts here.[46] The Riot Act (1715) made it a felony to gather in groups of twelve or more without prior approval. The Transportation Act (1719) mandated fourteen years slave labor in the colonies in the West Indies or North America for anyone who was pardoned for a capital crime, and it assigned seven years for anyone convicted of a felony, with the added stipulation that those returning from transportation early were subject to hanging. The Combination Act (1721) was passed in response to a strike by tailors in London, making it illegal for tailors to enter into "combinations" for the purpose of securing higher wages. The Workhouse Act (1723) authorized any parish in the country to build its own workhouse and allowed parishes to deny their parishio-

---

43. John Walliss, *The Bloody Code in England and Wales, 1760–1830*, 1.

44. An analysis of court documents from several counties in England found that between the mid-1700s and early 1800s, 80% of court indictments were for some type of property offense, and convictions for property crimes were nearly twice that of crimes against a person (murder, rape). 38% of those convicted of property crimes were sentenced to death. Walliss, *The Bloody Code*.

45. Peter Linebaugh, *The London Hanged: Crime and Civil Society in the Eighteenth Century*, xx.

46. See Linebaugh, *The London Hanged*, for further detail of the legislation discussed in this section and more.

ners any poor relief and to instead commit them to the workhouse.[47] The Vagrancy Act (1744) allowed for the arrest, prosecution, and transportation of the itinerant poor, naming as vagrants those deemed the lowest of society: play actors, minstrels, anyone begging for alms, gypsies, fortune tellers, jugglers, those running betting games, those lodging in alehouses, prostitutes,[48] those pretending to be soldiers, mariners, or pretending to work in harvest.[49] The Black Act (1723), named for outlaws who blacked their faces and engaged in a sustained campaign of deer poaching, threats, and violence in the king's forests, created over 200 capital offenses and in all specified the death penalty for over 350 crimes.[50]

In all, the criminal legislation of this time repressed poor workers and those forced to break the law to earn a subsistence—while protecting the property and livelihoods of the ruling class. In place of a standing police force, "propertied Englishmen had a fat and swelling sheaf of laws which threatened thieves with death."[51] These laws were not passed in response to public campaigns or well-articulated statements of social problems by lawmakers; they were knee-jerk reactions to the threat to property.[52] The poor, however, had few options. In many cases, crimes against property were the difference between living and dying. Under such conditions, death sentences would not serve as a deterrent. If left with the choice of starvation or thievery, the answer for many was simple, and it was not uncommon for "the eighteenth-century pickpocket [to ply] his trade at the hanging of another pickpocket."[53] Thus, the poor during the eighteenth century found themselves being squeezed ever tighter between expropriation of

---

47. By the end of the century, there were some two thousand workhouses in England, with ninety in London alone. Infant death rates in these squalid city workhouses were as high as fifty percent. See Anthony Brundage, *The English Poor Laws, 1700*, ch. 2.

48. With the ever-present threat of starvation, violence, and disease, many women sold themselves into prostitution. For an examination of prostitution in London during the eighteenth century, see Hallie Rubenhold, *The Covent Garden Ladies: Pimp General Jack and the Extraordinary Story of Harris's List*.

49. Joanne McEwan and Pamela Sharpe, eds., *Accommodating Poverty: The Housing and Living Arrangements of the English Poor, c. 1600–1850*, ch. 5.

50. Linebaugh, *The London Hanged*, 16–18, 202, 321; E.P. Thompson, *Whigs and Hunters: The Origins of the Black Act*.

51. Douglas Hay, Peter Linebaugh, John G. Rule, E. P. Thompson, and Cal Winslow, *Albion's Fatal Tree: Crime and Society in Eighteenth-Century England*, 18.

52. Hay, *Albion's Fatal Tree*, 20.

53. Linebaugh, *The London Hanged*, xx.

their old forms of subsistence and criminalization of the means they were forced to take to survive.

Conquest and Colonialism

When European explorers stepped on the shores of what would come to be known as the American continent, they found a people that had lived and developed complex societies for thousands of years. The land was so full of abundance that it was insisted by some to be the location of the Garden of Eden.[54] Indeed, the architectural sophistication of the cities, with their causeways, bridges, roads, temples, and palaces, encountered by Spanish conquistadors in places like Tenochtitlan and Cuzco, was so magnificent it created a state of awe in them.[55]

Despite this awe, understanding or interacting with these societies was not what drove the explorers. The conquistadors, mostly men of small nobility or financial means, sought wealth and fame in the New World. Their efforts received divine approval, as the decree by Pope Alexander VI in 1493 gave Spain and Portugal exclusive right to "discover" the entirety of the American continent.[56] They were now free to conquer, convert, and plunder with divine sanction.

When these ragtag bands of marauders reached the New World, their single-minded focus was on appropriating land and finding wealth. Soldiers had been promised gold and jewels, and the monarchs that financed the first exploratory voyages looked to recoup their financial investments with the rumored massive amounts of wealth to be found in "riverbeds filled with nuggets and of boulders that shattered and poured forth gold when struck with a club."[57] The Europeans' thirst for gold was insatiable and ever-present in accounts of these expeditions. They roved about with vicious attack dogs, "stealing, killing, raping, and torturing natives, trying to force them to divulge the whereabouts of the imagined treasurehouses of gold."[58] The Culhua-Mexica (Aztec) people, when they brought Cortés gifts of gold and jewels, described the greed of the colonialists:

---

54. David E. Stannard, *American Holocaust: The Conquest of the New World*, 637.
55. Bernal Díaz del Castillo, *The Discovery and Conquest of Mexico*, 269–70, 298.
56. Pope Alexander VI, *Inter Caetera* - Papal bull 1493. This pronouncement is known as the "Doctrine of Discovery."
57. Stannard, *American Holocaust*, 213.
58. Stannard, 69.

They lifted up the gold as if they were monkeys, with expressions of joy, as if it put new life into them and lit up their hearts. As if it were certainly something for which they yearn with a great thirst. Their bodies fatten on it and they hunger violently for it. They crave gold like hungry swine.[59]

The thirst for gold is only equalled by the thirst for land—not just to possess it but for the ability to control the labor and product of the land. The conquistadors wanted fame and riches, but they also wanted power and a life of leisure.[60] They were aided and abetted in this by the decree that set up the land tenure system known as the *encomienda*. According to this, any explorer or conqueror who found land inhabited by non-Christians was entitled to claim the land and force the indigenous inhabitants to labor and extract tribute from them. Anyone who desired to appropriate land or to engage the natives in a military conflict had only to read a statement, the *Requerimiento*, in the presence of a notary public.[61] This statement ostensibly gave the natives the opportunity to acknowledge the sovereignty of the Spanish monarchs and the Catholic church before they were enslaved or killed and their lands seized. In actuality, since it was not translated or required to be read in the presence of any indigenous people, it was merely a legal and theological justification for the deaths, torture, and enslavement of the people. It was often done merely as a formality "after they had been put in chains."[62] Exploitation, rape, forced marriage, abuse, and violence were rampant. The people were worked to death and barely given enough food to survive. Indigenous populations were decimated.[63]

The conquistadors, who often funded their own expeditions, gathered their own forces and forged on into unknown territories with no real accountability to anyone but themselves. No legal or moral framework

---

59. Eduardo Galeano, *Open Veins of Latin America: Five Centuries of the Pillage of a Continent*, trans. Cedric Belfrage, 19.
60. Kim MacQuarrie, *The Last Days of the Incas*, 43.
61. *Requerimiento*, National Humanities Center Research Toolbox.
62. Tzvetan Todorov, *The Conquest of America: The Question of the Other*, 148.
63. Bartolomé de las Casas, a Dominican friar and priest who chronicled the devastation wrought by the Spanish, observed, "Both women and men were given only wild grasses to eat and other unnutritious foodstuffs. The mothers of young children promptly saw their milk dry up and their babies die; and, with the women and the men separated and never seeing each other, no new children were born. The men died down the mines from overwork and starvation, and the same was true of the women who perished out on the estates. The islanders, previously so numerous, began to die out." Bartolomé de las Casas, *A Short Account of the Destruction of the Indies*, 24.

existed to stem the slaughter. The letters from Cortés cooly describe the "progress" of his conquest.[64] Following the death of Montezuma during a riot, the Aztecs regathered their strength and drove Cortés from Tenochtitlan. He returned with reinforcements and laid siege to the city, which had been weakened substantially by a smallpox epidemic. Having cut off food and fresh water to the city, he hoped for a quick victory, but he was astounded by the continued resistance and refusal to surrender. His troops ventured into the city many times, killing tens of thousands, but still the people refused to surrender. He writes that he and his troops "could not but be saddened by their determination to die."[65]

By the time the siege was over, the starvation, suffering, and death was horrific. In their trips into the city to test the resistance and destroy buildings and infrastructure, Cortés and his men notice "that they suffered greatly from hunger, for in the streets we had found roots and strips of bark which had been gnawed. . . . We found the streets along which we passed full of women and children and other wretched people all starving to death, thin and exhausted."[66] Still they refused to surrender. On the last day of the siege, Cortés met with the captain of the indigenous force, who informed him that his superior would rather die than meet with Cortés. Cortés resolved to "attack and slay them all." The scene in the city was apocalyptic:

> The people of the city had to walk upon their dead while others swam or drowned in the waters of that wide lake where they had their canoes; indeed, so great was their suffering that it was beyond our understanding how they could endure it. Countless numbers of men, women and children came out toward us, and in their eagerness to escape many were pushed into the water where they drowned amid that multitude of corpses; and it seemed that more than fifty thousand had perished from the salt water they had drunk, their hunger and the vile stench.[67]

When the surrender finally came, at least one hundred thousand had been killed or starved in the city. The survivors were then strip-searched for gold: "The Christians searched all the refugees. They even opened the women's skirts and blouses and felt everywhere: their ears, their breasts,

---

64. Inga Clendinnen, "'Fierce and Unnatural Cruelty': Cortés and the Conquest of Mexico."
65. Hernan Cortés, *Letters from Mexico*, 233.
66. Cortés, 256–57.
67. Cortés, 263.

their hair."[68] Countless thousands of others had been killed by Cortés in his campaign against the Aztecs, and many thousands more were wiped out by smallpox and other diseases.

We see the dead mostly through the eyes of the conquerors, but some of their own voices have been recovered. They tell of prophecy, of omens, of massacres, of terror, of greed, and of death.[69] One such account tells of the horrific slaughter of celebrants at the Feast of Toxcatl in Tenochtitlan. Cortés had left the city, putting his deputy, Pedro de Alvarado, in charge. At the height of the feast, when the celebrants were singing and dancing in the courtyard of the temple, Alvarado attacked without warning.[70] The translation of the original account details the terror

> And when this was happening, when already the feast was being observed, when already there was dancing, and already there was singing, when already there was song with dance, the singing resounded like waves breaking.
>
> When it was already time, when the moment was opportune for the Spaniards to slay them, thereupon they came forth. They were arrayed for battle. They came everywhere to block each of the ways leading out and leading in.... [N]o one could go out.
>
> And when this had been done, thereupon they entered the temple courtyard to slay them.... Thereupon they surrounded the dancers. Thereupon they went among the drums. Then they struck the drummer's arms; they severed both his hands; then they struck his neck. Far off did his neck [and head] go to fall. Then they all pierced the people with iron lances and they struck them with iron swords. Of some they slashed their backs: then their entrails gushed out. Of some they cut their heads to pieces; they absolutely pulverized their heads; their heads were absolutely pulverized. And some they struck on the shoulder; they split openings, they broke openings in their bodies. Of some they struck repeatedly on the shanks; of some they struck repeatedly the thighs; of some they struck the belly; then their entrails gushed forth. And when in vain one would run, he would only drag his intestines like something raw as he tried to escape. Nowhere could he go.[71]

---

68. Miguel Leon-Portilla, ed., *The Broken Spears: The Aztec Account of the Conquest of Mexico*, 140.

69. Leon-Portilla, *The Broken Spears*.

70. Alvarado had ostensibly learned, through confessions of priests and nobles obtained under torture, of a planned revolt, which he used as a pretext for his assault. The attack on the festival killed thousands.

71. Fray Bernardino de Sahagún, *Florentine Codex: General History of the Things of New Spain: Book 12: The Conquest of Mexico*, 55–56.

We must likewise consider the slaughter of Native Americans that took place at the hands of the British colonists. Beginning in Virginia in the early seventeenth century, spreading into New England and the Northeast, and West to Texas and California in the centuries to come, military and mob forces waged a campaign of displacement, extermination, and terror that, combined with disease (often spread intentionally),[72] resulted in the decimation of the populations of hundreds of tribes.

The brutality and cruelty that accompanied this extermination campaign is well-documented but not as well known. Settlers routinely targeted women and children in villages while men were away. Women were raped, and children were used for shooting practice; they had their heads stove in with rifle butts, were torn from their mother's breasts and dashed against rocks, or were simply left to die. The victims were scalped and mutilated, their genitals, fingers, ears, and noses were cut off for jewelry, and their bodies were skinned as trophies with their flesh being used to make boots, hats, leggings, and bridle reins.[73] Official bounties were offered on heads and scalps, including of women and children.[74] "Damn any man who sympathizes with Indians. . . . I have come to kill Indians. . . . Kill 'em all, big and small. Nits make lice," was the command of Colonel Chivington before the massacre of Cheyenne at Sand Creek.[75]

This explicit disregard for the right to life and humanity of indigenous peoples goes back to the foundation of the United States. When it came to relations with the Native Americans, the lofty ideals of life, liberty, and the pursuit of happiness did not extend far. With the population of the colonies exploding from about two thousand to over two million within the first two centuries, settlers needed land, and indigenous people were

---

72. Colin G. Calloway, *The Scratch of a Pen: 1763 and the Transformation of North America*, 73.

73. Stannard, *American Holocaust*, 462.

74. See Cormac McCarthy, *Blood Meridian, or the Evening Redness in the West*, for a bleak and brutal fictional portrayal of a gang of scalp hunters based on historical events.

75. The targeting of women and children, suggests David Stannard, indicates intentional genocide: "The European habit of indiscriminately killing women and children when engaged in hostilities with the natives of the Americas was more than an atrocity. It was flatly and intentionally genocidal. For no population can survive if its women and children are destroyed." Stannard, *American Holocaust*, 119; See Benjamin Madley, "Reexamining the American Genocide Debate: Meaning, Historiography, and New Methods," 98–139, for further discussion and examples.

in the way.⁷⁶ At times seeming magnanimous towards the natives in their speech or public facing pronouncements, the private orders and communications of the founding fathers suggest much less noble intentions. In May of 1779, in regards to the Iroquois, George Washington instructed Major General John Sullivan

> to lay waste all the settlements around . . . that the country may not be merely *overrun* but *destroyed*. . . . But you will not by any means, listen to any overture of peace before the total ruin of their settlements is effected. . . . Our future security will be in their inability to injure us . . . and in the terror with which the severity of the chastizement they receive will inspire them.⁷⁷

For his "inspirational" campaigns, in which he utterly wasted most of the settlements of the Seneca, Mohawk, Onondaga, and Cayuga, Washington was known by the natives as "Town Destroyer." One of the Iroquois told Washington to his face in 1792, "To this day, when that name is heard, our women look behind them and turn pale, and our children cling close to the necks of their mothers."⁷⁸ In the area of New York known as the "burned over district," a campaign of raids, ordered in 1779 by Washington, had "destroyed Indian settlements by burning houses, cutting down apple and peach orchards, torching corn, squash, and bean, and incinerating hay fields."⁷⁹ The metaphor of the "fire" of rampant evangelism in Joseph Smith's day seems quaint and disrespectful in the face of this brutal historical reality.

Thomas Jefferson had a conflicted relationship with Native Americans. On the one hand, he expressed a paternal love and responsibility for them, referring to them to John Adams as "our Indians." He appears to have viewed them as equal in some ways with whites, and he advocated

---

76. This conflict over land between settlers and native peoples contributed directly to the American Revolution. Following the French and Indian War, the Treaty of Paris, signed in 1763, transferred huge areas of indigenous land from French to British imperial control. Britain's declaration of the Proclamation Line in response to continued conflict between natives and settlers forbade American colonists from freely settling, purchasing, or appropriating land west of the Appalachian Mountains. This move, and others by Britain to protect their economic interests in North America, was a primary motivation in the drive for the colonies to declare independence. See Calloway, *The Scratch of a Pen*.

77. Richard Drinnon, *Facing West: The Metaphysics of Indian-Hating and Empire-Building*, 331; emphasis in original.

78. Stannard, *American Holocaust*, 120.

79. Linebaugh, *Stop Thief!*, 242.

a program of assimilation.[80] But the peaceable campaign of assimilation continued to butt up against the harsh reality of the need for land by the American colonialists. Although he promised that "the lands . . . would remain yours, and shall never go from you but when you should be disposed to sell,"[81] Jefferson embarked on a covert campaign of pressuring chiefs to sell their lands against their will. In the case of those who refused to sell, he encouraged traders to entrap them with debts piled up at government trading posts that would require them to sell their lands to settle.[82] His officials bribed others. He explicitly affirmed the duplicitous nature of this campaign, telling the legislature "their disclosure might embarrass and defeat their effect"[83] and that his plans would be "improper to be understood by the Indians."[84] His goals for dealing with the natives can be summed up in a letter to then General Andrew Jackson, who would later become president and wage his own war of extermination and forced relocation: "1. The preservation of peace; 2. The obtaining lands."[85]

When the obtaining of lands conflicted with the preservation of peace, however, land won. When the cajoling, bribing, entrapment, and foreclosing failed to secure the needed lands, Jefferson turned to military force. Whatever the conflicted nature of his personal feelings towards Native Americans, his policy objectives were clear: Native Americans must either cede their lands or be exterminated. This objective was the official government position towards Native Americans from that time forward. Villages and tribes were decimated as the indigenous populations were hunted, killed, and forced off their lands and relocated in official government actions, such as the infamous "Trail of Tears." In addition to the well-known stories of peoples such as the Apache, Cherokee, Seminole, Cheyenne, Navajo, Lakota, Iroquois, and Sioux, we list a few here with the percentage of the original population destroyed: Abenaki (98), Mahican (92), Mohawk (75), Pocumtuck (95), Maliseet-Passamaquoddy (67), Quiripi-Unquachog (95), Massachusett (81), Illinois (96), Kansas (96), Kalapuya (99), Talowa (92), Zuni (50), Acoma (70), Hopi (80), Mandan (90), Quapaw (99).[86] These examples can be multiplied many times over.

---

80. Drinnon, *Facing West*, 83.
81. Drinnon, 86.
82. Drinnon, 87.
83. Drinnon, 86.
84. Drinnon, 88.
85. Drinnon, 87.
86. Stannard, *American Holocaust*, 449–52.

Indigenous people's inheritance at the hands of American colonialists is one of genocide and destruction of culture and identity, disenfranchisement, and exploitation.[87] All told, modern archeological and anthropological estimates put the number of dead indigenous people due to colonialism in the Americas at as high as 150 million.[88] David Stannard concludes, "Of all the horrific genocides that have occurred in the twentieth century . . . none has come close to destroying this many—or this great a proportion—of wholly innocent people."[89]

We have considered only a few instances related to colonialism in the centuries before the Industrial Revolution and the Restoration. We have omitted, not for lack of importance, discussion of the enslavement of Africans in the building of the American colonies and the generation of wealth that contributed to industry and manufacturing in England.[90] This history, perhaps more well known than that of the indigenous people, is no less tragic. Current estimates vary widely, from some 12.5 million to over 60 million people captured from their homes and forced into ships that transported them across the Atlantic. As many as half of these died of starvation and disease before arriving in the Americas due to the appalling conditions on the ships. The rest were forced to labor in the most brutal conditions on farms and plantations, treated as chattel and brutalized and killed *en masse*. The Atlantic slave trade has left a legacy of racism and prejuduce in the United States. Indeed, some refer to it as America's "original sin," the effects of which still reverberate today.[91] Those who remained

---

87. Our own religious tradition is foundationally entwined with colonialism. See Gina Colvin and Joanna Brooks, eds., *Decolonizing Mormonism: Approaching a Postcolonial Zion*, for an incisive and confronting examination of how colonialism has shaped the structure, doctrine, and culture of The Church of Jesus Christ of Latter-day Saints.

88. David Michael Smith, "Counting the Dead: Estimating the Loss of Life in the Indigenous Holocaust, 1492–Present."

89. Stannard, *American Holocaust*, 75.

90. Hugh Thomas, *The Slave Trade: The Story of the Atlantic Slave Trade, 1440–1870*.

91. Ibram X. Kendi, *Stamped From the Beginning: The Definitive History of Racist Ideas in America*. Sylvia Federici notes the entrenchment of colonial injustice in American society and politics: "No major political change will in fact be possible in the United States unless the two grand injustices on which this country is based—the dispossession and genocide of the Native Americans and the enslavement of millions of Africans, continued through post-Reconstruction and in many ways into the present—are confronted and reparations are provided." Sylvia Federici, *Re-enchanting the World: Feminism and the Politics of the Commons*, 265. See Toni

in Africa were not safe from the shadow of colonialism. In the century following the initial events of the Restoration, the "Scramble for Africa" would see European powers partition and conquer most of Africa, leading to the enslavement, torture, brutalization, and death of tens of millions of Africans and a legacy of debt and impoverishment.[92]

Nor have we explored the havoc and devastation wrought by the East India Company, which went from inauspicious beginnings at the turn of the seventeenth century as a little private English business venture jockeying for position with other European powers for trading privileges in the East, to a corporation that had legal authority over the many English colonies in India. According to William Dalrymple, they were able to

> claim jurisdiction over all English subjects in Asia, mint money, raise fortifications, make laws, wage war [they employed a standing army twice the size of the English state force], conduct an independent foreign policy, hold courts, issue punishment, imprison English subjects, and plant English settlements.[93]

They bribed parliament, monopolized trade, and took advantage of national disputes and strife to conquer and colonize huge parts of the Indian subcontinent. Expanding their reach beyond India, they used their trade advantages to encourage the addiction of millions of Chinese people to opium, and then they declared war when the Chinese tried to revoke their trade privileges. All told, the imperialism and colonialism of the East India Company cost from several hundred thousand to upwards of ten million lives, with British colonial policy in India claiming tens of millions more due to famine.

The effects of colonialism have brutalized the entire world. From Aotearoa (New Zealand) in the South to Alyeska (Alaska) and Kalaallit Nunaat (Greenland) in the North, the seizure of lands, labor, and bodies

---

Morrison, *Beloved;* Colson Whitehead, *The Underground Railroad*; and Colson Whitehead, *The Nickel Boys*, for beautifully devastating fictional portrayals of the legacy of trauma and evil left by slavery.

92. Thomas Pakenham, *The Scramble for Africa: The White Man's Conquest of the Dark Continent from 1876 to 1912*; Adam Hochschild, *King Leopold's Ghost: A Story of Greed, Terror, and Heroism in Colonial Africa*; Walter Rodney, *How Europe Underdeveloped Africa*; Joseph R. Gibson, *How Europe and America are Still Underdeveloping Africa: Neocolonialism and the Scramble for Strategic Resources in 21st Century Africa*; and see Barbara Kingsolver, *The Poisonwood Bible*, for an elegant fictional treatment of the damage wrought by the intersection of colonialism and Christianity in Africa.

93. William Dalrymple, *The Anarchy: The East India Company, Corporate Violence, and the Pillage of an Empire*, 9.

and the erasure of indigenous culture and identity has irrevocably changed the course of history and shaped the trajectory and politics of our current day. Depicting the full scope and atrocity of the global indigenous genocide that accompanied the rise of imperial European powers between the fifteenth and twentieth centuries is beyond the scope of this chapter, or even this book or dozens of such studies. Indeed, it seems impossible, try as we might, to be able to capture the full breadth and depth of the massacre that took place at the hands of European colonialists. If we can't contemplate the staggering totality, perhaps reflecting on some of these examples will help us feel the experience of the one. After all, if Christianity has taught us anything, it is the depth of feeling that can come from contemplating the suffering, torture, and death of a single individual. We owe it to those who have suffered and died to feel the weight and horror of these deaths.

A Creation Groaning

We have seen that in the centuries leading up to both the Industrial Revolution and the Restoration, the shift from a feudal to a capitalist economy required the expropriation of land and resources on an unprecedented scale. This was accompanied by the immiseration and death of tens of millions of people. This atrocity has continued apace in the centuries since the Industrial Revolution.[94] The daily-expanding toll is hidden

---

94. Any discussion of the human toll of political and economic systems in the two centuries since the Restoration must reckon with the fact that tens of millions of lives have been lost under the banner of communism, which is, at least ideologically, opposed to capitalism. The two most obvious examples of this are Stalin's Russia and Mao's China. In both cases, the goal was rapid industrialization in order to compete with Britain and the US as a military and economic power. This was accomplished via forced labor and expropriation of peasant lands and livelihood on a massive scale. Both dictators also conducted campaigns to rid their nations of those with questionable loyalty or who stood in the way of the state's economic and military goals. Stalin's regime is estimated to have deliberately killed at least six million people, with at least three million more as the casualties of his policies (some total estimates as high as twenty million). Mao's policies and campaigns contributed to the deaths of forty-five to seventy million of his people. While usually cited as evidence against communism in favor of capitalism, in the context of the present study these atrocities are further evidence of the modern calamity caused by economic systems which prioritize profits or "progress" over human lives and livelihoods. For perspectives on Stalin's Russia, see James Harris, *The Great Fear: Stalin's Terror of the 1930s*; Anne Applebaum, *Red Famine: Stalin's*

behind the statistics of government agencies and propagandist think tanks who put a rosy hue on a global economic system that depends on the voracious consumption of lives and labor for its survival.

Those of us who live our lives in relative comfort and luxury often do not make the connection between our way of life and the misery and starvation of much of the Global South. As is always the case, it is the poor and marginalized—particularly women and children—who suffer the most.[95] When faced with the massive suffering of humankind, governments and corporations throw up their hands, feign concern, and manufacture statistics to hide the devastating reality that 60 percent of the world is living in poverty while the richest 10 percent own 82 percent of the world's wealth, the top 1 percent own 46 percent, and the bottom half of the human population own less than 1 percent.[96] Politicians foment culture wars—themselves the product of nationalist, white-supremacist, racist, homophobic, and misogynist ideologies—to distract from the rampant exploitation, abuse, and corruption of corporations. International courts protect corporate trade privileges and levy penalties on countries that try to extract themselves from the corporate death grip, while domestic legislative bodies and courts strip rights from indigenous people, racial minorities, women, and any other marginalized groups whose claim to

---

War on Ukraine. See Aleksandr Solzhenitsyn, *The Gulag Archipelago 1918–1956*, for a classic first-person account of Stalin's state apparatus of terror. For Mao's China, see Frank Dikötter, *Mao's Great Famine: The History of China's Most Devastating Catastrophe 1958–1962*; Jung Chan and Jon Halliday, *Mao: The Unknown Story*. See Yiyun Li, *The Vagrants*, for an unsparing fictional account of the fracturing of social and familial bonds that resulted from the Cultural Revolution.

95. Arundhati Roy, *Capitalism: A Ghost Story*; Maria Mies, *Patriarchy and Accumulation on a World Scale: Women in the International Division of Labour*.

96. Credit Suisse Institute, "Global Wealth Report 2022." According to the World Bank's statistics, the percentage of the world's population living below the international poverty line ($1.90 per day; around $694 per year) has decreased substantially under global capitalism. However, researchers have calculated more meaningful metrics, such as the "ethical poverty line" or the "basic needs poverty line" which take into account other aspects of health and well-being other than mere survival and found that by that standard, the World Bank grossly underestimates poverty rates. In 2015, over 60% of the world's population lived under the ethical poverty line. See Peter Joseph, *The New Human Rights Movement: Reinventing the Economy to End Oppression*, 487–89; Peter Edward, "The Ethical Poverty Line: A Moral Quantification of Absolute Poverty," 377–93.

humanity stands in the way of total corporate hegemony and the assurance of a perpetual source of disposable labor.

Corporations, freed from regulation, oversight, and accountability to anyone but their shareholders, with the help of complicit and corrupt governments, seek to privatize and extract profit from all aspects of our lives from conception to death: maternity, infant, child, retiree, and hospice care, basic dental and healthcare, food, water, housing, heating, cooling, electricity, internet, waste disposal, education, transportation, parking, infrastructure, mail and package delivery, life-saving drugs, treatments and operations, prisons, incarceration, probation, home confinement, residential treatment and rehabilitation, youth and mental health services, and exercise and recreation—with more avenues for and approaches to privatization and exploitation being continuously explored, developed, and implemented.[97] Social media companies mimic real human relationships, endlessly multiplying their fraud of emotional connection via newly improved reaction emojis as they profit from the emaciated and distorted bodies of "influencers"—while their algorithms sink users into echo chambers that amplify misogyny, racism, political extremism, conspiracy theorism, and tribalism. In a twisted irony that is the grotesque yet logical end to a society obsessed with both celebrity and wealth, we can now pay "entrepreneurs" or "coaches" who sell charismatic enthusiasm combined with prepackaged, meme-ready banality, promising us the key to more fulfilling lives or making our own millions.

The greed of the West has plundered the nations of the Global South and left them destitute and in debt, forever chasing a mirage of "progress" or "development." The condition of loans from the International Monetary Fund and the World Bank is to impose "structural adjustments," an innocuous-sounding term which in reality means austerity, enclosure, and privatization, leading to an endless cycle of poverty and more debt, and creating social and economic conditions that fracture communities, give rise to targeted actions against marginalized and vulnerable women, and restructure economies around intentional immiseration and poverty.[98] Modern-day

---

97. Donald Cohen and Allen Mikaelian, *The Privatization of Everything: How the Plunder of Public Goods Transformed America and How We Can Fight Back*; Lauren-Brooke Eisen, *Inside Private Prisons: An American Dilemma in the Age of Mass Incarceration*.

98. Sylvia Federici, *Caliban*, 236–39; *Witches, Witch-Hunting, and Women*, chs. 6–7. See Jamie Martin, *The Meddlers: Sovereignty, Empire, and the Birth of Global Economic Governance*, for discussion of how the world economic system was

slavery is practiced in "free trade zones" that gather the debris of offshored jobs to set up huge plantation-style factories that exploit women and children for wages of $1 per day or less.[99] Any country or citizenry that dares to challenge the international corporate hegemony or speak up for the right of its people to be free from exploitation is crushed by sanctions, union busting, blockades, and other economic or political tools of suppression. If all else fails, Western governments are ever ready, under the guise of "spreading freedom," to war against, undermine, and overthrow democratically elected governments in order to protect corporate interests.[100] Natural disasters and civil conflicts and unrest are viewed as opportunities for corporations to fill the vacuum created by social and political destabilization.[101]

The never-ending search for profits is on the verge of turning the earth itself into a desiccated husk. Human-driven climate change, caused by the greed of the fossil fuel industry which pumps tens of billions of tons of carbon dioxide into the atmosphere each year while cheerfully spearheading campaigns calling for individuals to reduce their carbon footprint, is causing more powerful hurricanes, flooding, global droughts, devastating fires, and ravaging biodiversity with its pollutions of natural ecosystems.[102]

---

developed to stabilize global capitalism at a time of systemic crisis after the First World War and how this system has perpetuated Western capitalist hegemony in the past century. See also Quinn Slobodian, *Globalists: The End of Empire and the Birth of Neoliberalism*, for a discussion of how intellectual "free market" thinkers did not envision a libertarian realization of small government and unregulated free markets, but rather specific policies and proactive international regulation to encase and protect the global flow of goods and capital from democratic and state interference.

99. Naomi Klein, *No Logo*; Joseph, *The New Human Rights Movement*.

100. The United States is by far the worst offender in this regard. Stephen Kinzer, in his book *Overthrow: America's Century of Regime Change from Hawaii to Iraq*, indicates that the United States was directly involved in the overthrow of thirteen foreign governments from 1893 to 2003. The number is likely much higher, as in her survey of regime change during the Cold War, Lindsey A. O'Rourke, "The Strategy of Covert Regime Change: US-Backed Regime Change Campaigns During the Cold War," 92–127, found that although the US only participated in six overt regime-change campaigns, they engaged in sixty-four covert actions designed to overthrow governments in other countries. See also Walter F. LaFeber, *Inevitable Revolutions: The United States in Central America*; Tim Weiner, *Legacy of Ashes: The History of the CIA*.

101. Naomi Klein, *The Shock Doctrine: The Rise of Disaster Capitalism*.

102. Naomi Klein, *This Changes Everything: Capitalism vs The Climate*; Michael E. Mann, *The Hockey Stick and the Climate Wars: Dispatches from the Front Lines*.

The Calamity Which Should Come: The Restoration in Historical Context   135

We are currently in the middle of a mass extinction, the sixth on record. This one is called the Anthropocene extinction, on account of it being caused by humans.[103] At least five hundred species have gone extinct in the last one hundred years, with more dying out daily. Global ice melting and warming seas are pushing the earth towards unrecoverable tipping points, breaking down fragile ecosystems, which will multiply and lead to disaster and humanitarian crisis on a global scale.[104] Our addiction to consumption has produced five gigantic islands of plastic in the ocean, the largest of which is twice the size of Texas and three times the size of France, in addition to at least twenty-four trillion pieces of microplastics, which are now so pervasive they have been found in the placentas and breastmilk of expectant and nursing mothers.[105]

This is the calamity that God foresaw, which was precipitated by the events in the centuries leading up to the Restoration events of 1820. *This* was the violation of the covenant that was so egregious that it required a redirection of nearly two thousand years of Christian tradition. A massive reset. Apostasy—*a falling away from the justice and equity of the covenant community*—had led to the inextricable entwinement of church and Empire. Christianity itself had become co-opted by the wealthy and powerful. Colonialism was sanctioned under the guise of conversion of "savages" or of bringing in the apocalypse which would usher in the second coming of Christ.[106] The church propped up the status quo, urging peasants and the poor to submit to their God-given inferior status, plying them with tales of heavenly riches in the life to come to offset their misery in their current circumstances and threatening damnation for any who questioned their rulers. In our own day, Christianity has too often become the face of racism, white supremacy, intolerance, nationalism, homophobia, misogyny, and greed; it too often sows violence and chaos instead of love

---

103. Elizabeth Kolbert, *The Sixth Extinction: An Unnatural History.*

104. *IPCC, 2022: Climate Change 2022: Impacts, Adaptation, and Vulnerability*; Mark Lynas, *Six Degrees: Our Future on a Hotter Planet.*

105. L. Lebreton et al., "Evidence that the Great Pacific Garbage Patch Is Rapidly Accumulating Plastic"; Atsuhiko Isobe et al., "A Multilevel Dataset of Microplastic Abundance in the World's Upper Ocean and the Laurentian Great Lakes"; Antonio Ragusa et al., "Plasticenta: First Evidence Of Microplastics In Human Placenta"; Antonio Ragusa et al., "Raman Microspectroscopy Detection and Characterisation of Microplastics in Human Breastmilk."

106. Stannard, *American Holocaust*, 748.

and community.[107] Jesus himself has been twisted into a grotesque idol to wealth and power, representations of him as a white European used implicitly or explicitly to sanction campaigns of violence, displacement, and slaughter of indigenous peoples and exploitation of the most poor and vulnerable, blaming them for their poverty and misery, leaving scores traumatized, dislocated, and dispossessed for generations.

Staring at the horror that would result from the imperial opening of this Pandora's box, God could not bear to look any longer. God had to act and move against the powers and systems of injustice and oppression. In response to the past and present immiseration and death of innumerable poor and oppressed people that has accompanied the rise and reign of economic systems which prioritize accumulation of wealth over human life, God spoke once again from heaven to proclaim salvation, brought forth new scripture, and reminded us of the "everlasting covenant" that includes all of humanity and creation. With globalization to follow in the centuries to come, the exportation of war, poverty, oppression, and exploitation would fill the whole earth with suffering. The timing of the Restoration was not a coincidence. It was an explicit answer to the past and future "blood of the saints" crying from the earth, God's emphatic and direct response to this greatest of all calamities.

---

107. Emmanuel M. Katongole, *Mirror to the Church: Resurrecting Faith After Genocide in Rwanda*; C. S. Song, *Jesus in the Power of the Spirit*; Brian D. McLaren, *Do I Stay Christian? A Guide for the Doubters, the Disappointed, and the Disillusioned*; Robert P. Jones, *White Too Long: The Legacy of White Supremacy in American Christianity*. Jones discusses how the American white evangelical Christian movement (strongest in the South) began to view the role of the church as providing individual salvation in the next life rather than collective action towards an improved and just society when it became clear that their hopes for a present-day white Christian ethnostate were frustrated by the "humiliating and decisive" defeat of the Confederacy in the Civil War and the African-American emancipation that followed; 93–95. See Mark A. Noll, *The Civil War as a Theological Crisis*, for further historical and theological context for this shift.

Chapter 5

The Book of Mormon: Liberation and Salvation Retold

And from that time forth they did have their goods and their substance no more common among them. And they began to be divided in classes.
— 4 Nephi 1:25–26

During the Middle Ages the idea of salvation as covenant community was superseded by a new focus on salvation as a transaction between God and individuals. Though there were many philosophical and cultural influences on the development of individualism during these centuries, the Western concept is specifically tied to the adoption and legal protection of private property and the resulting atomizing and isolation of groups and village collectives who had historically lived in communal relationships. This individualism went hand in hand with the development of the "Protestant Ethic" that became deeply ingrained in the social consciousness in the centuries following the Protestant Reformation. This ethic consisted of the idea that a life spent working was the only worthwhile pursuit, that people had a moral obligation to be "contributing members of society," that leisure was lazy and of the devil, and that accumulation of wealth was a sign of hard work, superior moral fiber, and divine providence.[1] These ideas provided a moral justification for a massive expropriation of land, resources, lives, and livelihood. Through the events discussed in the previous chapter, the poor, oppressed, and marginalized were fed to the engine of industrialization.

I suggest that the Restoration was a direct intervention by God to reject and push back against the widescale adoption of the capitalist ethic and ideology during the Industrial Revolution.[2] At its foundation, capitalism as a social and economic system of living is incompatible with the

---

1. Christopher Hill, *The World Turned Upside Down: Radical Ideas During the English Revolution*, 324–31; Keith Thomas, "Work and Leisure in Pre-Industrial Society," 50–66.

2. For a brief but thorough overview of the development and structure of capitalism as a global economic system, see Immanuel Wallerstein, *Historical Capitalism with Capitalist Civilization*.

type of covenant relationship for which God's salvation is the goal.³ It posits that individuals working towards their own self-interest will somehow turn into an aggregate good for all in society.⁴ It lionizes and requires "competition" of all sorts, between individuals for goods, services, and jobs, between businesses for a share of the market, between nations for access to products and resources. It commodifies and monetizes everything and encourages endless purchasing of frivolities, excess, waste, and displays of wealth. It champions the false idea of meritocracy, in which those who work hardest or have the best and most innovative ideas become successful, while those who are poor are poor because of their lack of effort, creativity, or moral fiber.⁵ It profits from the misery of the masses.⁶ The goal and measure of capitalist success—the accumulation of wealth—directly erodes community. As observed by Byung-Chul Han, "Money, by itself, has an individualizing and isolating effect. It increases my individual freedom by liberating me from any personal bond with others."⁷ Capitalism is then, by its very nature, antithetical to covenant community.

If God viewed the globalization of economic systems that prioritize accumulation of profits over life as a "calamity"—so much so that God directly intervened in the course of human affairs by calling a prophet and beginning a new dispensation—a primary focus of the Restoration would be a reminder of the nature of the covenant community that was God's goal for humanity. We have this reminder in the first major work of the Restoration, the Book of Mormon. Its importance in the Restoration chain

---

3. See Nancy Fraser, *Cannibal Capitalism: How Our System is Devouring Democracy, Care, and the Planet–and What We Can Do About It*, for an incisive discussion of how modern-day capitalism consumes everything in its quest for endless accumulation and expansion, thereby destroying "social reproduction—the forms of provisioning, caregiving, and interaction that produce and sustain human beings and social bonds," 46–47.

4. See Ernest J.P. Benn, *The Confessions of a Capitalist*, for a lengthy rationale and justification for this line of thinking. Benn justifies the unequal distribution of wealth this philosophy produces in that "my income is merely the index of the much bigger income enjoyed by a very large number of my fellow-men who, all of them, would lose such amenities as they now possess if my income were to go" (p. 19).

5. Wallerstein, *Historical Capitalism*.

6. This is not just a figure of speech. Peter Joseph, in his book *The New Human Rights Movement: Reinventing the Economy to End Oppression*, discusses how if businesses had to pay for the externalities (short and long term economic, social, health, and environmental harms) they cause, no major industries would be profitable.

7. Byung-Chul Han, *The Disappearance of Rituals: A Topology of the Present*, 43.

of events is clearly evident in that it was published *before* the official founding of the Church. Joseph Smith's preparation for bringing forth the Book of Mormon began in 1823 with the visit of Moroni and continued for four years with additional instruction and preparation before he was able to obtain the record from which he produced the book. Smith referred to the book as "the keystone of our religion" and a critical foundation for the Church, stating that without it, "where is our religion? We have none."[8]

If temporal liberation is the fundamental meaning of salvation, and if the Restoration is God's response and revelation of the fundamental nature of this covenant relationship, then the Book of Mormon should contain a powerful testimony of salvation as liberation and an emphasis on covenant community. We don't have to read far into the book to see just such an emphasis. On the title page of the 1830 edition, the primary purpose of the book is stated as "to show unto the remnant of the House of Israel how great things the Lord hath done for their fathers; and that they may know the covenants of the Lord, that they are not cast off forever." Here the Book of Mormon makes clear that its purpose is to awaken and remind Israel of their covenant status and obligations, but also, more importantly, of God's faithfulness to this covenant relationship. It will do so by demonstrating God's liberation for their ancestors. The additional fact that the book is not a historical curiosity, but was buried up to be brought forth in our day, indicates that *we* are those who are to be reminded of God's mercy in liberating these people. The second stated purpose of "convincing of the Jew and the Gentile that Jesus is the Christ, the Eternal God, manifesting himself unto all nations," should be contextualized within this reminder of the covenant status of Israel and God's temporal salvation in their history.[9] The Book of Mormon reminds us that a crucial aspect of Jesus's life, ministry, and ongoing salvific activity is the expansion of the borders of the covenant community. It makes clear that the borders are to expand to encompass all nations.

Initial Acts of Deliverance

Further underscoring this intention of proving God's mercy and salvation by way of temporal liberation, the first chapter of the book immediately

---

8. Joseph Smith et al., *History of the Church of Jesus Christ of Latter-day Saints*, 2:52.
9. See Joseph M. Spencer, *The Vision of All: Twenty-five Lectures on Isaiah in Nephi's Record*, for discussion of the Book of Mormon and the Restoration's specific role in bringing about the salvation of Israel at the hands of the Gentiles.

sets up a scenario of imminent peril for Lehi, a contemporary of the Old Testament prophet Jeremiah who had seen a vision and prophesied the destruction of Jerusalem. This places him in the tradition of other prophets who have been "cast out, stoned, or slain; and they also sought his life, that they might take it away." Having set up these dire conditions, the chapter ends by saying, "But behold, I Nephi, will show unto you that the tender mercies of the Lord are over all those whom he hath chosen, because of their faith, to make them mighty even unto the power of deliverance" (1 Ne. 1:20). Thus, the first indication we have of God's saving activity in the Book of Mormon is in relation to temporal deliverance from a mortal threat, and Nephi frames his account of his and his family's dealings with God in explicitly temporal terms.

Almost immediately following God's first act of liberation and deliverance, in which Lehi is commanded in a dream to take his family and leave Jerusalem, thereby saving him from those who sought to kill him, God commanded Lehi to send his sons back to Jerusalem to retrieve the brass plates. This sets up another scenario of mortal peril from which God delivers Nephi and his brothers. After escaping Laban's soldiers and following the rebuke of the angel in the cave, Nephi explicitly referenced the Exodus in exhorting his brothers to continue trying to obtain the plates:

> Therefore let us go up; let us be strong like unto Moses; for he truly spake to the waters of the Red Sea and they divided hither and thither, and our fathers came through, out of captivity, on dry ground, and the armies of Pharaoh did follow and were drowned in the Red Sea. Now behold ye know that this is true. . . . Let us go up; the Lord is able to deliver us, even as our fathers, and to destroy Laban, even as the Egyptians. (1 Ne. 4:2–3)

Here Nephi invokes the memory of God's initial triumphal act of deliverance, casting himself and his brothers in the role of Israel, and casting their adversary, Laban, in the shoes of Pharaoh. Already we can see the profound impact that this original, iconic act of liberation has on the minds and memories of God's people. It serves as a type with which to approach and understand other situations which pit the people against seemingly insurmountable odds.

Back at the camp, Nephi's mother Sariah has reached her breaking point. Already having left her home, inheritance, and likely her other family in Jerusalem, she "truly mourns" the loss of her sons, fearing the worst of their return to Laban. Her despondency was such that she questioned the inspiration of her husband Lehi. Despite his efforts to comfort her, it was not until her sons returned unharmed that she found that comfort. Her response when she finally was able to speak reveals the specific effect of God's temporal deliverance for her at this critical juncture: "Now I know of a surety that the Lord hath commanded my husband to flee into the wilderness" (1 Ne. 5:8). For Sariah, God's deliverance was proof of God's purpose for her and her family. God's other commandments were understood and believed through the lens of deliverance and protection of her sons.

After securing the brass plates, Nephi and his brothers were again commanded to return to Jerusalem, this time to recruit Ishmael and his family to their cause. However, upon returning to the wilderness it was not long before some of Ishmael's children joined with Nephi's elder brothers to rebel against their parents and desire to return to Jerusalem. In his attempt to change their minds, Nephi explicitly hearkened back to their recent deliverance from the hands of Laban: "how is it that ye have forgotten what great things the Lord hath done for us, in delivering us out of the hands of Laban, and also that we should obtain the record?" (1 Ne. 7:11). But his words were to no avail, and they bound him and left him to die in the wilderness. Nephi, however, plead with the Lord to be given the strength to break the bands, and God responded by loosening those bands and freeing him. This serves as yet another explicit example of God's liberation, deepening and expanding the view of the circumstances in which God is able to intervene to save and deliver.

These initial examples of deliverance are followed by others: the Lord provided the Liahona for direction and saved the families from starvation (1 Ne. 16), fortified the women to be able to sustain the lives of their children who had been born in the wilderness (1 Ne. 17), saved the family from destruction and shipwreck during their voyage, and once again delivered Nephi from his brothers' violence (1 Ne. 18). Throughout the initial pages of the narrative, Lehi's family holds onto the hope of a future "promised land" where they will rest from their travels and live in the providence of the Lord (17:13–14). Having been forced to leave the original promised land of their ancestors, their faith in God's ability to lead them to a new chosen place was sure. These historical and present acts of temporal deliverance provide mounting evidence of God's ability and willingness to save.

A Great and Terrible Gulf Divideth Them

Lehi's vision of the Tree of Life is one of the most iconic scenes in the Book of Mormon. It has been dissected and interpreted endlessly, both for its symbolism and for its literary richness.[10] There are many symbols in this vision, but from a liberation perspective, the one that looms largest is the gulf that separates the occupants of the great and spacious building from those who are partaking of the fruit of the tree of life. Here we have a scenario where two groups of people are explicitly juxtaposed, those who have come "through the mist of darkness, clinging to the rod of iron, even until they did come forth and partake of the fruit of the tree" (1 Ne. 8:24) and those in the great and spacious building "both old and young, both male and female; and their manner of dress was exceedingly fine; and they were in the attitude of mocking and pointing their fingers towards those who had come at and were partaking of the fruit" (1 Ne. 8:27).

When Nephi received his own vision of the tree of life, he was told that "the large and spacious building, which thy father saw, is vain imagination and the pride of the children of men. And a great and terrible gulf divideth them; yea, even the word of the justice of the Eternal God" (1 Ne. 12:18). Nephi later elaborated in his interpretation for Laman and Lemuel:

> And I said unto them that it was an awful gulf, which separated the wicked from the tree of life, and also from the saints of God. . . . And I said unto them that our father also saw that the justice of God did also divide the wicked from the righteous; and the brightness thereof was like unto the brightness of a flaming fire, which ascendeth up unto God forever and ever, and hath no end. (1 Ne. 15:28, 30)

These passages refer explicitly to the justice of God as standing between two groups of people: the rich and the saints of God. How is the justice of God to be understood here? It is easy for us, with our twenty-first-century eyes and religious understanding, to think of God's justice as referring to punishment. In our contemporary Christian understanding, God's justice is dispensed in a court setting, where our acts are weighed on a balance, and blessings and punishment are meted out according to our righteousness and wickedness. Justice, then, consists of God rewarding the righteous and punishing the wicked.[11] We are encouraged in this view by the discussion of justice in the Book of Mormon itself, particularly in

---

10. Charles Swift, "Lehi's Vision of the Tree of Life: Understanding the Dream as Visionary Literature," 52–63; Daniel L. Belnap, Gaye Strathearn, and Stanley A. Johnson, eds., *The Things Which My Father Saw: Approaches to Lehi's Dream and Nephi's Vision*; John W. Welch and Donald W. Parry, *The Tree of Life: From Eden to Eternity*; Corbin T. Volluz, "Lehi's Dream of the Tree of Life: Springboard to Prophecy," 14–38.

11. See discussion in Chapter 3.

our common reading of the discourse of Alma to his son Corianton (Alma 42). Nephi, in his explanation of the vision to his brothers, equated the gulf, or the justice of God, with the river: "And I said unto them that it was a representation of that awful hell, which the angel said unto me was prepared for the wicked" (1 Ne. 12:29). Our job is done, then. It seems clear that the gulf, or the justice of God, is that awful hell that waits to torment and torture the wicked.

Contemporary Latter-day Saint scholars seem to agree with this interpretation, and great efforts have been made to locate both the journey of Lehi's family, and the imagery in his vision of the tree of life, within the context of the ancient Near East. For example, S. Kent Brown argues that "as soon as we focus on certain aspects of Lehi's dream, we find ourselves staring into the ancient world of Arabia."[12] Understanding the geography of the area sheds helpful light as well. Focusing on one conspicuous geographic feature of the area, the frequent *wadis*, or canyons that cut across areas of the desert, Hugh Nibley further cements the interpretation of the gulf as hell:

> All who have traveled in the desert know the feeling of utter helplessness and frustration at finding one's way suddenly cut off by one of those appalling canyons with perpendicular sides—nothing could be more abrupt, more absolute, more baffling to one's plans, and so will it be with the wicked in a day of reckoning.[13]

By placing Lehi's dream in its appropriate historical and geographical context, these scholars expand the images and symbolic import of the vision. Hell is, after all, like an impassable canyon for those sentenced there. And so, once again, the justice of God seems safely ensconced in its retributive clothing.

We should resist this interpretation, and not just because it might make us uncomfortable. In fact, between Lehi's vision and Nephi's interpretation, there are several features that suggest that the river of water, hell, and the great gulf of God's justice have been wrongly equated.[14] Careful

---

12. S. Kent Brown, "New Light from Arabia on Lehi's Trail," 55–125.

13. Hugh Nibley, *Lehi in the Desert, The World of the Jaredites, There Were Jaredites*, 46; see also Larry E. Dahl, "The Concept of Hell," 262–79.

14. Nephi's mention of hell here is curious for an ancient inhabitant of Jerusalem. As mentioned in Chapter 1, the Protestant definition and concept of hell that we are familiar with where the wicked are punished eternally did not exist in ancient Israel, nor did the idea of a personified devil who opposed God and tempted humankind to commit evil acts. See Philip C. Almond, *The Devil: A New Biography*; and Gerald Messadié, *A History of the Devil*. Thus, the many mentions and discussions of hell and the devil in the Book of Mormon (as well

reading of the narrative suggests a slight but significant shift in interpretation between Lehi and Nephi. As noted, Lehi saw the tree, he saw the building, and he saw that they were separated by a river of water. When Nephi received his own vision of the tree of life several chapters later, he was told by the angel to "behold the fountain of filthy water which thy father saw; yea, even the river of which he spake; and the depths thereof are the depths of hell" (1 Ne. 12:16). Then the angel spoke of the "great and terrible gulf" that was the justice of God. When Nephi interpreted the vision for Laman and Lemuel, they asked him specifically about the river:

> And they said unto me: What meaneth the river of water which our father saw? . . . And I said unto them that it was an awful gulf, which separated the wicked from the tree of life, and also from the saints of God. And I said unto them that it was a representation of that awful hell, which the angel said unto me was prepared for the wicked. (1 Ne. 15:26, 28–29)

If we read carefully here, we can see that Nephi has conflated the river, which he has been told is a representation of hell, with the gulf, which we know is the justice of God. But never before in the narrative have these things been equated. In fact, Lehi never mentions the gulf, and the angel explicitly separates the two concepts in his explanation of the vision. Nephi, however, has equated these concepts in his interpretation. As a result, when we think of the vision, we also equate the river, the gulf, hell, and God's justice. Grant Hardy suggests that this interpretive move reflects the difference in perspective between Lehi and Nephi. Lehi saw an open invitation to come and partake of the fruit, where Nephi saw the need to safeguard the purity of the tree, and therefore to keep those who are unworthy away.[15] Whatever the reason, this move, which was occasioned by Nephi taking a subtle, but significant liberty with his interpretation, has disastrous consequences for our understanding of God's justice.

If God's justice is not to be understood as hell and punishment, what can the gulf represent? How are we to understand this division between the wealthy and the saints of God? The footnote to the use of the word gulf in both chapters 12 and 15 refers us to Luke 16:26, which speaks of another gulf fixed between two groups of people. This verse is situated within Jesus's

---

as ideas of salvation, atonement, and resurrection, among others) likely reflect the contemporary religious climate in which Joseph Smith produced the book. For a thorough and elegant treatment of the influence of Joseph Smith's religious and political climate on the content of the Book of Mormon, see Blake T. Ostler, "The Book of Mormon as a Modern Expansion of an Ancient Source," 66–123.

15. See Grant Hardy, *Understanding the Book of Mormon: A Reader's Guide*, 53–54.

parable of the rich man and Lazarus, and it can provide critical insight into understanding the gulf as seen in the vision of the tree of life:

> There was a rich man who was dressed in purple and fine linen and who feasted sumptuously every day. And at his gate lay a poor man named Lazarus, covered with sores, who longed to satisfy his hunger with what fell from the rich man's table; even dogs would come and lick his sores. The poor man died and was carried away by the angels to be with Abraham. The rich man also died and was buried. In Hades [Sheol], where he was being tormented, he looked up and saw Abraham far away with Lazarus by his side. He called out, "Father Abraham, have mercy on me, and send Lazarus to dip the tip of his finger in water and cool my tongue; for I am in agony in these flames." But Abraham said, "Child, remember that during your lifetime you received your good things, and Lazarus in like manner received evil things; but now he is comforted here, and you are in agony. Besides all this, between you and us a great chasm [gulf in KJV] has been fixed, so that those who might want to pass from here to you cannot do so, and no one can cross from there to us." (Luke 16:19–26)

As discussed in chapter 2, Jesus would be using this parable to teach his followers something about the social and economic conditions of their lives. In just a few deft strokes, Jesus painted the picture of a wealthy elite, who is clothed in the finest linen, dyed purple—the most expensive dye—and has more food than he can possibly eat. Contrast this with the beggar Lazarus, who is starving. His malnutrition has resulted in chronic festering wounds; he is so emaciated that he cannot even stop dogs from licking his sores. Lazarus is likely a member of the class of expendables, those poor who have been evicted from their homes and forced to beg after failing to find work as day laborers. Lazarus lies under the rich man's gate, a further symbol of wealth and prestige, and hopes to feed himself from scraps from the man's table. At this stage, he is no longer even begging; he has become too weak and diseased.[16]

It is important to once again note the explicit juxtaposition of two classes of people who would not generally have met in real life. Beggars would not be allowed to sit under a wealthy person's gate. They would have been cleared out into another quarter of the city, their presence deemed unsightly, and their uncleanliness feared as a possible source of pollution and disease.

---

16. William R. Herzog II, *Parables as Subversive Speech: Jesus as Pedagogue of the Oppressed*, 119.

Both Lazarus and the rich man die, and they find their fortunes reversed. Now Lazarus is held "in the bosom" of Abraham (a reference to covenant relationship), while the rich man finds himself in torment. Between the rich man and Lazarus is an enormous chasm (or gulf) which separates them from one another. William Herzog suggests that this gulf represents the huge economic divide between the rich man and Lazarus, such that in Jesus's parable "the invisible chasm that separated the rich man and Lazarus has become visible."[17] In other words, Jesus's purpose in illustrating the gulf was to call explicit attention to the social reality that separated the rich man from Lazarus. It is an uncrossable reality. The rich man will never stoop to Lazarus's level or refrain from exploiting the poor, and Lazarus can never dream of ascending to the rich man's position of prestige and wealth. There are powerful economic and ideological forces which hold the chasm in place.

With this added context, the meaning of the gulf—or the justice of God, in Lehi's vision—becomes clearer. It is important to note the difference in the condition of the rich in Lehi's dream from the rich man in Jesus's parable. In the latter, the gulf is fixed between Lazarus and the rich man *after death*, and God's justice seems to be reflected in Lazarus's rest and the rich man's torment. However, in Lehi's vision, the occupants of the spacious building are not in a state of torment; they are actively persecuting the saints of God. This suggests, contrary to some contemporary interpretations of the vision, that what Lehi was seeing is a depiction of the state of the different groups *as unfolding in history* and not a summation of the status of righteous and wicked after death and judgment. The distinction is critical, because it inverts the meaning of the justice of God in the parable and the vision. In Jesus's parable, justice is the levelling of circumstances after death, in that Lazarus is compensated for being poor and destitute, and the rich man is punished for his wealth, which would have depended on the exploitation of the peasants and poor. In Lehi's vision, the justice of God is the *requirement* that such a levelling take place. But this is impossible under the historical circumstances that have given rise and prominence to exploitive economic systems that create huge wealth disparities between the rich and poor. As long as these systems are supported or actively participated in, the levelling that comprises God's justice cannot occur, and so the wealthy are forever separated from the

---

17. Herzog, 122.

poor.[18] Thus, the gulf that separates rich from poor can be thought of as the vacuum of justice created by the presence of sin that fractures relationship and community. The fellowship that comprises the kingdom of God cannot exist under such conditions. The justice of God, currently unrealized, stands between such covenant relationship.

We must consider one more aspect of Lehi's vision. The building in which the wealthy reside is defined as the "vain imaginations and the pride of the children of men" (1 Ne. 12:18). In the context of our current discussion, these can be understood as the ideologies that prop up economic and social systems that prioritize accumulation of wealth over human lives.[19] They are vain imaginations because economists and others have convinced themselves that a dogged pursuit of individual self-interest will benefit all of humanity.[20] Massive profits and wealth for the rich are predicted by some economists to trickle down to everyone else through

---

18. Although Lehi and Nephi's visions indicate that those in the building are wealthy, that does not necessarily require that those who are at the tree are poor. We can, however, invoke Jesus's equating of the poor with those who are actively realizing and participating in the kingdom of God (Luke 6:20), making the explicit juxtaposition between wealthy and poor not only a feasible, but an appropriate interpretation.

19. See Adam Kotsko, *Neoliberalism's Demons: The Political Theology of Late Capital*, for an illuminating treatment of how this ideology has co-opted and corrupted the concepts of freedom and agency to support political and economic systems of exploitation. Freedom, in this view, is the inalienable human right to act as an economic agent in pursuit of one's own self-interest. This leads to a society "in which your freedom may flourish only at the expense of mine." Terry Eagleton, *Why Marx Was Right*, 169. See also Jessica Whyte, *The Morals of the Market: Human Rights and the Rise of Neoliberalism*. The work of Michael Novak, the Catholic theologian colloquially known as "capitalism's theologian," was dedicated to theological justification of "democratic capitalism" as the only political and economic system capable of manifesting the kingdom of God in the world and fulfilling Christian social and moral obligations. This political theology was proposed and developed in his work *The Spirit of Democratic Capitalism* and reached a frankly astounding culmination in *Toward a Theology of the Corporation*, in which he proposes the modern multinational corporation as the Suffering Servant of Isaiah 53:2–3: "a much-despised incarnation of God's presence in the world" (p. 39).

20. See Jonathan Schlefer, *The Assumptions Economists Make*, ch. 4, for a discussion of how neoclassical economic models which posit maximization of individual utility as the fundamental tenet of economics were developed by economists/politicians in a social and political climate in which classical models

greater investment and job creation, a prediction that has been repeatedly demonstrated as false.[21] Delusions of meritocracy are used to justify cutting support and safety nets for the poor and exploited. Thus, the great and spacious building in which the wealthy reside is the ideologies that give rise to oppressive and dominating economic and political systems. These ideologies are the "principalities and powers" of which the apostle Paul spoke.[22] Nephi saw their fall in the collapse of another great and spacious building that represents the "wisdom and pride of the world": "and it fell, and the fall thereof was exceedingly great" (1 Ne. 11:36). The great levelling is inevitable. God's justice cannot be staved off forever.

Remember the Captivity of Your Fathers

One of the most remarkable conversion stories in the Book of Mormon is that of Alma the Younger. He and the four sons of king Mosiah actively sought to "destroy the church" (Mosiah 27:10), with Alma seeming to be the leader of this group (vv. 8–9). While they were going about "rebelling against God," in a moment very reminiscent of Paul's experience on the road to Damascus, they were struck down by the power of an angel. The angel, in a voice of thunder, commanded Alma to stand and then rebuked him, telling Alma that his father had "prayed with much faith concerning thee that thou mightest be brought to the knowledge of the truth; therefore for this purpose have I come to convince thee of the power and authority of God" (v. 14).

The angel's strategy seems to have been to shake Alma and his friends with a demonstration of raw power and to convince them that God was the god that Alma's father claimed. The angel's parting statement to Alma can thus be interpreted within this context of proving God's power and bringing him to a knowledge of the truth. The statement also reveals the specific mechanism that can catalyze such a shift in understanding: "Now

---

emphasized that society, and therefore societal values, determine how income is distributed between labor and capital.

21. "Trickle-down economics" is a colloquialism for supply-side economics, an economic theory that posits that economic growth is most likely to be achieved by tax cuts, deregulation, and free trade, thus increasing the supply of purchasable commodities. It was popularized in the present era during the Reagan administration and recoined as "Reaganomics."

22. Walter Wink, *Unmasking the Powers: The Invisible Forces that Determine Human Existence*; Walter Wink, *Engaging the Powers: Discernment and Resistance in a World of Domination*.

I say unto thee: Go, and remember the captivity of thy fathers in the land of Helam, and in the land of Nephi; and remember how great things he has done for them; for they were in bondage, and he has delivered them" (Mosiah 27:16).

It is important to note here that the captivity that the angel was referring to is not the traditionally invoked bondage of Israel to Egypt but to acts of deliverance that likely occurred within Alma's lifetime or shortly before. The first was the deliverance of King Limhi and his people who had been brought into bondage to the Lamanites following the overthrow of Limhi's father, Noah's, kingdom. Through a series of escalating conflicts, Limhi's kingdom moved from being an independent tributary kingdom to a servile outlet for the aggression and hostility of the Lamanites, who stopped just short of outright extermination of his people (Mosiah 21).

Limhi's people attempted on several occasions to throw off their yoke of oppression through military confrontation, but they were repeatedly defeated, resulting in "a great mourning and lamentation among the people of Limhi, the widow mourning for her husband, the son and the daughter mourning for their father, and the brothers for their brethren" (Mosiah 21:9). The terror of the Lamanites was ever present: "Now there were a great many widows in the land, and they did cry mightily from day to day, for a great fear of the Lamanites had come upon them" (v. 10). Finally, they resign themselves to their bondage (v. 13).

Deliverance eventually came, but this proved to be disastrous for the people of Alma (Alma the Younger's father), who had previously fled the land at the time of Abinidi's execution. After providing the Lamanite guards with ample wine, Limhi's people snuck out the back while the guards were drunk and asleep (Mosiah 22). When the guards awoke in the morning, they gathered an army and pursued Limhi's people, who had fled to Zarahemla to join with the people of King Mosiah. However, after pursuing them for two days, the army of the Lamanites became lost and happened upon the city of Helam, which had been established by the elder Alma and his people following their exile from Noah's kingdom. The Lamanites occupied the city of Helam and placed Amulon, one of King Noah's priests, as ruler over the people.

Amulon, incensed by the social and political upheaval that stripped him of his position and exiled him and his fellow priests, held Alma responsible and subjected the refugees to persecution and forced labor (Mosiah 24:8–10). In a particularly cruel edict, Amulon further declared that any who were found calling upon God in prayer were to be put to death. Having stripped Alma's people of their freedom and dignity, he now attempted to remove the solace of their religion. However, Alma's people

> did pour out their hearts to him [God]; and he did know the thoughts of their hearts. And it came to pass that the voice of the Lord came to them in their afflictions, saying: Lift up your heads and be of good comfort, for I know of the covenant which ye have made unto me; and I will covenant with my people and deliver them out of bondage. (Mosiah 24:12–13)

Here, God affirms the liberating nature of the divine covenant. This was the covenant God made with Israel, and this was the covenant that was reaffirmed by Alma's people via their baptism at the waters of Mormon. It was a covenant of comfort, deliverance, and liberation.

Liberation is sure, but God provided yet another assurance of salvific love to Alma and his people by seeing that "the burdens which were laid upon Alma and his brethren were made light," making their forced labor easy (Mosiah 24:14–15). Although this act is generally viewed as a miraculous subjective lessening of physical burdens, given the nature of their baptismal covenant to "bear one another's burdens, that they may be light" (18:8–10), it is likely that this reflected God ensuring the natural result of living up to this commitment. Casting Alma in the role of Moses, God then resolved to liberate the people: "And he said unto Alma: Thou shalt go before this people, and I will go with thee and deliver this people out of bondage" (24:17). The Lord then caused a deep sleep to come over the Lamanites, and Alma and his people were able to leave and make their way to Zarahemla to join Limhi's people as subjects of King Mosiah.

These recent historical acts of deliverance are what Alma was commanded to remember. This command indicates something fundamentally transformative about reflecting on human bondage and the ability of God to liberate. As members of the Church, we believe that a central pillar of the Plan of Salvation is agency, the ability to act. Joseph Smith would go on to say in a later revelation that without agency "there is no existence" (D&C 93:30). Thus, the ability to freely act is a fundamental aspect of human existence. To take away this agency is to compromise our divine nature and potential as humans and children of God. For one human to subject another to bondage is a complete denial of that person's right to self-determination and authentic existence. It is a denial of their humanity in the starkest terms. It is an "othering" that shatters the communal bonds which dictate covenant existence.

Reflection on such captivity and on divine liberation reveals to us the true nature of God, God's purpose for humanity, and the fundamentally corrupting nature of human bondage and oppression. This is an act of repentance, in the true sense of the word. It catalyzes a reorientation, a new view of reality, of God, of ourselves, and of the world. We understand what God being a god of love means. This love is a love that is manifest in God's desire and resolve to alleviate suffering and liberate us from anything that holds us captive. In the throes and suffering of captivity and oppression is where God is yearned for and felt most keenly. The liberation is an assurance that God remembers the divine covenant, but importantly, that the terms of that covenant have not changed—that God's love can be trusted in and relied on. This is the change in perspective and the assurance that "remembering the captivity of the fathers" gifts us. Finally, and this may be the critical point, remembering the captivity of the fathers forces our definitions of God to be constantly contextualized and critiqued from the viewpoint of historical acts of salvation and liberation—specifically from the viewpoint of the victims—ensuring we do not lapse into thinking about or codifying ideas of God or doctrine in ways that damage or marginalize those who are most in need of God's salvation and liberation in our own day.

When recalling his experience with the angel and his own conversion to his son Helaman, Alma says that it was the angel's declaration "if thou wilt of thyself be destroyed, seek no more to destroy the church of God" that weighed most heavily on his mind in his conversion experience. But his own teaching, including to his son in this same chapter, suggests both that it was his reflection on the captivity and liberation of his fathers that was the catalyst for conversion, and that his ongoing reflection on these liberative acts plays a crucial role in his ongoing religious praxis. In fact, following his renunciation of his career as the chief judge to devote himself to full-time ministry, Alma settled on this specific line of preaching as the opening pronouncement in the messages he delivered throughout the land. While discussions of Alma's discourse to the city of Zarahemla in Alma 5 generally focus on the later questions he asks the people regarding faith, judgment, and works, it is significant that he began this litany of questions by reminding and asking them to reflect on the captivity of their fathers and on God's deliverance of them. He refers the people back to the time when his father Alma established a church among them at the waters of Mormon:

> And behold, I say unto you, they were delivered out of the hands of the people of king Noah, by the mercy and power of God. And behold, after that, they were brought into bondage by the hands of the Lamanites in the

wilderness; yea, I say unto you, they were in captivity, and again the Lord did deliver them out of bondage by the power of his word. . . . And now behold, I say unto you, my brethren, you that belong to this church, have you sufficiently retained in remembrance the captivity of your fathers? Yea, and have you sufficiently retained in remembrance his mercy and long-suffering towards them? (Alma 5:4–6)

Later, in his lament for the wickedness of his people and his desire to cry repentance with the voice of an angel, Alma again explicitly refers to the impact that remembering God's liberation has had on his faith, this time drawing an explicit connection between God's acts of liberation for his fathers with the initial act of deliverance in Egypt:

Yea, and I also remember the captivity of my fathers; for I surely do know that . . . the Lord God, the God of Abraham, the God of Isaac, and the God of Jacob, did deliver them out of bondage. Yea, I have always remembered the captivity of my fathers; and that same God who delivered them out of the hands of the Egyptians did deliver them out of bondage. (Alma 29:11–12)

Finally, in his counsel to his son Helaman, he again opens with this injunction:

I would that ye should do as I have done, in remembering the captivity of our fathers; for they were in bondage, and none could deliver them except it was the God of Abraham, and the God of Isaac, and the God of Jacob; and he surely did deliver them in their afflictions. (Alma 36:2)

He then recounts his own captivity and deliverance: "God has delivered me from prison and from bonds and from death; yea, and I do put my trust in him, and he will still deliver me" (Alma 36:27). This he does before reminding Helaman once again of the bondage and liberation of Israel and of Sariah and Lehi's family and descendants and admonishing him to "retain in remembrance, as I have done, their captivity" (vv. 28–29).

For Alma, there seems to have been no greater tool to bring about conversion than to reflect on the reality of the bondage that was suffered by his fathers, so much so that he recommended this course of action to the majority of those he preached to. The remembering and pondering on this captivity, and the liberation that was effected by God, seems to play a pivotal role in the conversion process. Alma's references to a "mighty change of heart," being "born again," and "singing the song of redeeming love" suggest a profound change that resulted from remembering and contemplating these profoundly human and humanizing acts of divine liberation.

Are We Not All Beggars?

As the end of his life neared, King Benjamin (whose father, Mosiah, received the refugees from Limhi) called all his people together in order to give them one last address and to declare his successor. In his address, he took great pains to emphasize the utter dependence of humanity on God for their lives and livelihoods. Humans have merited nothing of themselves and thus are in debt to God for their very lives (Mosiah 2:21, 25). His purpose in doing this seems to be to get his subjects to reflect on their dependence on and need for God. He also spoke of keeping commandments, of sin, of blessings, of the Atonement of Christ, and of salvation. This set off a massive conversion event within the community who had gathered to hear him (Mosiah 4:2–3). Thus, Benjamin's words awakened the people to the true nature of their relationship with God. Their state is one of dependence on God, and God freely offers salvation to those who will receive it.

But salvation is an ongoing concern. Benjamin makes clear that all is not done. In order for those who have "tasted of his [God's] love" to maintain a remission of their sins, there is an explicitly temporal, economic requirement:

> And also, ye yourselves will succor those that stand in need of your succor; ye will administer of your substance unto him that standeth in need; and ye will not suffer that the beggar putteth up his petition to you in vain, and turn him out to perish. Perhaps thou shalt say: The man has brought upon himself his misery; therefore I will stay my hand, and will not give unto him of my food, nor impart unto him of my substance that he may not suffer, for his punishments are just—But I say unto you, O man, whosoever doeth this the same hath great cause to repent; and except he repenteth of that which he hath done he perisheth forever, and hath no interest in the kingdom of God. For behold, are we not all beggars? Do we not all depend upon the same Being, even God, for all the substance which we have, for both food and raiment, and for gold, and for silver, and for all the riches which we have of every kind?. . . . O then, how ye ought to impart of the substance that ye have one to another. And if ye judge the man who putteth up his petition to you for your substance that he perish not, and condemn him, how much more just will be your condemnation for withholding your substance, which doth not belong to you but to God. . . . I say unto you, wo be unto that man, for his substance shall perish with him. (Mosiah 4:16–23)

Here we can see Benjamin's reason for hitting so hard earlier in his address the utter dependence of humankind on God. It is not to emphasize the depravity and worthlessness of humanity, as is done in some Christian traditions, but it is rather to undercut two fundamental pillars of economic inequality: meritocracy and private property.

Meritocracy is a pernicious and pervasive fallacy in the Western, capitalist world. It asserts that an individual's social and economic standing is solely a result of their individual effort and has nothing to do with the circumstances of their birth or the political or economic context in which they grow up. It is the doctrine that has led to demonization of African Americans in the inner city. It blames their lack of achievement on their "ghetto culture."[23] It views immigrants as "freeloaders." It justifies cuts to social spending and imposes means testing on social programs and gives rise to the perennial image of the "welfare queen."[24] It points to those in positions of privilege and power as hardworking people who have realized "the American dream," and it chides those who live in abject poverty for their lack of motivation or lazy lifestyle and reliance on "handouts." It justifies the obscene salaries of corporate CEOs, who make between one hundred and over twenty thousand times the amount they pay their workers,[25] on the basis of their inherent ingenuity, creativity, and noble undertaking of "business risks." It demonizes those who argue that society should provide for the needs of all, and it labels "equality of outcome" as inherently undemocratic, somehow not a desirable aspect of a civilized society.[26]

Benjamin forcefully and utterly refutes this line of thinking and makes clear that those in a position of wealth and privilege have not merited this of themselves or by their own efforts. Those in the position of poverty who are forced to beg also are not responsible for their plight; their punishments are not just, meaning they have not reaped the rewards of any laziness or lack of moral fiber on their part.

---

23. Thomas Sowell, *Black Rednecks and White Liberals*; *Discrimination and Disparities*; see also James B. Stewart, "Thomas Sowell's Quixotic Quest to Denigrate African American Culture: A Critique," 459–66.

24. The term was popularized by Ronald Reagan during his 1976 presidential campaign, and refers to the supposed epidemic of poor who defraud the welfare system while living lavish lifestyles. The term is often used to denigrate black single mothers.

25. Sarah Anderson, Sam Pizzagati, Brian Wakamo, *Executive Excess 2022: 28th Annual IPS Executive Compensation Report*. This report found that for the three hundred publicly traded US corporations with the lowest median wage in 2020, the average CEO to worker pay ratio was 670:1. Forty-nine corporations had a ratio of greater than 1000:1. Only six corporations had ratios below 100:1.

26. See Kelli Potter, "Liberation Theology in the Book of Mormon," 175–92, for similar discussion.

But it is not enough to impart of our substance to the poor liberally. No, Benjamin goes even further. He wants not just to dispel judgment of those who were poor and begging. In a stunning move, he emphasizes that nothing we "own" is ours at all. Thus far in the sermon, we could be forgiven for thinking that our property has been given to us by God, and because of this, we need to be generous with it. But Benjamin realizes how easy it is to rationalize away such generosity, particularly in our era of "prosperity gospel," where wealth and status are taken to be direct blessings from God for our demonstrated righteousness and obedience. The flip side of this is, of course, that those who are poor are poor as punishment from God for their wickedness and disobedience.

This will not do. To head this off, Benjamin doubles down and repudiates the entire concept of private property. He clarifies that our "substance" has not been given to us by God; God has never given over ownership of it. In other words, nothing we possess is ours. It all belongs to God, and we are obligated to redistribute it to those in need. Furthermore, anyone who does not do this "hath no interest in the kingdom of God," and "his substance will perish with him." Here Benjamin unequivocally emphasizes the connection between redistribution of wealth and the kingdom of God. Living in love and community with goods and substance in common is the type of existence that comprises the kingdom. Here he hearkens back to Jesus's encounter with the rich young man (Mark 10), in which Jesus tells him that despite keeping all the commandments, he must sell all his possessions and give the money to the poor in order to inherit eternal life. This explicit economic requirement from Jesus has often been rationalized away by saying that what Jesus was condemning was not wealth *per se* but an unhealthy focus on wealth that blinds one to the needs of others. But we have no evidence that this is what Jesus meant. In the context of Benjamin's address, the rich young man symbolizes those who hold to their personal religious piety while participating in, and benefiting from, economic systems of oppression and exploitation. William Herzog explains the critical shortsightedness of such living:

> Perhaps it has not occurred to the rich ruler that, while he has never killed a man face to face, he has most likely degraded peasant farmers to the status of day laborers, and from the time a peasant becomes a day laborer, devoid of the safety net of the village and with nothing left to sell but his animal energy, to the time he dies of malnutrition is a matter of a few years at most. Every time he alienates a peasant family from their land, he has pronounced a death sentence upon them. He has destroyed a family and killed its members. It

may never have occurred to the rich man that, while he has not borne false witness in a court, he has defrauded the people of the land. Every time he has blamed his victims for the plight that he and his class have visited upon them, he is bearing false witness against them. It probably has not occurred to the rich man that while he has never mugged anyone on the street and taken their money, he has used the system to rob the poor blind. He could not achieve his prominence and wealth except at the expense of others, but he does not see this as stealing. It is called getting ahead and climbing the ladder of power and prestige.[27]

Here we can see that any attempt at personal piety is dwarfed by the collateral damage produced by systems that depend on, and produce, economic inequality. Like the rich young man, are we unaware of the misery visited upon those whose labor and lives support our lifestyles? Do we consider the exploitation behind our consumption of popular brands? Do we think that God tallies our temple attendance while the lives and livelihoods of the poor are ruined by our excess? In this context, Jesus's statement, "How hard it will be for those who have wealth to enter the kingdom of God!" (Mark 10:23), can be read not as a pronouncement about a future salvation in the world to come but as a statement of the economic reality of the gulf between rich and poor. The kingdom of God, or living in community with others, cannot be realized if some have wealth while others are poor and destitute. This is antithetical to the kind of community that comprises God's kingdom.

With this as context, we can better understand Benjamin's discussion of "the natural man" earlier in the sermon. If living in community and common comprises the kingdom of God, then the absence of this community is our "natural" or fallen state. The relationship between community, communion, and fallen man is articulated by Kelli Potter. She observes,

> Before the fall, Adam and Eve are in perfect communion with God. The fall takes them out of this communion; the fall is their falling out of communion with God. Instead of being in a community with God, they are "thrown out" on their own. They are made responsible for themselves. The material substance that they need is no longer provided. They have to struggle just to survive. They are like the animals. They are "natural." This struggle comes from the breakdown of community. And conversely, true community eliminates the need for the struggle. . . . Being a natural enemy to God is being an enemy to community. On this reading, the "natural man" is not a metaphysical state of an individual. Instead, it has a social character. It is the state of rejecting communion with God and neighbor. It is the

---

27. William R. Herzog II, *Jesus, Justice, and the Reign of God*, 165–66. See also Walter Rauschenbush, *Christianity and the Social Crisis*, 218–19.

state of rejecting our radical dependence on our community. . . . This also explains how we can take part in the fall without individually doing it. We are complicit in the institutional structures of our society. Our failure to act against them is an action in their favor. And these institutional structures, in part, cause the breakdown of the community. Capitalism essentially rejects the utter dependence of the individual on the community and thus is the (current) economic form of the fall of humanity.[28]

This take on the fall and natural man suggests that social and political systems that atomize family and community, and that stress individual merit and accomplishment outside the bonds and well-being of community, are opposed to God and God's plans for creation. The natural man, reflected in systems which pit people against one another in a race to amass wealth and status, is an enemy to God. Capitalism, as currently implemented in Western society, is fundamentally opposed to community. Its logic depends on positing that all humans are individual economic actors who seek to maximize their own personal benefit. The market must be allowed maximum freedom. As explained by Bruce Alexander,

> The exchange of labour, land, currency, and consumer goods must not be encumbered by clan loyalties, village responsibilities, guild rights, charity, family obligations, social roles, or religious values. Since cultural traditions "distort" the free play of the laws of supply and demand, they must be suppressed to establish a free market society.[29]

We have seen in the last chapter how the ushering in of capitalist economic systems required expropriation of lives, resources, and labor on a massive scale and destroyed communal and common bonds. The acceleration of industry, technology, and corporate exploitation is fracturing these bonds at an ever-growing pace in our day, leading to inequality, suffering, misery, and death.[30] King Benjamin, speaking to us from the dust, provides a prophetic voice of warning. This is a gross iniquity, for which the entire creation suffers. This is the fall of man writ large upon history, a grotesque and mutating sin in which we are all complicit. Coming on the heels of

---

28. Potter, "Liberation Theology in the Book of Mormon," 189–90. See also John Dominic Crossan, *God and Empire: Jesus Against Rome, Then and Now*, 68–70.

29. Bruce K. Alexander, *The Roots of Addiction in Free Market Society*, 9; see also Alexander, *The Globalization of Addiction: A Study in Poverty of the Spirit*.

30. In the United States, where this economic fracturing of community is at an advanced stage, these "deaths of despair" have been directly linked to the societal impacts of unregulated capitalism. See Anne Case and Angus Deaton, *Deaths of Despair and the Future of Capitalism*.

this social and economic commandment, Benjamin's exhortation that his subjects "take upon [them] the name of Christ" (Mosiah 5:9) takes on new meaning. The explicit economic message in his sermon underlines both the inextricable nature of salvation, from the temporal prosperity and security of all, and the demands of justice on any society or community striving to realize the kingdom of God.

Pride, Wealth, and Boundary Markers

Mormon, writing to his son Moroni shortly before the rout of the Nephites by the Lamanites, provided this summation of the Nephite civilization: "Behold, the pride of this nation, or the people of the Nephites, hath proven their destruction except they should repent" (Moroni 8:27). This is a serious accusation. But moreover, it is a highly specific one. Mormon didn't say that the "wickedness" or "sin" of the Nephites had proven their destruction. He said it was their pride. This specific diagnosis indicates that we, for whom the record was preserved, should pay special attention to the descriptions of pride in the Book of Mormon. Thankfully, we have many opportunities to do so, as Mormon, the book's primary editor, maintains a throughline of the effects of pride on Nephite society over the course of his record.

This repetition of the effects of pride in the Book of Mormon has become generally known as the "pride cycle." It is the familiar progression from righteousness to wealth to wickedness to destruction to humility and repentance, then back to righteousness. This pattern is repeated throughout the book, until the end, when the cyclical pattern leads not to repentance but to the utter annihilation of the Nephite people. Mormon, having edited and compiled so many instances of this cycle, desperately hoped for one more cycle of repentance and renewal, but it was not to be; as Grant Hardy observes, "Nephite history has become linear rather than cyclical."[31]

In order to understand why Mormon placed such emphasis on pride as the downfall of the Nephites, we need to pay special attention to the ways in which he used the word when describing the degeneration of society. After all, as the editor, we can assume that Mormon would have been particular in his use of the term. Furthermore, we can be sure that he would have described the critical features of pride that he viewed as responsible for the Nephite destruction. So, what does Mormon say about pride?

The words "pride" or "proud" occur 82 times in the Book of Mormon. Of these, 53 explicitly connect pride with riches and wealth. Furthermore,

---

31. Hardy, *Understanding the Book of Mormon*, 114.

whenever a specific reason for pride is given, it is nearly always tied to prosperity and riches: the people are prideful *because* of their wealth (e.g., Jacob 2:13, Alma 4:6, Hel. 3:36; 3 Ne. 6:10). Thus, in his compilation and editorializing, Mormon seems to have taken special care to explicitly emphasize the link between wealth and pride.

We are still a long ways away from the total destruction of the Nephite nation. So far we know that according to Mormon, riches and wealth can cause pride. How do we get from there to societal collapse? The answer can be found in the particular sin that results from pride, which is specifically tied to wealth. Mormon reports that when they were righteous, the people under Alma "were all equal. . . . And they did impart of their substance, every man according to that which he had, to the poor, and the needy, and the sick, and the afflicted; and they did not wear costly apparel, yet they were neat and comely" (Alma 1:26–27). This system of living leads to stability and to their prosperity:

> And now, because of the steadiness of the church they began to be exceedingly rich, having abundance of all things whatsoever they stood in need— an abundance of flocks and herds, and fatlings of every kind, and also abundance of grain, and of gold, and of silver, and of precious things, and abundance of silk and fine-twined linen, and all manner of good homely cloth. And thus, in their prosperous circumstances, they did not send away any who were naked, or that were hungry, or that were athirst, or that were sick, or that had not been nourished; and they did not set their hearts upon riches. (Alma 1:29–30)

This arrangement lasted for seven years, but then pride crept in:

> And it came to pass in the eighth year of the reign of the judges, that the people of the church began to wax proud, because of their exceeding riches, and their fine silks, and their fine-twined linen, and because of their many flocks and herds, and their gold and their silver, and all manner of precious things, which they had obtained by their industry; and in all these things were they lifted up in the pride of their eyes, for they began to wear very costly apparel. (Alma 4:6)

We can highlight a few things here. First, Mormon makes it clear that prosperity is not the problem. He is careful to name every form of wealth in this verse that he had named above. The list of raw materials, animals, and fabric is repeated with one significant difference: here, "good homely cloth" with which the people had adorned themselves in "neat and comely" dress has been replaced with "very costly apparel." This designation indicates that the Nephites' industry had moved from the purpose of producing "whatsoever they stood in need" to producing wealth to be displayed in conspicuous consumption. This is wealth for wealth's sake, and it is pursued for the sole purpose of status and privilege. Once production turns from need to excess, there are any number of ways to display such status. Mormon's most common way of referring to this is by mentioning "costly" or "very fine" apparel, but we also have mention of "ringlets, bracelets, ornaments of gold" (Alma 31:28), and "all manner of fine pearls" (4 Ne. 1:24). Nephi, quoting Isaiah, gave us a sample of the many ways that pride was evidenced by conspicuous consumption and displays of wealth (although we must admit our discomfort with his singular critique of women):

> tinkling ornaments, and cauls, and round tires like the moon; The chains and the bracelets, and the mufflers; The bonnets, and the ornaments of the legs, and the headbands, and the tablets, and the ear-rings; The rings, and nose jewels; The changeable suits of apparel, and the mantles, and the wimples, and the crisping-pins; The glasses, and the fine linen, and hoods, and the veils. (2 Ne. 18:23)

The prophets in the Book of Mormon who focused on this aspect of pride do so for a very specific reason. They recognized the grave threat. As we mentioned, they were not so concerned with wealth *per se*. They were not ascetics, advocating a life of poverty and debasement. Mormon gives the reason for the deep concern in his account of Alma leaving the government to focus exclusively on the ministry:

> Yea, he saw great *inequality* among the people, some lifting themselves up with their pride, despising others, turning their backs upon the needy and the naked and those who were hungry, and those who were athirst, and those who were sick and afflicted. Now this was a great cause for lamentations among the people, while others were abasing themselves, succoring those who stood in need of their succor, such as imparting their substance to the poor and the needy, feeding the hungry, and suffering all manner of afflictions. . . . And now it came to pass that Alma, having seen the afflictions of the humble followers of God, and the persecutions which were heaped upon them by the remainder of his people, and seeing all their inequality, began to be very sorrowful. (Alma 4:12–15; emphasis added)

Here we can see that the pride of the people had led them to neglect their covenant obligation to the poor and needy and had led to inequality. This is the great sin that so concerns the prophets[32]—the pride that results from

---

32. For an extended and insightful treatment of inequality in the Book of Mormon, see Robert F. Schwartz, "Inequality and Narrative in the Book of Mormon," 31–75.

wealth severs the bonds of community that are so crucial to the covenant. It does so in a most insidious fashion. To understand, we must think in terms of the covenant obligations and outward practices that signified God's covenant with Israel. In doing so, we will see how pride not only threatens the covenant community but actually initiates a new covenant of division that is in opposition to the community that constitutes the kingdom of God.

To illustrate, allow me a personal example from my time in high school. In Rexburg Idaho, at Madison High, we had identifiably different groups of students. This, I suspect, is the case at every high school. Among the different groups, there were the cowboys, who were denoted by their boots, cowboy hats, and tight Wrangler jeans. There were the skaters, who wore skate shoes, baggy jeans, and band t-shirts. There was my group, the kids of middle-class parents, who had nice, though not top name-brand, clothes. Then there were the "rich" kids. These were generally the kids of farmers or professionals (doctors, lawyers), who owned the majority of land and industry in Rexburg. They were distinguished, among other things, by their name-brand clothes. Thus, clothing in my school served as one symbol of which group we belonged to.

The most conspicuous piece of clothing, at least to my memory, was Girbaud jeans. These jeans were alike to others in all respects but one: they had a small white tag across the fly with the name "Girbaud" stitched on it. They became popular in Idaho in the early 90s. It seemed that overnight, the rich kids all had them. They became a status symbol. They marked off those who were wealthy from those who weren't. The ranks of those who wore Girbaud jeans seemed impenetrable. I couldn't afford them (one pair cost over $100). I felt I wasn't cool enough or good enough at sports to hang out with the guys, and I certainly wasn't cool enough to ask any of the girls out. There was an invisible boundary between us, marked by that little white tag on the fly of those jeans.

This example from my own memory (though admittedly crude and stereotypical) illustrates just how symbols of wealth can serve as boundary markers between groups of people. This appears to have been what happened with the Nephites. Once the focus turned from providing for needs to accumulation and public display, wealth served to mark those who were rich off from those who were poor. The class distinctions between the people became sharply defined. Whereas before everyone was "familiar with all and free with [their] substance" (Jacob 2:17), those who were wealthy now started to group themselves and separate themselves from those who were not. The obligation to provide for the poor was lost in the pursuit of endlessly more wealth and ways to display it, and those with wealth began to persecute those who did not have as much. Nephi's brother Jacob faced this problem that had already arisen among the first generations of the Nephites, and he excoriated his people for "wear[ing] stiff necks and high heads because of the costliness of your apparel, and persecut[ing] your brethren because ye suppose that ye are better than they" (Jacob 2:13).

Once class distinctions arose, Nephite society became ordered to favor the rich. This led to ever-increasing opportunity and privilege for the already wealthy, and more and more inequality and poverty. Mormon records that in the twenty-ninth year of the reign of the judges

> there were many merchants in the land, and also many lawyers, and many officers. And the people began to be distinguished by ranks, according to their riches and their chances for learning; yea, some were ignorant *because* of their poverty, and others did receive great learning *because* of their riches. (3 Ne. 6:11–12, emphasis added)

Thus we can see that wealth leads to division, and privilege and opportunity become increasingly available only to the wealthy. This can be clearly seen in our own day. The children of the wealthiest families go to the best schools, which means they have the best educational opportunities, which means they end up in positions of power and influence, and very often, in government. And so you have the rich in charge of the government, and policy created to increase the wealth of the already wealthy, with no care for the needs and subsistence of the poor. In fact, as we saw in the last chapter, laws are passed to protect and increase the property and wealth of the rich at the expense of the poor and marginalized.

This is, in a very real sense, a covenant relationship that serves the needs of the wealthy at the expense of others. If we think of the covenant practices that served as boundary markers to designate Israel as God's people (such as circumcision and purity laws), all of these have their equivalents in the descriptions of Nephite pride and wealth and in the practices of the present-day wealthy. For the Nephites, their boundary markers consisted of fine clothes, jewelry, and so forth. For the wealthy in our day, we have name-brand clothing and accessories, jewelry, cars, yachts, mansions, jets, country clubs, botox treatments, breast augmentation, facelifts, lip fillers, tummy tucks, business associations, private fundraisers for politicians, foundations, stock portfolios, and now even space tourism. The list of boundary markers goes on and on. These conspicuous displays of wealth and practices serve both to mark off the wealthy from the poor and to entrench wealth and power within their ranks—precisely in opposition to the covenant community of justice and equity that should constitute the people of God.

In the Book of Mormon, we are given an example of this kind of covenant in the Gadianton robbers, who explicitly covenanted on pain of death to not reveal their secret combinations, which had as their goal the accumulation of wealth and power. Here, the boundary markers of the Gadianton robbers are described in detail, an evil corruption of the types of practices and rituals that should solemnize the unity of the covenant community:

> And now it had come to pass that there were many, even among the Nephites, of Gadianton's band. . . . [T]hey did unite with those bands of robbers, and did enter into their covenants and their oaths, that they would protect and preserve one another in whatsoever difficult circumstances they should be placed, that they should not suffer for their murders, and their plunderings, and their stealings. And it came to pass that they did have their signs, yea, their secret signs, and their secret words; and this that they might distinguish a brother who had entered into the covenant, that whatsoever wickedness his brother should do he should not be injured by his brother, nor by those who did belong to his band, who had taken this covenant. . . . And whosoever of those who belonged to their band should reveal unto the world of their wickedness and their abominations, should be tried, not according to the laws of their country, but according to the laws of their wickedness, which had been given by Gadianton and Kishkumen. (Hel. 6:18–24)

The Gadianton robbers eventually overthrew the government and nearly proved the destruction of the Nephite nation. Their single-minded focus on wealth led them not only to violate God's covenant with Israel but to substitute it with a covenant with their own god of wealth. This is the face of idolatry in the Book of Mormon. This is why pride is so deadly. As we saw in the Old Testament, once the covenant obligation to the poor and vulnerable is neglected, once the covenant bonds of community are shattered, the end is near.

We don't often focus on this aspect of pride in the Church. We sometimes mention that it is tied to wealth in the Book of Mormon, but the specific economic causes and consequences of pride are often glossed over and abstracted in favor of diagnosing general and individual spiritual maladies.[33] The danger of this approach is that it removes pride from the spe-

---

33. Speaking of this "dangerous privatization of spirituality," Gustavo Gutiérrez says that "the poor/rich opposition (a social fact) is reduced to the humble/proud opposition (something within the individual)." Gustavo Gutiérrez, *We Drink From Our Own Wells: The Spiritual Journey of a People*, 15.

cific context in which Mormon and the other Book of Mormon prophets placed it. Mormon makes clear that it is wealth, not personal spiritual failings, that leads to pride. He tells us that pride was caused by wealth and led to the separation of classes marked off by conspicuous displays of wealth as status. This led to greater class separation and control of society by the wealthy at the expense of the poor. Focusing on individual spiritual failings obscures the social context and origin that is so critical to understanding the fatal manifestation of pride in the Book of Mormon and in our day.

President Ezra Taft Benson, in his address "Beware of Pride" in April 1989, stated that the main element of pride is enmity. Placing pride in its appropriate social context helps us better understand the root and origin of this enmity. It is not a general animosity towards others, but it is the result of the way society is ordered. We are taught to hate people (the meaning of enmity) because of class distinctions and boundary markers. We are taught to be competitive because our society sets up scenarios where one can only prosper at the expense of others. Benson's closing statement shows the way forward to reclaim the understanding of pride as the antithesis of covenant community:

> My dear brethren and sisters, we must prepare to redeem Zion. It was essentially the sin of pride that kept us from establishing Zion in the days of the Prophet Joseph Smith. It was the same sin of pride that brought consecration to an end among the Nephites.[34]

This statement rightfully identifies pride as the culprit in the failure of these covenant communities that flourished after Christ's visit. Here again, Mormon is explicit in his detail as to the cause of their peace and communal bonds:

> And they had all things in common among them; therefore they were not rich and poor, bond and free, but they were all made free, and partakers of the heavenly gift. (4 Ne. 1:3)

Mormon makes clear that the reason for their peace was their full and total acceptance of the covenant community as their way of life. They lived in common. There was no private property. There were no class distinctions. They did not even distinguish themselves as separate peoples, no longer calling themselves Lamanites and Nephites. They all partook of the heavenly gift, the kingdom of God.

After nearly two hundred years, when all are rich and living in harmony, Mormon issued a foreboding statement:

---

34. Ezra Taft Benson, "Beware of Pride."

> There began to be those among them who were lifted up in pride, such as the wearing of costly apparel, and all manner of fine pearls, and of the fine things of the world. And from that time forth they did have their goods and their substance no more common among them. And they began to be divided in classes. (4 Ne. 1:24–26)

The covenant was broken. The downfall of society had begun. Note the degeneration did not come from the corruption of individual morality but from the pride that resulted in boundary marking and class division. Wealth and private property that leads to inequality are the culprits. Covenant community is the answer.

Placing pride in its appropriate context becomes even more important when we consider the social and political context in which Benson was giving his address. The United States had just come to the end of two terms of the Reagan administration. This presidency had seen the ushering in of a new era of corporate hegemony and a massive upwards transfer of wealth that has proven catastrophic in the last forty years. Reagan, following the blueprint of Margaret Thatcher in the United Kingdom, implemented widespread free-market economic reforms. He cut taxes on the wealthy and deregulated business, opening the door to monopolies and consolidation of markets in the hands of a few corporations. He busted unions, severely curtailing the rights and power of workers to challenge their exploitation. He began to envision and craft free-trade agreements that would be further honed and implemented in subsequent decades (most significantly the North American Free Trade Agreement under Clinton in 1994). These agreements further cemented corporate unaccountability and hegemony, leading to offshoring of jobs and exploitation of workers all over the world. Beginning under Reagan and accelerating through the Clinton administration and over the next few decades, the government slashed funding for public services, social programs, and welfare assistance, and privatized much of what was left, leading to more cuts to social spending, healthcare, and public support.[35] At the same time as prisons were being privatized, rates of imprisonment and the prison population increased in an unprecedented manner, fueled by increased racial disparity

---

35. Donald Cohen and Allen Mikaelian, *The Privatization of Everything: How the Plunder of Public Goods Transformed America and How We Can Fight Back*. In 1983 the Reagan administration released a twenty-three thousand page report that served as a blueprint for privatization of government functions over the next few decades.

in the criminal justice system.[36] The wealth gap between rich and poor began to yawn ever wider, a chasm that is still widening today.

Reagan, along with free-market economists, instituted the Washington Consensus, which required severe "structural adjustments" for developing countries devastated by civil and economic crises who sought loans from the IMF or World Bank, essentially turning these countries into corporate fronts and reducing them to generations of debt. His administration provided financial aid and training to the government in the Salvadoran civil war, leading to the slaughter of tens of thousands of civilians, and overthrew governments in Chad, Nicaragua, and Grenada. In the years since, US-led wars in the Middle East, Pakistan, Afghanistan, and other areas of the world have killed nearly one million people—with several hundred thousand of these being civilians—displaced tens of millions of refugees, and poisoned the environment, leaving generations afflicted with increased rates of cancers, radiation poisoning, and birth defects, all while generating trillions of dollars for the military-industrial complex.[37] Foreign trade policy and agreements have allowed corporations to run rampant in developing countries, exploiting workers and displacing indigenous people from their ancestral lands and homes.[38]

---

36. Michelle Alexander, *The New Jim Crow: Mass Incarceration in the Age of Colorblindness*; Tony Platt, "US Criminal Justice in the Reagan Era: An Assessment," 58–69; Lauren-Brooke Eisen, *Inside Private Prisons: An American Dilemma in the Age of Mass Incarceration*. While the carceral system began to expand under Reagan, it was Bill Clinton's signing of the Crime Bill in 1994 that entrenched racially driven arrests, prosecutions, and imprisonment.

37. The most current estimate of the total killed in US-led wars since September 11, 2001, is 929,000. Of these, 387,000 have been civilians. Thirty-eight million refugees have been displaced. Although the numbers are much harder to calculate, economic sanctions have also likely caused the deaths of many more civilians, on the order of millions, due to inadequate food and medical care. See M. Savabieasfahani, F. Basher Ahamadani, and A. Mahdavi Damghani, "Living Near an Active U.S. Military Base in Iraq Is Associated with Significantly Higher Hair Thorium and Increased Likelihood of Congenital Anomalies in Infants and Children"; M. Savabieasfahani et al., "Prenatal Metal Exposure in the Middle East: Imprint of War in Deciduous Teeth of Children," 505; Neta C. Crawford, *United States Budgetary Costs and Obligations of Post 9/11 Wars Through FY2020: $6.4 Trillion*; John Mueller and Karl Mueller, "Sanctions of Mass Destruction," 43–53; George Bisharat, "Sanctions As Genocide," 379–425.

38. Naomi Klein, *The Shock Doctrine: The Rise of Disaster Capitalism*; Naomi Klein, *No Logo*.

These social and political realities are the face of pride today. What can be done? How do we keep ourselves from giving in to the division and boundary marking that constitute the breaking of covenant community that is so common all around us? We need a way to force ourselves to cross the boundaries that are instituted by society and by our own prejudices. We need a way to look past the "otherness" of those around us who have different life stations and experiences. We need a way to put ourselves in their shoes, to suffer as they suffer, and to hope as they hope. God has provided such a way, and it is to this covenant that we now turn.

If This Be the Desire of Your Hearts

During Abinadi's trial, the elder Alma, one of king Noah's priests, felt convicted by his conscience. When Noah ordered the execution of Abinadi, Alma pled for the prophet's life. This, however, turned Noah against Alma, who was driven out of the city by Noah's soldiers. Inspired by Abinidi's preaching, Alma recorded as much as he could remember and then moved about among the people privately teaching what he had learned.

King Noah and his priests had glutted themselves off the labor of the people. Mormon writes that Noah levied a tax of one fifth of everything they possessed to support the "riotous living" of himself and his priests. We are not told much about how the kingdom functioned under Noah's father, Zeniff, but we are told that this taxing of the people "changed the affairs of the kingdom," suggesting that it was a new development with Noah (Mosiah 11:3–4). While there is much description in the previous chapters of Nephite industry, we are never told of taxation to support the king and his retainers. Rather, the industry seems to support the people in their basic needs. For example, we are told that they raised grain and produced cloth "to clothe [their] nakedness" (Mosiah 10:5). Thus, while the brief account of Zeniff's rule focuses heavily on the military conflict between the Nephites and Lamanites (Mosiah 9–10), what we do know of the arrangement of the kingdom never gives us the impression that there is exploitation or oppression of the people.

The description of Noah's kingdom, by contrast, is right away one of excess, greed, and exploitation. Once again, Mormon uses parallelisms in his writing to illustrate his point. In the description of the taxation, he says that Noah "laid a tax of one fifth part of all they possessed, a fifth part of their gold and of their silver, and a fifth part of their ziff, and of their copper, and of their brass and their iron" (Mosiah 11:3). This is then used by Noah to build "many elegant and spacious buildings." It is obvious here who was doing the building. The people were forced to labor on Noah's projects: "thus did the people labor exceedingly to support iniquity" (v. 6). Mormon is explicit that the "precious things" they were forced to ornament Noah's buildings with were the very things he had taken from them in taxes: "gold and of silver, and of iron, and of brass, and of ziff, and of copper" (v. 8).

The description of Noah's kingdom building reminds us of the description of the reign of Solomon. Noah built himself a huge palace, and the temple was remodeled during his reign with all manner of "fine work" (Mosiah 11:11). He planted vineyards and made "wine in abundance; and therefore he became a wine-bibber, and also his people" (v. 15). Thus, Mormon does not mince words in portraying the excess of Noah and his priests. His taxation would have been onerous, and his forced labor would have taken people away from their own fields and subsistence. Though Mormon describes the sins of "the people," he makes it clear that it is Noah and his priests that were responsible for the degeneration of the kingdom: "and he did cause his people to commit sin, and do that which was abominable in the sight of the Lord. . . . [T]hey also became idolatrous, because they were deceived by the vain and flattering words of the king and priests" (vv. 2, 7). The idolatry spoken of here is what results when religious teaching is corrupted to serve the needs of the ruling class. Noah's priests would have taught the people that the rulers ruled by divine right and were favored and blessed by God, signified by their wealth. This would have in turn caused the people to prioritize wealth themselves, having been convinced that the accumulation of wealth was a sign of divine favor. The people idolized and mimicked the behavior of their rulers. Many of the so-called "harlots" that Noah and his priests sexually exploited would have been driven into prostitution by the demands on their families for subsistence due to the burden of taxation and forced labor. Thus, the king and his excess led to the sin and ruin of his people.

This is the social and political environment that Abinadi preached in. The first thing he said to the people was that if they would not repent, the Lord would deliver them into bondage to their enemies. He issued this threat repeatedly as he tried desperately to wake the people up to the dreadful reality of their situation (Mosiah 11–12). They had been told by their king and priests that their social arrangements were divinely ordained, and Abinadi worked to pull the veil from off their eyes and did so by invoking the memory of Israel in bondage to Egypt. But it was to no avail. The "eyes of the people were blinded" by the flattery of their king and priests (11:29). When Abinadi was finally captured, put on trial, and killed, it was the people who brought him before the king—an indication of the hold that the idolatrous ideology had over their hearts and minds. Within a few years, the kingdom would be conquered, with many killed and taken captive by the Lamanites. In this case, the prophesied slaughter and bondage took less than a generation to be fulfilled. This scenario set up the liberation of Limhi and Alma's people that would play a central role in Alma the Younger's attempts to wake up his own people.

Between Abinadi's execution and the bondage of Noah's people to the Lamanites is the account of a small group of Alma's followers who form a church at the waters of Mormon:

> Now, there was in Mormon a fountain of pure water, and Alma resorted thither, there being near the water a thicket of small trees, where he did hide himself in the daytime from the searches of the king. And it came to pass that as many as believed him went thither to hear his words. And it came to pass after many days there were a goodly number gathered together at the place of Mormon, to hear the words of Alma. Yea, all were gathered together that believed on his word, to hear him. And he did teach them, and did preach unto them repentance, and redemption, and faith on the Lord. And it came to pass that he said unto them: Behold, here are the waters of Mormon (for thus were they called) and now, as ye are desirous to come into the fold of God, and to be called his people, and are willing to bear one another's burdens, that they may be light; Yea, and are willing to mourn with those that mourn; yea, and comfort those that stand in need of comfort, and to stand as witnesses of God at all times and in all things, and in all places that ye may be in, even until death, that ye may be redeemed of God, and be numbered with those of the first resurrection, that ye may have eternal life— Now I say unto you, if this be the desire of your hearts, what have you against being baptized in the name of the Lord, as a witness before him that ye have entered into a covenant with him, that ye will serve him and keep his commandments, that he may pour out his Spirit more abundantly upon you? And now when the people had heard these words, they clapped their hands for joy, and exclaimed: This is the desire of our hearts. (Mosiah 18:5–11)

There are several things to consider in this brief but remarkable passage. First, Alma was in mortal danger. He had been exiled by king Noah, and the king routinely sent out his soldiers to search for his former priest. If found, Alma would have been killed. Nevertheless, Alma felt compelled to risk his own life to share what he learned from Abinadi. This is an indication of a significant conversion event in Alma's own life. Second, Alma's preaching produced a following. It appears that the characterization of

Noah's people as being beyond reaching was not entirely correct. There are, at least by Mormon's accounting, several hundred who believed Alma and came to hear his preaching. These people would have been aware that their coming to hear Alma put them at risk of being taken by the king's soldiers. Thus, the idyllic, peaceful setting of the waters of Mormon that we normally see in our mind's eye should be reconceptualized as a covert operation at imminent risk of discovery and tragedy for this small band of believers. Why did they keep returning at the risk of their lives?

We don't know the specifics of what Alma taught the people at the water's edge. The verse says that he preached unto the people "repentance, and redemption, and faith on the Lord" (Mosiah 18:7). This seems standard Christian boilerplate fare. But the enthusiasm with which these people accept baptism suggests that something in them had fundamentally changed. This is an indication, yet again, of a conversion event, in some respects similar to that described at the speech of King Benjamin. However, we get a sense that the conversion had already come some time earlier for these people. At the waters of Mormon there was no unified petition for Jesus to save; there was no dramatic episode of falling down and prostrating themselves. Instead, Alma seems to have sensed in his followers that something had already changed them and put new desires into their hearts. His articulation of their desires was so accurate they could not help but clap their hands for joy at his suggestion of baptism as a way of solemnizing what was already in their hearts. What are they so ecstatic about?

Alma's invitation to his followers essentially consists of two activities that are necessary aspects of a life of discipleship: to suffer and to witness. Alma was not talking here about suffering generally. The people already knew such suffering. Famine, conflict, poverty, and disease all entail suffering, and they were in some sense the unavoidable experience of a mortal life, especially for the poor.[39] However, here Alma was talking about a very specific type of suffering. His shorthand for it is bearing burdens, mourning, and comforting. This is suffering *with* others—the essence of Christian discipleship.[40] The Latin word *compati*, from which the word compassion derives, is literally translated as "suffer with." Thus, in the

---

39. For an elegant treatment of the reality of human suffering and what it does, and does not, reveal about God, see Gustavo Gutiérrez, *On Job: God-Talk and the Suffering of the Innocent*.

40. The critical importance of suffering with others in true discipleship is made clear by the fact that the three Nephites are to be spared any mortal pain or suffering while they tarry *except* sorrow "for the sins of the world" (3 Ne. 28:9).

scriptures when we read accounts of Jesus having compassion on people, we should understand the text as implying that Jesus "suffered with" people. We are helped further by considering the Greek word that is translated as "to feel or be moved with compassion" in the New Testament. This word, σπλαγχνίζομαι, or *splagchnizomai*, refers to an emotional response that is so intense that it is felt in the bowels.[41] This is an emotional response of such intensity that it requires action on the part of the one feeling it. The word is used sparingly in the New Testament (only twelve times), and eight of those uses refer to the response of Jesus to those he encountered in his ministry. Thus, encountering suffering and need filled Jesus with a consuming response of love and solidarity that required action from him (see 3 Nephi 17:5–10). This seems to be what Alma was sensing in his little band of followers. A love of humanity and an emotional pull that manifests itself in the desire to suffer with others and do what can be done to alleviate such suffering. Sometimes we are able to bear a burden; sometimes we can offer comfort; sometimes all we can do is mourn.

This passage indicates the deep commitment that discipleship involves. It is a commitment to throw oneself unreservedly and wholeheartedly into what makes us truly human. By committing, even covenanting, to support one another in our mutual suffering, we embrace our mortality, our humanity, and our divinity. Experiencing the extremes of existence reminds us just how fragile life is, and we are never closer to our own mortality than when we experience death, disease, or illness. Our shared humanity is revealed in our response to the suffering of our fellow human family. A response of true compassion is different from a response of sympathy or even empathy. Sympathy and empathy both involve feeling something for the one who suffers, but such feeling is experienced at a safe remove, a distance that doesn't risk being too affected by the suffering. Douglas John Hall explains:

> To feel compassion, deeply and sincerely, is to overcome the subject/object division; it is to suffer with the other. Not just to have a certain fellow feeling for him or her, and certainly not only to look with pity on another—a pity that in its actualization accentuates one's distance from the other. Rather, it means to be thrust into solidarity of spirit with the other—to experience, in one's own person, the highest possible degree of identity with the other.[42]

---

41. The bowels, or guts, were thought to be the location of emotions such as love in ancient Greece, hence the reference to this part of the body.
42. Douglas John Hall, *The Cross in Our Context: Jesus and the Suffering World*, 22.

Here we can see why the commitment to suffer with others is protective against the boundary markers that accompany pride. In demonstrating compassion, the boundary between ourselves and those around us disintegrates. By throwing ourselves wholly into the suffering of others, we experience their lives and realities, their pains, their hopes, and their fears. The "otherness" that separates us has been transcended in a solidarity that results from a truly shared humanity.

Suffering with others, however, is not Alma's only invitation. He also invited his followers to "stand as witnesses of God at all times, and in all things, and in all places" (Mosiah 18:9). We often think of this as a reference to standing boldly and declaring our belief in God, Jesus, and the Church. We feel this reminds us that we need to stand up for what we believe in, and we need to do it in an uncompromising and fearless fashion. But if we think about the connection between suffering with others and standing as a witness, we can discern a different meaning. In fact, suffering with others provides a powerful—and maybe the most explicit—witness of God in the world. In suffering, we come to see and know the nature of God. We truly *witness* God.

This reality is illustrated powerfully by the Japanese author Shūsaku Endō in his masterful novel *The Samurai*. It tells the story of a lesser noble in feudal Japan during the early seventeenth century who was sent on a diplomatic mission to negotiate more favorable trade relations with Spain. His travels to Mexico and eventually Rome exposed him to Christianity, and he encountered representations of the crucified Christ everywhere he went—in homes, churches, and monasteries. At first he was repulsed. He could not understand how anyone could worship "such a miserable, wretched fellow . . . someone so ugly and emaciated." However, he then encountered a renegade Japanese priest in Mexico who explained,

> In the old days . . . I had the same doubts. But I can believe in Him now because the life He lived in this world was more wretched than any other man's. Because He was ugly and emaciated. He knew all there was to know about the sorrows of this world. He could not close His eyes to the grief and agony of mankind. That is what made Him emaciated and ugly. Had He lived an exalted, powerful life beyond our grasp, I would not feel like this about Him.[43]

The mission and voyage of the samurai was haunted by the image of the crucified Jesus, but still he could not bring himself to believe. His own

---

43. Shūsaku Endō, *The Samurai*, 220. He explores similar themes in his novel *Silence*.

fortunes turned sour after his diplomatic mission was refused in Rome due to growing tensions between Japan, who was accelerating their purge of Christians, and the Catholic Church. By the novel's end, he was left bereft of land and prestige, his own life a casualty of imperial politics. It was only then that he began to understand how this pathetic man could be worthy of reverence and worship. It was in his own identification with Jesus *as poor, wretched, emaciated, ugly, and suffering that this revelation came.* His own suffering had led him to Jesus. Our suffering, and suffering with others, can do the same. It is in the extremity of life that we understand the depth of God's love for us manifest in a willingness to suffer the pains of mortality. And when we come to see Jesus's suffering in our own suffering and the suffering of those around us, we come to witness God in the world.

As Christians, we hold that the ultimate manifestation of the nature of God is in the life and Atonement of Jesus Christ. This is known traditionally as the incarnation. Jesus was God in human form. Or rather, God became human in Jesus. At the last supper, when asked by Philip to "show us the father," Jesus replied, "Have I been with you all this time, Philip, and you still do not know me? Whoever has seen me has seen the Father" (John 14:8–9). When we think of Jesus's mortality and suffering, however, we often focus only on what it means for the suffering we experience in our lives. Because of Jesus's suffering, he understands how to "succor" us better, and this provides solace and comfort in our moments of distress. We need help to bear our suffering, and as Dietrich Bonhoeffer, the German theologian who was hanged by the Nazis for his alleged role in a plot to assassinate Hitler, wrote while awaiting execution in prison, "Only the suffering God can help."[44] Thus, Jesus's suffering is a comfort to us because we believe it demonstrates that he can identify with our own suffering in every particular.

But do we ever consider the converse? If Jesus experienced all that humankind would suffer, then our own suffering and the suffering of those with whom we stand in solidarity must by necessity also help us come to know and understand him—and by extension, God—better. Put another way, because God, in Jesus, suffered the pains of humanity, the more human pain we suffer, the better we come to know God. Thus, when we commit ourselves to suffering with others, we become more attuned to the experience of the suffering Jesus in those around us. And herein the critical relation between suffering and witnessing becomes clear. It is precisely

---

44. Dietrich Bonhoeffer, *Letters and Papers from Prison*, 164.

because there is so much suffering in the world that the covenant to bear one another's burdens, mourn with those that mourn, and comfort those who stand in need of comfort allows us to stand as witnesses of God *at all times, and in all things, and in all places.*

This must have been what Alma's little band of saints understood at the waters of Mormon. This must have been why they were so excited about throwing themselves into a covenant community of shared suffering. Their eyes had been opened to the humanity of those around them, in all its beauty and ugliness and contradictions. They felt moved by their faith in the life and humanity of Jesus to suffer in solidarity with them. And somewhere in those fearful, broken, weeping, and tearstained faces, they had found God. Their covenant, made in full awareness and understanding of the sacrifice it would require, was nothing less than a covenant to participate with God in the redemption and liberation, indeed the salvation, of humanity.

An Infinite and Eternal Reconciliation

The Book of Mormon is a story of the catastrophic effects of estrangement without reconciliation, wherein the familial bond that is broken shortly after the arrival of Lehi's family in the promised land is never fully mended.[45] Throughout their history, the rare occasions of peace between the Nephites and Lamanites are fleeting and short-lived; instead, the majority of the narrative chronicles a state of constant warfare between the two peoples. This ongoing violence is largely rooted in the perpetuation of a simple narrative that is exemplified in Zeniff's description of the Lamanites:

> They were a wild, and ferocious, and a blood-thirsty people, believing in the tradition of their fathers, which is this—Believing that they were driven out of the land of Jerusalem because of the iniquities of their fathers, and that they were wronged in the wilderness by their brethren, and they were also wronged while crossing the sea; And again, that they were wronged while in the land of their first inheritance, after they had crossed the sea, and all this because that Nephi was more faithful in keeping the commandments of the Lord—therefore he was favored of the Lord, for the Lord heard his prayers and answered them, and he took the lead of their journey in the wilderness. And his brethren were wroth with him because they understood not the dealings of the Lord; they were also wroth with him upon the waters because

---

45. See Patrick Q. Mason and J. David Pulsipher, *Proclaim Peace: The Restoration's Answer to an Age of Conflict*, for an in-depth exploration of the effects of this "festering, unreconciled grievance" (epub, 292).

they hardened their hearts against the Lord. And again, they were wroth with him when they had arrived in the promised land, because they said that he had taken the ruling of the people out of their hands; and they sought to kill him. And again, they were wroth with him because he departed into the wilderness as the Lord had commanded him, and took the records which were engraven on the plates of brass, for they said that he robbed them. And thus they have taught their children that they should hate them, and that they should murder them, and that they should rob and plunder them, and do all they could to destroy them; therefore they have an eternal hatred towards the children of Nephi. (Mosiah 10:12–17)

Here we can see that Zeniff has summarized the history of the Lamanites and Nephites as a simple duality: the Lamanites are wicked, and the Nephites are righteous.[46] His characterization of the conflict denies the complexity of the family history and attributes only the most rudimentary motivations to those on each side of the argument.[47] The Lamanites believed they were wronged, whereas the Nephites know that God had favored them on account of their greater faithfulness. Throughout the rest of the book, the main features of this duality are maintained (although the Nephites and Lamanites experience several role reversals). In other words, the narrative establishes a clearly defined "us vs. them" mentality. Nephi portrayed the Lamanites as a monolithic antagonist whose sole purpose was to "be a scourge unto thy [Nephi's] seed" (1 Ne. 2:24; 2 Ne. 5:25). He and his descendants thus wholly and completely "othered" the Lamanites. The tragic effects of this "othering" reverberated across generations.

At its heart, the estrangement in the Book of Mormon has to do with the perpetuation of grievances from generation to generation. Both sides defined themselves as victims. The Lamanites' entire identity seems to revolve around getting revenge for their mistreatment at the hands of Nephi, whereas the Nephites viewed themselves as victims of the Lamanites' unjustified hatred. These were competing narratives for which there was no easy solution. The Nephites and Lamanites had adopted and repeatedly affirmed identities that were at odds with one another. Community and fellowship under such circumstances is impossible. Reconciliation requires a wholesale shifting of

---

46. This is a curious position for Zeniff to take, given he had just refused to slaughter the Lamanites due to "having seen that which was good among them" (Mosiah 9:1).

47. See Hardy, *Understanding the Book of Mormon*, ch. 2, for a detailed discussion of this as it pertains to Nephi's narration. See also Richard L. Bushman, "The Lamanite View of Book of Mormon History," 52–72.

understanding of the situation, a rewriting of history, and a breaking down of the barriers that have been erected and reinforced. The people, long divided, needed to become one again. In a word, reconciliation requires *atonement*.

When we view Jesus's Atonement through the lens of reconciliation, a significant shift in our understanding occurs. No longer do we view it as a payment for our individual sins.[48] Instead, we view it as the means to mend the breach in relationships that results from sin. The word "atonement" is mentioned more than twice as many times in the Old Testament as in the Book of Mormon (it is only mentioned once in the New Testament). It is always mentioned in the context of the covenant and sacrificial practices of ancient Israel. Recall that the purpose of these practices was to solemnize the continual salvation experienced through God's covenant relationship and to keep Israel, as a body, free from sin and in right relationship with God. As discussed in Chapter 1, the Law of Moses and the Ten Commandments had as their focus the safeguarding of relationships within the covenant community. When these relationships were broken, atonement had to be made. While we tend to think of atonement as performing a cleansing function, Mary Douglas argues that given its role within the context of the covenant, the Hebrew verb *kipper* (translated as "atone" or "expiate") is more accurately defined as:

> To cover, or recover, cover again, to repair a hole, cure a sickness, mend a rift, make good a torn or broken covering. . . . [I]t means making good an outer layer that has rotted or been pierced. . . . When the covering of the universe has been rent, it is not the person who did the deed who needs urgently to be washed but the covering that needs repair.[49]

Thus, God's protective covenant covering was torn by sin, which fractured relationships within the community via exploitation or violence. God provided a way for this tear to be mended.[50] Atonement, then, James

---

48. See discussion in Chapter 3.

49. Mary Douglas, "Atonement in Leviticus," 117–18, 123. See also Margaret Barker, *Temple Theology: An Introduction*, 68–70.

50. It is critical to note here that the many sacrificial rites specified in Leviticus indicate a god who is anxious for the breach in relationship to be mended. This can be clearly seen in the case of bodily impurities that result in ritual uncleanliness for an extended period of time. James Greenberg notes "sacrifice seems to be required for some bodily impurities because these impurities have caused an excessive time of separation between the infected person, the sanctuary and thus YHWH's presence." James A. Greenberg, *A New Look at Atonement in Leviticus: The Meaning and Purpose of Kipper Revisited*, 100. In all of these cases,

Greenberg notes, "repairs the protective [covenant] connection that was broken"[51] by sin.

But sin is not a one-way street. We tend to think of sins as singular violations of some moral imperative that we accumulate throughout our lives, and that Christ's Atonement provides a way for us to forego the punishment for these infractions that offend God or violate God's law. In fact, this conceptualization is a distortion. As noted by Douglas John Hall, "There has been no more effective way of erasing the profundity of this term [sin], which refers to a quality of relationship, than to quantify it. The result is a petty moralism that no longer speaks to the great and abiding conflicts of human persons in their complex intermingling."[52]

Andrew Sung Park, a Korean-American theologian, relates the Korean term *han* (恨) to an understanding of sin. He defines *han* as the "critical wound of the heart"[53]:

> [*Han* is] the hardened heart that is grieved by oppression and injustice. . . . When the heart is hurt so much, it ruptures symbolically; it aches. When the aching heart is wounded again by external violence, the victim suffers a yet deeper pain. The wound produced by such repeated abuse and injustice is han in the heart.[54]

Han can be generated by

> social, political, economic, or cultural oppression. It is entrenched in the hearts of the victims of sin and violence, and is expressed through such diverse reactions as sadness, helplessness, resentment, hatred, and the will to revenge. Han reverberates in the souls of survivors of the Holocaust, Palestinians in the occupied territories, victims of racial discrimination, battered wives, victims of child molestation, the unemployed and exploited workers.[55]

This understanding of sin complicates things considerably. Here, sin is an endemic feature of social and political systems and structures. Furthermore, because sin refers to a quality of human relationship, there is no one-sided fix. Atonement cannot simply mean absolving one or more

---

sacrifice is offered *after* the ritual purification has been completed, thus providing a formal way to solemnize the mending of the relationship, rather than a way to cleanse a person of their impurities.

51. Greenberg, 42.
52. Hall, *The Cross in Our Context*, 104.
53. Andrew Sung Park, *The Wounded Heart of God: The Asian Concept of Han and the Christian Doctrine of Sin*, 10.
54. Park, 20.
55. Park, 10.

parties of their infraction, because it is the relationship that is damaged. Relationship, by its very nature, is a complex and dynamic interaction between multiple parties. Sin causes, according to Marjorie Suchocki, "an intertwining of victim and violator through the very nature of violation."[56] In order for the sin to be mended, for the *han* to be undone, the relationship has to be mended. This is why atonement and reconciliation are one and the same. Christ's Atonement, rather than being a once-for-all-time payment for individual sins, makes possible an ongoing and future reconciliation from the relationship-shattering effects of sin.

As mentioned above, the thing that stood in the way of reconciliation between the Nephites and Lamanites was the constant refreshing of generational grievances. This led to a perpetual cycle of violence. Thus, each new generation had a reason to hate their enemies even more. Add to the perceived historical injustice the cumulative effects of grief and the psychological and emotional damage from those killed, wounded, or traumatized in battle, raids, and conflict (this is the *han*, if you will, of the Nephites and Lamanites), and you have a recipe for intergenerational hatred, violence, and retribution leading to further suffering. Under these conditions, reconciliation is impossible.

So how does the Atonement of Jesus make this seemingly impossible reconciliation a possibility, let alone a reality? The answer can be found by contemplating the symbolism of the cross.[57] Jesus himself emphasizes the critical nature of such reflection when he appeared to the Nephites following his death: "And my Father sent me that I might be lifted up upon the cross; and after that I had been lifted up upon the cross, that I might draw all men unto me" (3 Ne. 27:14). How does reflection on the cross draw us to Jesus, and how does this enable reconciliation? Jesus was

---

56. Marjorie Hewitt Suchocki, *The Fall to Violence: Original Sin in Relational Theology*, 147.

57. Martin Luther's original development of this theological approach, following from his reading of the apostle Paul, is known as *theologia crucis* (theology of the cross). Examples of the development of this theology in contemporary Christian scholarship can be found in Douglas John Hall, *Lighten our Darkness: Towards an Indigenous Theology of the Cross*; Douglas John Hall, *God and Human Suffering: An Exercise in the Theology of the Cross*; Douglas John Hall, *The Cross in our Context*; Dorothee Soelle, *Suffering*; Jürgen Moltmann, *The Crucified God: The Cross of Christ as the Foundation and Criticism of Christian Theology*; S. Mark Heim, *Saved from Sacrifice: A Theology of the Cross*; James H. Cone, *The Cross and the Lynching Tree*; and Kazoh Kitamori, *Theology of the Pain of God: The First Original Theology from Japan*.

killed on the cross as a political criminal. His life and ministry threatened the ruling class. His solidarity with, and attempt to wake up, the poor and marginalized to the reality of their oppression and exploitation threatened the institutional religious hegemony. His expansion of the covenant community outside of the business of sacrifice and temple ritual threatened the high-priestly life of luxury. He had to die. From a liberation perspective then, the cross represents the institutional powers that violently resist the ushering in of the reign, or kingdom, of God. God's justice is not easily established in the world, in Jesus's day or ours. Jesus's love for and life dedicated to liberating the poor was bound to bring him into violent conflict with the ruling powers. As Dorothee Soelle observes,

> Love does not 'require' the cross, but *de facto* it ends up on the cross. *De facto* Jesus of Nazareth was crucified. . . . The cross is no theological invention, but the world's answer, given a thousand times over, to attempts at liberation.[58]

It seems that in the cross, the ruling powers have won. Jesus was dead and buried, another threat neutralized.

Most horrifically, it seems clear that in his most desperate hour, Jesus was abandoned even by God, crying in his last excruciating moments, "Eli, Eli, lema sabachthani?"—that is, "My God, my God, why have you forsaken me?" (Matt. 27:46). In that cry is the crying of billions of poor and oppressed throughout history who have been chewed up and spit out by Empire. Why have you abandoned us to torture, starvation, and death? Where is your power to liberate? Where is salvation?

The lesson of the cross, however, is not one of abandonment. It is one of solidarity. Jesus was not abandoned by God on the cross. Rather, Jesus, as ever, was Emmanuel—*God with us*—on the cross. Jon Sobrino clarifies the significance of Jesus dying in this way: "If God was on the cross of Jesus, if God shared in the horrors of history in this way, then God's closeness to us, begun at the incarnation and made present to us in Jesus's life, has been consummated."[59] God, in Jesus, had demonstrated solidarity with the poor and oppressed by suffering even unto death. This is hugely consequential for the poor in its own right because, as Sobrino again notes, "the cross, in itself, already speaks of closeness to their own situation. And as they, besides being poor and oppressed, are those who

---

58. Soelle, *Suffering*, 163–64; emphasis in original.
59. Jon Sobrino, *Christ the Liberator: A View from the Victims*, 87.

are distanced and marginalized, anything that means closeness already brings something of salvation with it."[60]

Jesus is not only God's solidarity with the poor and oppressed; he is God's solidarity with humanity. This is because the cross also symbolizes God's willingness to die for the sins of the world—or, we could say, *because* of the sins of the world. Due to humanity's collective failure to protect and care for "the least of these," the covenant had been broken, and an atonement was desperately needed: "therefore God himself atoneth for the sins of the world" (Alma 42:15). According to Miroslav Volf, during the initial covenant with Abraham,

> Abraham cut the sacrificial animal in two, and "a smoking fire pot and a flaming torch" [symbolizing the presence of God] . . . passed between the halves. The unique ritual act performed by God was a pledge that God would rather "die" than break the covenant, much like the animals through which God passed died. The thought of a living God dying is difficult enough—as difficult as the thought of a faithful God breaking the covenant. At the foot of the cross, however, a veritable abyss opens up for the thought. For the narrative of the cross is not a . . . story of a God who "died" because God broke the covenant, but a truly incredible story of God doing what God should neither have been able nor willing to do—a story of God who "died" because God's all too human *covenant partner* broke the covenant.[61]

The cross, however, does not only reveal both the true nature of sin as broken covenant community and God's willingness to die because of humanity's breach of that covenant relationship. Jesus's willingness to die on the cross at the hands of the ruling powers rather than engage in violent struggle shows the only truly effective strategy towards reconciliation. Jesus had refused to be a political messiah. He had refused to take power by force. His resistance was one of nonviolence. He showed the people that the kingdom of God was not something to be won by violence, but that it could only be realized as lives and hearts are knit together as one. His recognition and nurturing of the humanity in all around him broke down the barriers between "us and them." His unbounded love showed the way to the undoing of the enmity of "othering" that constituted the "original sin" (Gen. 3:12; Moses 4:18) and led to the fall of humankind into systems

---

60. Sobrino, 272.

61. Miroslav Volf, *Exclusion and Embrace: A Theological Exploration of Identity, Otherness, and Reconciliation*, 112; emphasis in original.

of violence, domination, oppression, and death.⁶² As noted by Volf, "The cross is the giving up of God's self in order not to give up on humanity; it is the consequence of God's desire to break the power of human enmity without violence and receive human beings into divine communion."⁶³

Jesus's death on the cross was his final witness that liberation and justice cannot be won by violence. As demonstrated over and over again throughout history, justice won by violence only recreates and recapitulates the violent systems it replaces—the oppressed become the oppressors. Justice means retribution. In the process, ideologies become entrenched, such that even those who struggle for liberation succumb to using institutional power to oppress others. As Paul said to the Ephesians, "For we wrestle not against flesh and blood, but against principalities, against powers, against the rulers of the darkness of this world, against spiritual wickedness in high places" (Eph. 6:12 KJV). Thus, violence, no matter how "justified" it is, always begets more violence.⁶⁴

This cycle of violence is clearly shown in the Book of Mormon struggle between the Nephites and Lamanites. The so-called "war chapters" in the book of Alma are an explicit example of the cycle of violence that degenerates into more and more violence and brutality that makes reconciliation impossible.⁶⁵ These chapters depict a constant military struggle with no real peace. From the perspective of the Nephites, the Lamanites were the aggressors, while the Lamanites felt they are fighting to reclaim their stolen lands and rights to rule. Under these conditions there can be no compromise.

The stalemate is explicitly illustrated in the volley of epistles between the Lamanite king Ammoron and Nephite captain Moroni following the assassination of Amalikiah. Moroni accused Ammoron "concerning this

---

62. Suchocki, *The Fall to Violence*. The story of Cain and Abel graphically illustrates the violence that accompanies "civilization" and "progress." As John Dominic Crossan puts it, "That inaugural fratricide was the murder of a shepherd by a farmer on his own land. . . . The farmer displaces the shepherd and builds a city." Crossan, *God and Empire*, 60–61.

63. Volf, *Exclusion and Embrace*, 89.

64. See Mason, *Proclaim Peace*, for development of a Latter-day Saint theology of peace and nonviolence and an exploration of the power of nonviolence to change hearts and societies.

65. This cycle is perhaps illustrated most horrifically in the Jaredite apocalypse in Ether 13–15 and in the debased sadism, sexual violence, and lack of humanity depicted in Moroni 9.

war which ye have waged against my people, or rather which thy brother hath waged against them, and which ye are still determined to carry on after his death" (Alma 54:5). He spoke of the "justice of God, and the sword of his almighty wrath" (Alma 54:6) that would utterly destroy the Lamanites if they did not retreat. He then threatened Ammoron "concerning that awful hell that awaits to receive such murderers as thou and thy brother have been" (Alma 54:7). He once again made clear that if the Lamanites did not retreat, they would "pull down the wrath of that God whom you have rejected upon you, even to your utter destruction" (Alma 54:9).

Moroni himself, however, was caught up in the spiral of violence. So convinced was he of the righteousness of his position that he succumbed to bloodlust. Rather than let God destroy the Lamanites, Moroni cast himself as the embodiment of God's wrath. And this wrath would not be appeased with Lamanite retreat. He further warned Ammoron that if he did not exchange prisoners on his terms and withdraw the Lamanite claim to the government,

> I will come against you with my armies; yea, even I will arm my women and my children, and I will come against you, and I will follow you even into your own land, which is the land of our first inheritance; yea, and it shall be blood for blood, yea, life for life; and I will give you battle even until you are destroyed from off the face of the earth. (Alma 54:12)

Up until now, Moroni had only sought for the Lamanite retreat. Here, caught up in the spiral of violence and retribution, he threatened to engage his entire population, women and children included, in a campaign of genocide against the Lamanites.

Moroni's epistle did not have its intended effect—far from it. Ammoron's grief had turned to fury, and he called Moroni out for murdering his brother, vowing to "avenge his blood upon you, yea, and I will come upon you with my armies for I fear not your threatenings" (Alma 54:16). He then repeated the age-old Lamanite grievance: "For behold, your fathers did wrong their brethren, insomuch that they did rob them of their right to the government when it rightly belonged unto them" (Alma 54:17). Like Moroni, his terms for peace were no less than a complete surrender and subjection of the Nephites: "And now behold, if ye will lay down your arms, and subject yourselves to be governed by those to whom the government doth rightly belong, then will I cause that my people shall lay down their weapons and shall be at war no more" (Alma 54:18). Failing this, Ammoron warned that he would "wage a war which shall be eternal, either to the subjecting the Nephites to our authority or to their eternal extinction" (Alma 54:20). He then called Moroni on the carpet for his hypocrisy in threatening Ammoron with hell for murder after himself orchestrating the murder of Amalikiah, appealing to the equality of the Lamanites and Nephites in the eyes of God: "And if it so be that there is a devil and a hell, behold will he not send you there to dwell with my brother whom ye have murdered, whom ye have hinted that he hath gone to such a place?" (Alma 54:22). His closing statement displays how entrenched the opposing narratives have become, rewriting history (at least according to Nephi's account): "I am Ammoron, and a descendant of Zoram, whom your fathers pressed and brought out of Jerusalem. And behold now, I am a bold Lamanite; behold, this war hath been waged to avenge their wrongs, and to maintain and to obtain their rights to the government" (Alma 54:23–24). This fiery and volatile exchange between Moroni and Ammoron exemplifies the utter intractability of the situation.

Miroslav Volf, in his book *Exclusion and Embrace*, examines in depth the extreme difficulty of true reconciliation in a world of appalling violence and injustice.[66] Volf struggles from a place of profound personal experience. He is a Croatian national who was deeply impacted by the ethnic conflicts in the region. His father was tortured in a concentration camp, and Volf himself was exposed to prolonged interrogation by secret police. For Volf, true reconciliation requires forgiveness. In order to break the cycle of retributive violence, there must come a time where we let go of our desire for revenge, either human or divine. Reconciliation, therefore, requires that we strive to be "more than conquerors" (Rom. 8:37). Jesus requires this of his followers. To a group of people who would have been very aware of the injustice of their situation of oppression and exploitation, and very justified in wishing harm or revenge on their oppressors, he stated, "Ye have heard that it hath been said, Thou shalt love thy neighbour, and hate thine enemy. But I say unto you, Love your enemies, bless them that curse you, do good to them that hate you, and pray for them which despitefully use you, and persecute you" (Matt. 5:43–44 KJV). As Howard Thurman puts it, "Jesus says to the disinherited: 'Love your enemy. Take the initiative in seeking ways by which you can have the experience of a common sharing of mutual worth and value. It may be hazardous, but you must do it.'"[67]

---

66. Volf explores these themes further in his books *Free of Charge: Giving and Forgiving in a Culture Stripped of Grace* and *The End of Memory: Remembering Rightly in a Violent World*.

67. Howard Thurman, *Jesus and the Disinherited*, 100.

Jesus himself illustrated this in his plea during his crucifixion for his crucifiers: "Father, forgive them; for they know not what they do" (Luke 23:34 KJV). Notice that Jesus does not say we should dismiss the violence done to us as a mere trifle. As discussed above, violence and sin reverberate far beyond the moment of any discrete occurrence. It is far from trivial in its immediate effects and extended damage. What forgiveness entails, according to Marjorie Suchocki, is "willing the well-being of victim(s) and violator(s) in the context of the fullest possible knowledge of the nature of the violation."[68] Only in fully excavating and understanding the causes and effects of violence can we begin to see the humanity, the brokenness, of the perpetrators. This shift in perspective and feeling is necessary because Jesus doesn't tell us only to refrain from hurting our enemies in violent retribution. He tells us to love them, to bless them, to do good to them, and to pray for them.[69] In the context of the present discussion, we can see why this is so crucial. Forgiveness is the only way to break the cycle of enmity and retributive violence and to heal the broken hearts, suffering, and pain of intergenerational *han*. Without it, grievances will never die and will instead be passed on and nourished for generations in an unending spiral of violence. Volf, quoting Serbian journalist Zeljko Vukovic, illustrates the heartbreaking generational trauma and corrosive effects of the inability to forgive horrific injustice:

> One of the most distressing stories from the war in former Yugoslavia comes from a Muslim woman. Here is how she tells it:
>
> I am a Muslim, and I am thirty five years old. To my second son who was just born, I gave the name "Jihad." So he would not forget the testament of his mother-revenge. The first time I put my baby at my breast I told him, "May this milk choke you if you forget." So be it. The Serbs taught me to hate. For the last two months there was nothing in me. No pain, no bitterness. Only hatred. I taught these children to love. I did. I am a teacher of literature. I was born in Ilijas and I almost died there. My student, Zoran, the only son of my neighbor, urinated into my mouth. As the bearded hooligans standing around laughed, he told me: "You are good for nothing else, you stinking Muslim woman . . ." I do not know whether I first heard the cry or felt the blow. My former colleague, a teacher of physics, was yelling

---

68. Suchocki, *The Fall to Violence*, 144.

69. We must be absolutely clear here, that forgiveness does not require us to subject ourselves to further abuse or violence. In many cases of serious abuse or violence, it is appropriate, even necessary, to separate oneself from the abuser to protect the physical, emotional, and mental health and well being of oneself or other affected parties.

like mad, "Ustasha, ustasha...." And kept hitting me. Wherever he could. I have become insensitive to pain. But my soul? It hurts. I taught them to love and all the while they were making preparations to destroy everything that is not of the Orthodox faith. Jihad-war. This is the only way.[70]

What can be done in such a case? How is the cycle of violence to be broken? What good does Jesus's death on the cross do for people such as these? Where is God's salvation? More importantly, how can such oppression be overcome by nonviolent resistance?[71] In the face of such hatred, wouldn't that approach be tantamount to lying down and bearing our necks to the swords of our slaughterers, to submit ourselves willingly to annihilation? What hope, what real hope, not some pie-in-the-sky moralizing, do we have of reconciliation in such a scenario? How is forgiveness possible in the face of continual atrocity?

The story of the people of Ammon shows the power, and the very real risk, of pursuing a strategy of nonviolent resistance as a means of reconciliation. The people, having been converted, refused to take up weapons any more. Instead, they buried their weapons in the earth:

> And thus we see that they buried their weapons of peace, or they buried the weapons of war, for peace. And it came to pass that their brethren, the Lamanites, made preparations for war, and came up to the land of Nephi.... Now when the people saw that they were coming against them they went out to meet them, and prostrated themselves before them to the earth, and began to call on the name of the Lord; and thus they were in this attitude when the Lamanites began to fall upon them, and began to slay them with the sword. And thus without meeting any resistance, they did slay a thousand and five of them;.... Now when the Lamanites saw that their brethren would not flee from the sword, neither would they turn aside to the right hand or to the left, but that they would lie down and perish, and praised God even in the very act of perishing under the sword—Now when the Lamanites saw this they did forbear from slaying them; and there were many whose hearts had swollen in them for those of their brethren who had fallen under the sword, for they repented of the things which they had done. And it came to pass that they threw down their weapons of war, and they would not take them

---

70. Volf, *Exclusion and Embrace*, 76–77.

71. This issue demands more exploration than can be undertaken here. The question of the ethics of violent resistance in the context of the American struggle of oppressed blacks for liberation from white oppressors is addressed with nuance and force in James H. Cone, *God of the Oppressed*, particularly chapter 9. See also Oscar Romero's discussion of violence in *Voice of the Voiceless: The Four Pastoral Letters and Other Statements*, 105–10; Mason, *Proclaim Peace*, ch. 6.

again, for they were stung for the murders which they had committed; and they came down even as their brethren, relying upon the mercies of those whose arms were lifted to slay them. (Alma 24:19–25)

This remarkable and tragic, yet ultimately hopeful and beautiful, account represents the only true way towards breaking the cycle of violence: relying on the power of shared humanity to "swell the hearts" of our enemies. It is to continue Jesus's mission of atonement and reconciliation as his living body in the world. It is to remember his broken and torn body in those we encounter in our daily lives and interactions. It is to suffer with, and alleviate the suffering of, "the crucified people of the world"[72] despite personal risk. Indeed, it is to take up our own cross and follow him. This is what the Korean-American theologian Wonhee Joh calls "living in fullness of *jeong*." *Jeong* (정) is a difficult-to-define term that involves a deep sense of identity with another, a transcendence of boundaries in a shared mutual compassion and feeling. Joh observes,

> Jeong is powerful precisely because it is an emancipatory and healing power even in relationships that have been reduced to simple binarism, as is often the case between oppressor and oppressed. . . . Ultimately, it is this intimate existential recognition of the self mirrored in the other that leads to transformation of the heart.[73]

Thus, *jeong* breaks down the enmity between the sinner and the sinned against, and allows forgiveness of the *han* that results from generational violence and trauma. For Joh, this fullness of *jeong* was personified by Jesus on the cross. Feeling this *jeong* was what caused the people of Ammon to bury their weapons despite the risk of death at the hands of their enemies. This is what spilled over the invading Lamanites and caused their hearts to swell, stopping their slaughter. Viewing one another in their shared humanity had allowed God to make good on the promise: "A new heart I will give you, and a new spirit I will put within you; and I will remove from your body the heart of stone and give you a heart of flesh" (Ezek. 36:26).

This is the meaning of the cross. This is the real and potential "cost of discipleship."[74] This is why we covenant to suffer with one another

---

72. The phrase was coined by Ignacio Ellacuría, a Salvadoran Jesuit priest, in reference to the peasants killed and tortured in the Salvadoran civil war and other poor and oppressed people throughout history. See Ignacio Ellacuría, "The Crucified People," 257–78. Ellacuría was assassinated on November 16, 1989.

73. Wonhee Anne Joh, *The Heart of the Cross: A Postcolonial Christology*, 97.

74. The term is the title of the most well-known work by Dietrich Bonhoeffer, *The Cost of Discipleship*.

in the world as the foundation of our church community. This is God's promise of salvation. The cross, however, is not the end of the story. The culmination of the passion, the resurrection of Jesus, in addition to being a triumphant vindication and validation of his life and mission for the poor and oppressed, is the hope and surety of a new day, even for those who die in bringing about God's kingdom. It is "the conviction that God did indeed perform the impossible, gave life to one crucified and will give life to all the crucified,"[75] and it is the hope for a new dawn for truth and justice, for peace and equity. The resurrection is "absolute fulfilment and salvation, and thereby absolute liberation."[76] As the "firstfruits of them that slept" (1 Cor. 15:20 KJV), the risen Jesus is an explicit witness that Empire and evil cannot thwart God's plan for liberation and renewal: "so that, just as Christ was raised from the dead by the glory of the Father, so we too might walk in newness of life" (Rom. 6:4). *This is atonement.* The ongoing gift and responsibility of reconciliation as one in Christ as we work to eliminate any and all imposed boundaries on the building of, and participation in, God's covenant community: "the redemptive task of bringing the achievement of the cross to bear on the world."[77] The struggle for, faith in, and promise of a future for humanity where "all shall be well, and all shall be well, and all manner of things shall be well."[78]

---

75. Jon Sobrino, *Christ the Liberator*, 49.
76. Jon Sobrino, "The Central Position of the Reign of God in Liberation Theology," 178.
77. N. T. Wright, *The Challenge of Jesus: Rediscovering Who Jesus Was and Is*, 95.
78. Julian of Norwich, *Revelations of Divine Love*, 79.

Chapter 6

Zion:
And There Was No Poor Among Them

But it is not given that one man should possess that which is above another, wherefore the world lieth in sin.
— D&C 49:20

The Book of Mormon makes clear that living in covenant community is central to the establishment of the kingdom of God and that deviating from this course has catastrophic effects on societies and nations. It serves as "the voice of one crying from the dust" to warn us of the consequences of wealth, inequality, and pride. True to the prophetic pattern that was established anciently, in Joseph Smith, God had called a prophet whose job it was to wake the people up to the reality of their situation, to help them contemplate and understand a new vision of reality, to liberate them from anything that would keep them from entering into covenant community with one another, and to establish laws and ordinances to solemnize this relationship and protect the communities it established.

The Restoration functioned as a reset from the prevailing Christian orthodoxy that had become entangled with individualistic accounts of salvation and had supported capitalist expansion and exploitation. God needed to remind the people of their covenant obligations to one another and to creation, an obligation that had been abandoned in the pursuit of wealth and personal salvation in opposition to the fellowship of covenant community. A clean break was needed, and a framework within which the new covenant community—really a return to the old covenant community—could be developed was required. The well-known events surrounding the formation of the Church—such as the appearances of heavenly messengers to confer priesthood authority on Joseph and Oliver and the explicit tying of this authority to ancient patriarchal orders—served to reinforce this break from the orthodoxy of the Protestant traditions and provided a framework for the new church to view itself as an authoritative continuation of an ancient religious order. This established a crucial linkage from which to understand and interpret the prophetic tradition of Israel.[1] In addition, it grounded the organization of the Church with a structure which would allow the flexibility needed for geographically diverse groups to function, while at the same time ensuring a uniformity of doctrine and practice that would help to avoid the splintering that was so common in religious sects of the day. The Book of Mormon was another authoritative evidence of the divinity of the work, a unique scripture that clarified and deepened understanding of traditional Christian doctrine and provided a warning about the damning and destructive effects of wealth inequality and pride.

Thus, much of the early activity recorded in Church history seems to have functioned to both set the Church off from other Christian sects and provide an authoritative basis from which to begin the building of the kingdom. Following the founding of the Church, establishing Zion as this covenant community was to become the central focus of Joseph Smith, and those who willingly chose to enter into covenant relationship with God and one another constituted the kingdom of God on the earth. Setting the theological basis and directing the practical application of this "new and everlasting covenant" would then be a recurring feature of the Prophet's revelations during the early years of the Church.[2] Thus, the Restoration is God's ongoing authoritative rejection of ideas of individual salvation outside of community and of the inherent nobility of and freedom to pursue our own self-interest at the expense of the poor and marginalized. It is a rejection of ideologies that champion economic systems that exploit and

---

1. Viewing the Restoration as a continuation of the prophetic tradition of Israel suggests a reframing of the meaning of the "Spirit of Elijah." While understood within Latter-day Saint tradition as being primarily (if not exclusively) related to genealogy and temple work, situating it within the covenant salvation history of Israel suggests a more temporal and economic purpose of "planting in the hearts of the children the promises made to the fathers" (D&C 2:2–3) and turning the hearts of the children to the fathers. The prominence given Moroni's version of this prophecy in the Restoration chain of events suggests the critical and foundational importance of restoring covenantal justice, the lack of which has resulted in the earth being "utterly wasted" in our day.

2. In a fascinating study, Joseph Spencer suggests that the purpose of the Restoration was to fulfill the Hebrew prophecy of the salvation of Israel as realized in the support and nurture made possible by the redistribution of wealth from the Gentiles. See Joseph M. Spencer, *For Zion: A Mormon Theology of Hope*. Spencer makes an explicit connection between Joseph Smith's consecration project and the collection of Gentile funds taken up by Paul at the beginning of his ministry in order to "remember the poor" (D&C 42:30; Gal. 2:10).

ruin huge numbers of people. As an explicit rebuke of these systems and ideologies, the Restoration invites all to remember the original covenant God made with humanity and creation, to enter into community with one another, and by so doing, enter into communion with God.

There I Will Give Unto You My Law

By December 1830, less than a year after the founding of the Church, the Saints were in a precarious position. Animosity towards Joseph Smith and the fledgling church had continued to grow. His life was in danger, and the lives and livelihoods of the Church members were threatened. A few months prior, Joseph had received a revelation indicating that a gathering of God's people was to take place: "ye are called to bring to pass the gathering of mine elect. . . . [T]hey shall be gathered into one place on the face of this land" (D&C 29:7–8). Joseph had sent out missionaries to scout out the location of the city to which the people of God would be gathered, and on December 2, he received another revelation indicating that the Church was to "assemble together at the Ohio" (D&C 37:3). God was aware of plots against Joseph, Sidney Rigdon, and the Saints by "the enemy in the secret chambers" who sought their lives (D&C 38:28), and thus we can see the first of many modern examples from the Restoration of God's deliverance from a temporal threat, much like the deliverance of Lehi and his family. In this revelation, God uses language very similar to that used in the covenant promise with both Israel and Lehi's family that promises an inheritance in a rich land of promise:

> And for your salvation I give unto you a commandment, for I have heard your prayers, and the poor have complained before me, and the rich have I made, and all flesh is mine, and I am no respecter of persons. And I have made the earth rich. . . . And I hold forth and deign to give unto you greater riches, even a land of promise, a land flowing with milk and honey, upon which there shall be no curse when the Lord cometh; And I will give it unto you for the land of your inheritance, if you seek it with all your hearts. And this shall be my covenant with you, ye shall have it for the land of your inheritance, and for the inheritance of your children forever, while the earth shall stand, and ye shall possess it again in eternity, no more to pass away. . . . And that ye might escape the power of the enemy, and be gathered unto me a righteous people, without spot and blameless—Wherefore, for this cause I gave unto you the commandment that ye should go to the Ohio; and there I will give unto you my law; and there you shall be endowed with power from on high. (D&C 38:16–20, 31–32)

There is a foreboding warning, however, along with the promise of a rich inheritance. The Saints who had read the recently published Book of Mormon could not have missed it: "And if ye seek the riches which it is the will of the Father to give unto you, ye shall be the richest of all people, for ye shall have the riches of eternity; and it must needs be that the riches of the earth are mine to give; but beware of pride, lest ye become as the Nephites of old" (D&C 38:39).

After selling their property and journeying to Kirtland, the promised law came in the form of a revelation on February 9.[3] Here, following a summary of the Ten Commandments, the Lord tells the Saints, "Thou knowest my laws concerning these things are given in the scriptures. . . . [I]f thou lovest me thou shalt serve me and keep all my commandments" (D&C 42:28–29). This contextualizes what comes next as being in fulfillment of the first great commandment to "love the Lord thy God with all thy heart, and with all thy soul, and with all thy mind" and the second to "love thy neighbour as thyself" (Matt. 22:37–39 KJV). Aware of the challenges that the Saints would face, God reiterates the laws of relationship that will govern the covenant community. As with Israel, an economic system to ensure justice and equity is set forth. Those who belong to the Church were to consecrate their property by deeding it to the bishop, who then would redistribute it according to the needs of each family. Those who received property or goods according to this system were not owners; they were instead "stewards." After this first consecration, any wealth or income "more than is necessary for their support" was also to be consecrated: "It shall be kept to administer to those who have not, from time to time, that every man who has need may be amply supplied and receive according to his wants" (D&C 42:33).

This covenant system of economics had as an explicit purpose to provide for the needs of the poor: "And behold, thou wilt remember the poor, and consecrate of thy properties for their support that which thou hast to impart unto them, with a covenant and a deed which cannot be broken. And inasmuch as ye impart of your substance unto the poor, ye will do it unto me" (D&C 42:30–31; Matt 25:40). The Lord makes clear here that

---

3. Spencer, *For Zion*, ch. 11, discusses how the changes from the original text of the revelation made to the version that was canonized in 1835 (the current Section 42 in the Doctrine and Covenants) reflect changes in the practicalities of administering the law of consecration as well as misunderstandings of its intended fulfillment of God's covenant with Israel, issues that the Church leadership struggled with in the early attempts and failures of its implementation.

an essential feature of the gathering of God's people is providing for the poor. The repetition that follows underscores the gravity of this commandment: "Therefore, the residue shall be kept in my storehouse, to administer to the poor and the needy. . . . I will consecrate of the riches of those who embrace my gospel among the Gentiles unto the poor of my people who are of the house of Israel" (D&C 42:34, 39). The language referring to a "covenant and deed which cannot be broken" (v. 30), and the explicit invocation of Jesus's statement to his followers that those who serve and take care of the poor and afflicted are in reality doing so to him, underscores the seriousness and central nature of this practice in true discipleship.

The revelation further invokes the covenant language of God with Israel "that ye may be gathered in one, that ye may be my people and I will be your God" (D&C 42:9), mirroring the words of God to Moses before the liberation of Israel from Egypt: "I will redeem you with an outstretched arm and with mighty acts of judgment. I will take you as my people, and I will be your God" (Ex. 6:7). The purpose of the gathering is for the Church to become God's people—the body of Christ—which requires entering into covenant relationship with God and with one another.

In order for this relationship to be sustained, there are specific economic requirements, as God made clear to Israel following their deliverance (see Chapter 1). We saw how economic inequality led to the degeneration of covenant relationship in Nephite society (see Chapter 5). This was further clarified in the revelation about Enoch and the city of Zion that Joseph Smith received two months prior while working on his inspired revision of the Bible. This revelation had made explicit the only conditions upon which the Zion community could be realized: "And the Lord called his people Zion, because they were of one heart and one mind, and dwelt in righteousness; *and there was no poor among them*" (Moses 7:18; emphasis added). Here, God makes clear that in order to be God's people, there can be no poor among the Saints. The presence of poverty indicates an enmity and inequality that is antithetical to the kind of covenant community that comprises the kingdom of God. Thus, the law that God gives to the Saints upon arrival in Kirtland is an updated version of the economic code given to Israel by Moses following their deliverance, tailored for their specific circumstances but with the same goal of preserving the covenant relationship. Finally, God makes it clear that all this is to be done "for the salvation of my people" (D&C 42:36), thus making an explicit connection between the temporal welfare of Church members, the poor and needy, and salvation.[4] Later that month another revelation underscored the duty of the Church to care for the poor until the system of property consecration and redistribution could be fully enacted: "Behold, I say unto you, that ye must visit the poor and the needy and administer to their relief, that they may be kept until all things may be done according to my law which ye have received" (D&C 44:6). Thus, God's law to the Saints gathering in Kirtland reaffirms the central nature of the covenant community and sets forth a code of conduct and an economic system to maintain the covenant community in justice and equity.

If You Are Not Equal in Earthly Things

The law given to the Saints when they arrived in Kirtland, which was further developed and refined over the next few years and became known as the Law of Consecration, was designed explicitly to care for those in need and, according to Joseph Smith, to ensure that "rich men cannot have power to disinherit the poor."[5] This focus on righteousness as economic equality shares the sentiment of the stark and unequivocal statement attributed to the apostle Paul that "the love of money is the root of all evil" (1 Tim. 6:10). Drawing this connection even further, a revelation directed towards the Shakers, a utopian Christian group that had a communal settlement about twenty miles north of Kirtland, further expands this notion:

> For behold, the beasts of the field and the fowls of the air and that which cometh of the Earth is ordained for the use of man for food and for raiment and that he might have in abundance. But it is not given that one man should possess that which is above another, wherefore the world lieth in sin. (D&C 49:19–20)

Here God explicitly connects wealth inequality with sin and makes clear that such inequality is the direct cause of the proliferation of sin in the entire world. Recall that the true nature of sin is fractured relationships between God, humanity, and creation. When we remember this and survey the historical context of the Restoration—with its rampant exploitation and expropriation of lives, livelihoods, labor, and natural resources, all for the purpose of consolidating wealth in the hands of a ruling class—we

---

4. The Book of Mormon prophet Jacob affirms this temporal view of God's covenant promises when he emphasizes three times that the latter-day work is being initiated in order to fulfill God's promises to Israel "in the flesh" indicating a temporal understanding of the covenant fulfillment (2 Ne. 10:2, 15, 17).

5. Joseph Smith to Edward Partridge, 2 May 1833.

can begin to make sense of this revelation and understand the gravity and far-reaching spiritual effects of inequality.[6]

About a year later, another revelation, this one dictated for the purpose of organizing the Saints in Jackson County, Missouri, where they had gathered to build Zion, gives further clarity on the relationship between so-called temporal and spiritual matters. Earlier, God had indicated that all commandments had a spiritual function: "all things unto me are spiritual, and not at any time have I given unto you a law which was temporal" (D&C 29:34). Given the explicitly temporal nature of taking care of the poor and needy, we might ask what this has to do with spiritual matters. The revelation dictated by Joseph Smith on March 1, 1832, answers the question clearly and forcefully:

> For verily I say unto you, the time has come, and is now at hand; and behold, and lo, it must needs be that there be an organization of my people, in regulating and establishing the affairs of the storehouse for the poor of my people, both in this place and in the land of Zion—For a permanent and everlasting establishment and order unto my church, to advance the cause, which ye have espoused, to the salvation of man, and to the glory of your Father who is in heaven; That you may be equal in the bonds of heavenly things, yea, and earthly things also, for the obtaining of heavenly things. For if ye are not equal in earthly things ye cannot be equal in obtaining heavenly things; For if you will that I give unto you a place in the celestial world, you must prepare yourselves by doing the things which I have commanded you and required of you. (D&C 78:3–7)

Here God once again repeats the commandment to establish a storehouse of consecrated goods for taking care of the poor and needy among the Church. But the revelation goes further; not only does it state that inequality is the cause of sin in the world, it makes an explicit connection between taking care of the poor, the salvation of humanity, and inequality. The Lord does not mince words when saying, "if ye are not equal in earthly things ye cannot be equal in obtaining heavenly things" (v. 6). Thus, the economic status of the community relationships and not the mere piety of the individual is what dictates whether salvation is effected among the human family. This salvation is a covenant relationship, as evidenced by the reference to the "bonds of heavenly things."

To drive the point home further, this revelation invokes the language of another revelation received two weeks prior. This revelation, known as "The Vision" (D&C 76), exploded the Saints' understanding of salvation,

---

6. See Spencer, *For Zion*, 43–44, for similar discussion.

which according to contemporary Christian tradition at the time was understood to comprise only two options: heaven and hell.[7] In this revelation, however, the Prophet revealed that all humankind will be saved and that heaven is partitioned into three degrees of glory: telestial, terrestrial, and celestial, corresponding to different degrees of faithfulness and spiritual progression. It is within this context of the newly expanded vision of the afterlife that the importance of caring for the poor in Doctrine and Covenants 78 should be understood: in order to inherit the highest degree of glory, there cannot be inequality in temporal things.[8]

Two years later, another revelation was received that offers further clarity on the relationship between wealth inequality and salvation. The context of the revelation was the serious difficulty that the Church faced in Jackson County, Missouri. At this time, Church members had been driven from their homes, the storehouse was no longer in operation, and those in charge of managing it, Sidney Gilbert among others, had incurred debts.[9] The revelation dictates in exhaustive detail the allocation of property to the members of the United Firm, but it also clarifies further God's views on property, ownership, stewardship, and inequality. The seriousness with which God views the covenant relationship established by the law is underscored. God is displeased with those who "have broken the covenant through covetousness and with feigned words. . . . For I, the Lord, am not to be mocked in these things" (D&C 104:4, 6).

> For it is expedient that I, the Lord, should make every man accountable, as a steward over earthly blessings, which I have made and prepared for my creatures. I, the Lord, stretched out the heavens, and built the earth, my very handiwork; and all things therein are mine. And it is my purpose to provide for my saints, for all things are mine. But it must needs be done in mine own way; and behold this is the way that I, the Lord, have decreed to provide for my saints, that the poor shall be exalted, in that the rich are made low. For the earth is full, and there is enough and to spare;[10] yea, I

---

7. This dichotomy was also reinforced by Book of Mormon teachings.

8. While the three degrees of glory are generally interpreted as a description of the afterlife, Latter-day Saint theology clearly states that this earth will be transformed into the celestial kingdom (D&C 130:8–9). Thus the reference to the degrees of glory can instead be thought of as different degrees of covenant relationship, the highest of which requires equality in temporal things.

9. See Spencer, *For Zion*, chapter 10, for detailed discussion of the difficulties faced by the Church in administering the law of consecration during the early years.

10. This pronouncement of gratuitous abundance is diametrically opposed to the foundational premise of free-market economic theory, which is that resources

prepared all things, and have given unto the children of men to be agents unto themselves. Therefore, if any man shall take of the abundance which I have made, and impart not his portion, according to the law of my gospel, unto the poor and the needy, he shall, with the wicked, lift up his eyes in hell, being in torment. (vv. 13–18)

Here, emphasis is placed on the fact that God has created all things and is therefore the sole owner of the earth and its abundance. Twice God states this. Humans are made stewards of God's property, but they are not owners and cannot dispose of the gifts as they wish. Instead, they must do so according to God's purposes. And God makes clear that this purpose is to provide for the children of humanity, God's children. The provision, however, must be done in God's way. What is this way? "That the poor shall be exalted, in that the rich are made low" (v. 16). This is a levelling. It is God's purpose to provide for the poor by levelling the rich. We must make absolutely clear here that nowhere in this revelation (or scripture generally) is a distinction made between the rich who gain their wealth through "honest" means and those who amass wealth through explicit exploitation of the poor. In a world with "enough and to spare," if there are poor, the justice of God demands a levelling of the rich. The simultaneous existence of both rich and poor indicates an enmity and inequality that is contradictory to and incompatible with the kingdom of God.

The significance of this revelation is further underscored when we consider that the original copy that was transcribed by Orson Pratt had a slight but profound difference in the wording. The statement regarding the fate of those who "take of the abundance which I have made, and impart not his portion, according to the law of my gospel, unto the poor and needy" was originally dictated as "he shall, with *Dives*, lift up his eyes in hell, being in torment." This obscure reference seems inscrutable, but it is actually a Latin word that was translated in Joseph's day as "rich man." Furthermore, the capitalization indicates that this translation was held colloquially within Christian communities as the name of the rich man in Jesus's parable of the rich man and Lazarus.[11] Thus, here we have a revelation that details God's abhorrence of inequality and exploitation of the poor at the hands of the rich and that explicitly invokes the accepted folklore around Jesus's parable condemning such exploitation. There can

---

and means of subsistence are scarce. See Peter Joseph, *The New Human Rights Movement: Reinventing the Economy to End Oppression*.

11. Matthew C. Godfrey et al, eds., *Joseph Smith's Revelations: A Doctrine and Covenants Study Companion from the Joseph Smith Papers*.

be no mistaking the message conveyed here. The change from *Dives* to *the wicked*, though making the revelation more accessible, dilutes and generalizes the original intent as an explicit condemnation of the rich who directly oppress the poor through support of or participation in political and economic systems that entrench wealth inequality. Thus, the law of consecration can be viewed within a larger context of God's justice working to overcome inequality throughout the world. Zion is to be a light to the world—to show the world how to be God's people—and the defining characteristic of Zion is that there is no poor among them.

I Am Now Willing to Give All I Have to the Lord

In our day and age, when economic systems that prioritize accumulation of profits over human lives reign supreme, where we are forced to participate in such systems just to survive, and where our connection with and responsibility to the rest of creation has been so completely severed, it's difficult for us to fathom the very real stakes of the law of consecration in the lives of the early Saints. We tend to spiritualize this law, as is the case with so many other explicitly temporal commandments. In the same way we turn Jesus's condemnation of wealth in the encounter of the rich young man into a merely spiritual litmus test, we have turned the law of consecration into a barometer of our spiritual commitment to God and the Church. The practical economic requirements of the law have been excised. But for those early Saints who practiced the law, there was no separation of spiritual and temporal. The law required a specific economic sacrifice, and those who were willing to obey had to be willing to renounce all their property to the Church.

The historical records are scant, but those that exist reveal the personal stakes for these early faithful members of the Church who tried their best to obey the law at great cost to themselves and their families. Sherilyn Farnes and Mitchell Schaefer published twenty affidavits of consecration submitted to Brigham Young in Nauvoo in 1842.[12] These provide snapshots into the lives and livelihoods of these people who took seriously the injunction from the Lord through the prophet to "bind yourselves by this covenant . . . and you are to be equal . . . every man seeking the interest of his neighbor, and doing all things with an eye single to the glory of God."

---

12. Sherilyn Farnes and Mitchell K. Schaefer, "Myself . . . I Consecrate to the God of Heaven: Twenty Affidavits of Consecration in Nauvoo, June–July 1842," 101–32.

Some of these affidavits reflect a general willingness to consecrate property:

Augustus Stafford, June 29, 1842
Nauvoo Jun 29 1842

To Prest B Young
    This Certifies that I Augustus Stafford have furnature <goods> household Furnature including all I posess amounting to one hundred & Twenty five Dollars which is at the Dsposal of the twelve

Others go into great detail in enumerating the property to be consecrated. These affidavits show how seriously the Saints who entered into this covenant took their obligation to their fellow saints and the poor. They wanted to make sure they kept nothing back, taking great care to list every item in their possession:

> John S. Canfield,19 June 29, 1842
> Citty of Nauvoo June 29th 1842
>
> Schedule of property
>
> half of one lot with a small log Cabbin
> House hold furniture one bed and
> Clothing for the same. Wareing apperil
> one pair of pantaloons one pair of shooes
> one straw hat.
> one table and dishes to set the sa<me> for
> four persons. two small tin pai<l>s one
> s[o]up pan tin flour box two small butter
> boxes one lantern one b<a>nd box one
> trunk & chest 6 Baskets 3 barrells
> one stone churn one stone crock one wash
> tub one soap tub 2 tin milk pans
> one cradle one small bake pan one small
> stew kettle one tin kettle one fire shovel
> one flat iron one fri pan ◊◊◊ one iron
> one Book of mormon one Bible and testamen<t>
> one Book of Covenants 3 hymns Books
> melenial [millennial] poems 3 Glass bottles 6 phials
> one tunell 5 towels 2 table cloths.
> one Calico one Gingham one mull one Silk
> dress for my wife Children 2 dreses
> each 8 pairs of hose 2 Bonnets
> one Crape shawl 2 aprons 2 Capes
> and 23 hnkerchiefs 2 Caps 1 pair of

shoo<e>s. Myself Wife and two children
I Consecrat[e] to the God of He[a]ven
and for the Good of his Cause hoping
to keep the faith and endure to the<> end
is the p[r]ayer of your un worthy
servent
    John S Canfield

[Reverse Side of Affidavit:]

Things forgoten in
the list 3 Chairs 2 axes 2 drawing
k<ni>ive 3 Plains 5 Chissels
$845 cts due from Stephen Markam
$225 cts due to G W Pierce
2 Squares 2 handsaws with all
I possess I freely give to the Lord
and into thy hands for good.
to President Young
    Nauvoo

Without fail, the Saints consecrated not only their property but their own lives to the Church for the building of the kingdom of God. Families of every size and makeup, whether they were "cleanly clad" or "poorly clad," all willingly placed themselves "at the disposal of the church," "for the building of the kingdom," showing how fully these early Saints were dedicated to building the covenant community and the cause of Zion. It is impossible to read these affidavits without being moved by the sacrifice and commitment they represent. These are people who were following a prophet's call to consecrate their entire lives and livelihoods to the building of the kingdom. The stakes in the lives of these people were very real, but they acted in faith, trusting in God to provide. Such faith is truly remarkable.

Perhaps this commitment is illustrated most movingly in the affidavit of Elizabeth Stewart. It is only two lines, and she consecrates "bedding & clothing $17, cow and calf $15." It is signed "Elizabeth Stewart a widow." Here, a widow, likely dependent on others for her scant livelihood, offers the very bedding on her bed and the clothes on her back. The words of Jesus to his disciples ring here with timeless profundity: "Truly I tell you, this poor widow has put in more than all those who are contributing out of their abundance; but she out of her poverty has put in everything she had, all she had to live on" (Mark 12:43–44). Reading these affidavits provides a window into sacred moments in the lives of these early Saints.

For some, these affidavits are all we know of them, but they stand as clear evidence of lives transformed by their faith, people committed to building a community of equals and willing to sacrifice their all for the privilege of entering into, and sustaining, this covenant community.

Consecration, Emptying, and Atonement

The essence of the law of consecration is the giving of all we have and are—our own temporal means, but also our unique gifts and abilities—to the building of the kingdom of God. Although the commonly accepted wisdom in the Church is that the law of consecration was done away with no later than 1838, and the law of tithing was instituted in its place, there is no evidence, either in the writings of Joseph Smith or the official records of the Church, that this was the case.[13] We tend to think of the law of consecration as a "higher law" that we will live when we are ready, perhaps to be "instituted anew by the commanding word of the Church's current prophet"[14] or by Jesus when he returns. But prophets have repeatedly stressed that the law has not been done away with. The Saints have simply refused to live it. Brigham Young recounted his experience after he was put in charge of taking an inventory of the "surplus" property of the Saints following the revelation asking for consecration toward the temple in Far West, Missouri:

> I found the people said they were willing to do about as they were counseled, but, upon asking them about their surplus property, most of the men who owned land and cattle would say, "I have got so many hundred acres of land, and I have got so many boys, and I want each one of them to have eighty acres, therefore this is not surplus property." Again, "I have got so many girls, and I do not believe I shall be able to give them more than forty acres each." "Well, you have got two or three hundred acres left." "Yes, but I have a brother-in-law coming on, and he will depend on me for a living; my wife's nephew is also coming on, he is poor, and I shall have to furnish him a farm after he arrives here." I would go on to the next one, and he would have more land and cattle than he could make use of to advantage. It is a laughable idea, but is nevertheless true, men would tell me they were young and beginning the world, and would say, "We have no children, but our prospects are good, and we think we shall have a family of children, and if we do, we want to give them eighty acres of land each; we have no surplus property." "How many

---

13. Farnes and Schaefer, "Myself," 101–2; Spencer, *For Zion*, 119–20.
14. Spencer, *For Zion*, 144.

cattle have you?" "So many." "How many horses, &c?" "So many, but I have made provisions for all these, and I have use for everything I have got."[15]

Young stresses that there is a fundamental misunderstanding regarding what is being asked here. We are not being asked to give something of our possessions to the work of God's kingdom. We are being asked to recognize that nothing we "own" is actually ours at all. As made clear by King Benjamin in the Book of Mormon and the Lord himself in the revelations discussed above regarding consecration, we do not own "our" property. The law of consecration, then, was not conceived of and instituted by God in 1831; the revelation is rather a temporal instantiation of an eternal law. As Stephen Harper observed, "Just as the law of consecration, though revealed in February 1831, did not begin then, it did not end when some refused to obey and others were thwarted in their attempts. President Gordon B. Hinckley taught that 'the law of sacrifice and the law of consecration have not been done away with and are still in effect.'"[16]

The law of consecration is still deeply embedded into our cultural, if not practical, religious lives. Accepting this law is a crucial part of our covenant obligations in the temple endowment. We cannot withdraw our obligation to accept this covenant; "God will not be mocked" in this thing. It is a serious and binding commitment, and fulfilling this covenant obligation is required if we desire to live a celestial existence.

What can living the law of consecration look like in practice in our world? In a world where property is sought after, hoarded, protected by the rule of law, and guarded and seized by armies and navies, what does a real, practical consecration look like? We are required by the economic arrangements of society to participate in these systems. Are we to give away all our money to the Church or to the poor? Are we to become poor and destitute ourselves? How can we honor the inextricable entwinement of temporal and spiritual aspects of this covenant, refusing to cede the concrete material obligations to a diffuse, immaterial spiritual interpretation?

An answer can be found as we consider the fundamental relation between consecration and atonement. Consecration, as practiced by the early Saints, was the giving away of property and money, but it was also the realization that all these are only God's gifts over which they were stewards

---

15. Brigham Young, "Consecration," *Journal of Discourses*, Vol. 2, 306–7.

16. Matthew McBride and James Goldberg, eds., *Revelations in Context: The Stories Behind the Sections of the Doctrine and Covenants*.

to begin with.[17] In early American society, as today, money and property represented status and privilege. Therefore, in a very real way, consecration involves emptying oneself of wealth, status, and privilege. But the end goal is not just to divest the rich of their money. Such a transfer of wealth is the natural outcome of the rich seeing the humanity and suffering of their poor sisters and brothers. The result is a levelling of the rich and the poor, and the creation of equality. The fact that there is no coercion in the law indicates that it is only a voluntary emptying of privilege and wealth that will accomplish this levelling. Agency must be preserved, for without it "there is no existence" (D&C 93:30). And at a fundamental level, consecration cannot be forced, because so doing will not erase the enmity that has led to the inequality in the first place. The "othering" of the poor by the rich must be undone. Indeed, Zion only exists where there is "one heart and one mind."

The voluntary emptying of wealth and privilege does not come easily. Indeed, this can be seen from the Book of Mormon, where the entire book can be seen as a cautionary tale about the consequences of failure to engage in a consecrated covenant community. This is the conclusion of Kelli Potter, who speaks of this emptying of the rich appropriately as liberation:

> Liberation, in the Book of Mormon, is in the hands of the most powerful, just as atonement is in the hand of the almighty Son of God. And just as the almighty Son must give up that power and, in a very real sense, empty himself of his divinity, the powerful and "righteous" in the Americas must empty themselves of their pride. But instead of being a story of salvation in which the ideal of liberation is fulfilled, the Book of Mormon is a story of damnation in which the people of God are condemned and destroyed by the "wicked."[18]

Here Potter speaks of the Atonement of Christ as an emptying of his divinity. This doctrine is known in traditional Christian theology as *kenosis*,[19] and it refers to a passage in Paul's epistle to the Philippians, where he enjoins them to

> be of the same mind, having the same love, being in full accord and of one mind. Do nothing from selfish ambition or conceit, but in humility regard others as better than yourselves. Let each of you look not to your own inter-

---

17. See Spencer, *For Zion*, ch. 12, for a discussion of stewardship as it pertains to the various iterations of the law of consecration in the early Church and our understanding of this law today.

18. Kelli Potter, "Liberation Theology in the Book of Mormon," 176–77.

19. C. Stephen Evans, ed., *Exploring Kenotic Christology: The Self-Emptying of God*; Paul T. Nimmo and Keith L. Johnson, eds., *Kenosis: The Self-Emptying of Christ in Scripture and Theology*.

ests, but to the interests of others. Let the same mind be in you that was in Christ Jesus, who, though he was in the form of God, did not regard equality with God as something to be exploited, but emptied himself, taking the form of a slave, being born in human likeness. And being found in human form, he humbled himself and became obedient to the point of death—even death on a cross. (Philip. 2:2–8)

This passage speaks of what Nephi in the Book of Mormon refers to as "the condescension of God" (1 Ne. 11:16, 26). However, if we consider what is being said here, the reality of God's emptying becomes even more sobering. In Jesus, God had emptied themself of all power, privilege, and glory. This is not the way that gods are meant to act. Gods are meant to demand obedience and tribute and honor. Gods are meant to punish those who displease them, and they show their power in mighty acts of destruction, wiping out entire cities or nations. For a god to willingly empty itself of such power seems in opposition to the very idea of what a god is. And yet, in Jesus, God did just that. Jesus's life and ministry showed that God identifies, wholly and completely, with those in the world who have no power, privilege, and wealth. To the Saints in Corinth, Paul explicitly identifies Christ's emptying with the metaphor of wealth: "though he was rich, yet for your sakes he became poor" (2 Cor. 8:9). Jesus showed God's absolute solidarity with "the least of these," to the point of suffering and dying as one of them. As Gustavo Gutiérrez puts it, Christ emptied himself in order "to struggle against human selfishness and everything that divides persons and allows that there be rich and poor, possessors and dispossessed, oppressors and oppressed."[20]

What caused God's voluntary emptying of power and privilege? The answer comes in what is known as the Book of Moses that was revealed to Joseph Smith in 1830. The seventh chapter describes Enoch's encounter with God. Here, Enoch sees in a vision all the children of Eve and Adam, and after viewing the misery and suffering of those who fall into violence and wickedness,

> the God of heaven looked upon the residue of the people, and he wept; and Enoch bore record of it, saying: How is it that the heavens weep, and shed forth their tears as the rain upon the mountains? How is it that thou canst weep, seeing thou art holy, and from all eternity to all eternity? . . . how is it thou canst weep? (Moses 7:28–29, 31)

---

20. Gustavo Gutiérrez, *A Theology of Liberation*, 172.

Notice that Enoch does not ask why God is crying. He asks three times how it is possible that God *can* cry. When Enoch sees God's raw display of emotion and vulnerability, he cannot reconcile it with his view of God as an all-powerful, majestic being. God's answer is touching in its humanity, and it illustrates the depth of God's love and feeling for humanity:

> The Lord said unto Enoch: Behold these thy brethren; they are the workmanship of mine own hands, and I gave unto them their knowledge, in the day I created them; and in the Garden of Eden, gave I unto man his agency; And unto thy brethren have I said, and also given commandment, that they should love one another, and that they should choose me, their Father; but behold, they are without affection, and they hate their own blood.... [W]herefore should not the heavens weep, seeing these shall suffer? (Moses 7:32–33, 37)

Here Enoch sees that God not only cares about humanity; God actually weeps for their suffering.[21] Following this, God then describes to Enoch just what the suffering of humanity entails. Enoch is staggered by the enormity:

> Wherefore Enoch knew, and looked upon their wickedness, and their misery, and wept and stretched forth his arms, and his heart swelled wide as eternity; and his bowels yearned; and all eternity shook.... And as Enoch saw this, he had bitterness of soul, and wept over his brethren, and said unto the heavens: I will refuse to be comforted. (Moses 7:41, 44)

All is not lost, however; there is hope: "But the Lord said unto Enoch: Lift up your heart, and be glad; and look" (Moses 7:44). What does God show Enoch that causes him to lift up his heart and be glad? What good news, indeed, what gospel does God reveal? "And behold, Enoch saw the day of the coming of the Son of Man, even in the flesh; and his soul rejoiced" (Moses 7:47).

God's response to the suffering of humanity is to empty themself of power and privilege and to take on human form as Jesus. Indeed, so great is the suffering that, as stated by the prophet Abinadi, "God himself shall come down among the children of men, and shall redeem his people. And because he dwelleth in flesh he shall be called the Son of God" (Mosiah 15:1–2). Thus, the cause of God's emptying in the incarnation, life, ministry, and death of Jesus was God's desire to identify with, and participate in, the suffering of humanity. We have discussed this above as compassion, or suffering with others. In this compassion, God "descended below all

---

21. See Terryl Givens and Fiona Givens, *The God Who Weeps: How Mormonism Makes Sense of Life,* for an eloquent book-length treatment of the implications of this idea for an understanding of salvation, Latter-day Saint belief, and Christianity in general.

things" so that God might "comprehend all things" (D&C 88:6).[22] This is pure love. We know this also as charity. This is the only way towards true reconciliation—to view one another in our shared humanity. This is the *jeong* that the people of Ammon felt and by which the invading Lamanites were overcome. True and lasting reconciliation requires opening our hearts to this love.

Following Enoch's vision of humanity, he is shown another vision that reveals the sweeping and far-reaching scope of the consequences of humankind's sin for creation:

> And it came to pass that Enoch looked upon the earth; and he heard a voice from the bowels thereof, saying: Wo, wo is me, the mother of men; I am pained, I am weary, because of the wickedness of my children. When shall I rest, and be cleansed from the filthiness which is gone forth out of me? When will my Creator sanctify me, that I may rest, and righteousness for a season abide upon my face? And when Enoch heard the earth mourn, he wept, and cried unto the Lord, saying: O Lord, wilt thou not have compassion upon the earth? . . . And it came to pass that Enoch cried unto the Lord, saying: When the Son of Man cometh in the flesh, shall the earth rest? I pray thee, show me these things. And the Lord said unto Enoch: Look, and he looked and beheld the Son of Man lifted up on the cross, after the manner of men. . . . And again Enoch wept and cried unto the Lord, saying: When shall the earth rest? (Moses 7:48–49, 54–55, 58)

Enoch's question to God is a question, indeed an indictment, of humanity. When shall the earth rest? Enoch saw Jesus ascend into heaven and, realizing that his work on earth was not done, begged God, "Wilt thou not come again upon the earth?" (v. 59). With so much suffering remaining and so much more to come, how could he leave? Many members of our Church and other Christians in our day ask the same thing: "When is the second coming going to happen?" "I wish Jesus would just hurry up and come again already, the earth is so wicked." "Jesus will sort all of this out when he comes again." We are content, as usual, to leave the salvation to God at some point in the future.

But the message of the cross and atonement, as we discussed above, is not a once for all future salvation *for* humanity; it is a revelation of the way forward to an ongoing historical realization of salvation that *depends*

---

22. It is important here to note the usual usage of "comprehend" in Joseph Smith's day. Whereas today it is defined primarily as referring to the ability to understand the meaning of something, in Smith's day, the first definition listed in Webster's 1828 dictionary was "to contain; to include; to comprise."

on the participation of humanity. God's kingdom is "already but not yet."[23] Jesus revealed the way towards reconciliation for the poor and oppressed through non-violent resistance and the emptying of wealth and privilege. These are different—but crucial—acts of atonement. And such atonement, such reconciliation, cannot happen without our participation. Moreover, God's respect for agency indicates that God will not force us to do this. God "draws all men"—just as Christ's ministry led to him being "lifted up upon the cross, that [he] might draw all men unto [him]" (3 Ne. 27:14); God does not force them. Would it not also be a violation of agency for Jesus to come in power and glory and force justice and equity on the world via divine violence? The cross indicates that even God will not take power or force justice in this way. It is up to us to change our families, communities, cities, nations, and world. Doing so requires us to participate in the liberation of the poor and oppressed. Indeed, we must participate in God's salvation in the world if it is to happen. We covenant to take upon us the name of Christ. Doing so means acting in our own capacity as "Christs" (anointed ones) in a participatory atonement that must eventually encompass the entirety of humanity (Mosiah 5:7–10). As stated by Kelli Potter,

> The atonement is not merely an act in which Jesus, despite his power and divine prestige, gives up his life for the lives of others. It is an atonement that is meant to be present in the community of God. It is uniquely crafted for a people of power and economic privilege, and it demands their emptying themselves, with Christ, into the oppressed.[24]

The poor and oppressed in the world are our constant reminder that God's salvation is wanting, unfulfilled, on the earth. Like the wounds of the crucifixion in the risen Jesus, they are a tangible, physical witness of the need for an ongoing, historical fulfillment of the resurrection that began in the garden tomb. As such, God identifies in particular with them. This is known in liberation theology as God's "preferential option for the poor."[25] This position is taken by some to be a political move by those who look to give moral weight to their arguments against current economic and political systems, but God being for the oppressed has nothing to do with empty political rhetoric. If God is a god of life, then God's presence will be most needed, and most clearly and urgently manifest, in situations in

---

23. The concept was proposed by Dutch-American theologian Geerhardus Vos, and suggests that Christians are actively participating in the realization of the kingdom of God on the earth even though the kingdom is not realized fully at present.

24. Potter, "Liberation Theology," 176.

25. Gustavo Gutiérrez, "Option for the Poor."

which life is denied, in which liberation to life is demanded. The poor and oppressed, who are denied the right to live their lives to the fullest—and in very many cases denied the right to simply even exist[26]—are the most clear and pressing example of this need.[27] God's preferential option for the poor reflects the literal reality of both God and the world we live in.

If we accept this fact, how can we not view the current instantiation of capitalism and economic systems that prioritize profits over human lives, and all the horror they have and continue to visit on the world, as evil? How can we not view the huge gulf that separates wealthy from poor as an unacceptable economic reality in dire need of correcting? How can we view exploitation of workers, in developed and undeveloped nations, as "smart business"? How can we justify and support the huge salaries of CEOs when their employees cannot even afford healthcare or housing and struggle to put food on the table? How can we content ourselves with exorbitant lifestyles, made possible by extracting limited resources, filling landfills with excess waste, and deforesting the planet to maximize farming profits, when millions of people starve to death each year? When we wake to this reality, the lesson of the cross can no longer be viewed as an example of individual piety or the means for individual salvation. We see the cross present in the lives of the poor, in the video footage of migrants and refugees, in the decimated civilians in war-torn nations, in the exploited women and children in free-trade zones, in those who are trafficked for sex or labor, in the drug addicts, in the homeless and incarcerated, in the victims of police and gun violence, in those poisoned by toxic waste, chemical, and oil spills, in those displaced by brushfires and floods, in farmers who commit suicide after losing their land to the ruthless expansion of corporate farming and incurring unrepayable debts, and in lives devastated by our reckless planetary exploitation. *This* is "where it is that the crucifixion is happening today."[28] *These* are the faces and bodies of the crucified Christ in the world today, and economic and political systems that exploit and destroy for profit are the crucifiers.

---

26. Jon Sobrino, "Poverty Means Death to the Poor," 267–76; Gustavo Gutiérrez, *We Drink From Our Own Wells: The Spiritual Journey of a People*, 9–10.

27. As stated with eloquence and force by the 1979 conference of Latin American Catholic bishops at Puebla, Mexico; "Made in the image and likeness of God to be his children, this image is dimmed and even defiled. That is why God takes on their defense and loves them." Quoted in Jon Sobrino, *Christ the Liberator: A View from the Victims*, 189.

28. Dorothee Soelle, *Suffering*, 3.

We cannot turn inward in the face of such suffering. It is not a personal emptying and reconciliation that is required. Indeed, such emptying, consecration, and reconciliation must flood our communities and world. We must consider seriously what consecration and emptying looks like on the community, national, and world level. Wealthy nations in the West must empty themselves of their wealth and privilege. They must make reparations for generations of colonialism, exploitation, and abandonment of the Global South. Indigenous peoples, African Americans, and other victims of colonialism and colonization must be compensated for bodies, lands, freedom, culture, and livelihoods stolen, destroyed, or poisoned; for slavery, beatings, rapes, and lynchings; for separate stores, drinking fountains, and schools; for forced relocation, assimilation, and ghettoization; for languages beaten out of school children; for families torn apart by forced placement, boarding, or adoption; for children's bewilderment and hurt at the hatred directed at them from peers and strangers alike, for being forced far too young to bear burdens far too heavy; for enmity instilled by parents, nurtured by children, and reinforced by politics and policy; for generations of trauma and inequality perpetrated. This is only a gross and vulgar approximation of the reconciliation and justice that is required, but it is a start. Policy and laws that favor the wealthy and privileged must be changed to ensure justice and equity. Political systems in which policymakers are beholden to corporate interests must be upended. Economic policy must reflect the basic humanity of the entirety of the world, not prioritize the rights and trading privileges of transnational corporations. We must affirm our mutual dependence on and relationship with the earth and creation and cease viewing it as a resource to be exploited.

We must finally come to the painful realization that Western civilization was built on white supremacist, nationalist, and patriarchal ideologies. The perpetuation of these ideologies through colonialism under the guise of "progress," "enlightenment," and "Christian moral values" has led to inconceivable suffering throughout history and in the present day. This is the "great and abominable church" seen by Nephi (1 Ne. 14). These are the tares that have choked the wheat and driven the church into the wilderness (D&C 86:3). We must relentlessly examine and interrogate our own doctrine, policy, and practices for any traces of these biases and remove any of our own imposed barriers to the building of, and equal access to, covenant community.[29] We must seriously open and engage in

---

29. Gina Colvin and Joanna Brooks, eds., *Decolonizing Mormonism: Approaching a Postcolonial Zion*.

dialogue with those of our faith community who have been marginalized by our self-imposed boundaries and officially apologize for the hurt these boundaries have caused. We must critically and constantly examine our own ideals and lifestyles and vigilantly guard against infiltration of ideologies and attitudes that lead to consumerism, vanity, pride, or acceptance or support of political, social, and economic systems of domination, exploitation, and oppression.[30] The undoing of these pernicious ideologies and the harmful impacts of their infiltration into our own faith tradition and culture will be a long, torturous, and arduous process. Indeed, "enduring to the end"[31] of this confronting self-examination and institutional repentance, of laying bare, opening, and reopening our wounds will constitute painful and ongoing work, but we must begin, and we must begin now.

In the final analysis, the meaning of the Restoration is a hearkening back to God's liberation from oppression and God's establishment of the covenant community. This has been the historical meaning of salvation, and this is the reality and necessity of salvation in our day. We must reclaim this vision of salvation in the Church. We must extend our focus outside of ourselves, our families, and our congregations. God requires us to consecrate everything with which we have been blessed, or with which we may be blessed in the future, to the building up of the kingdom of God on the earth and the establishment of Zion.

After all of the practicalities and failed implementations in the early period of the Church, Joseph Smith received a startling revelation about the nature of Zion: "Therefore, thus saith the Lord, let Zion rejoice, for this is Zion—THE PURE IN HEART" (D&C 97:21; emphasis in original). We cannot realize God's intended covenant community unless our hearts are purified in shared love for one another. In the Sermon on the Mount, Jesus proclaimed, "Blessed are the pure in heart, for they shall see God" (Matt. 5:8). To the extent we become so by sharing in one another's sufferings and emptying ourselves of everything that stops us from viewing each other in our shared humanity—taking seriously our symbolic burial with Jesus by baptism "in a death like his" so that we can be raised as a community of Saints by the spirit "in a resurrection like his" (Rom. 6:5) as his living body in the world—we will witness God in the world, and we will become witnesses of God to those in the world who have yet to yield themselves to God's love. Our efforts are in the hope of an

---

30. Hugh Nibley, *Approaching Zion*.

31. I am grateful to Rolf Straubhaar for shining new, revelatory light on this concept in his contribution to Colvin and Brooks, *Decolonizing Mormonism*, 103–13.

eventual yielding, even for our enemies. We work towards a day when we shall "meet them there, and we will receive them into our bosom, and they shall see us; and we will fall upon their necks, and they shall fall upon our necks, and we will kiss each other" (Moses 7:63).

We work and hope for a day when all are seen for who they truly are, when we know one another "as we are known" (1 Cor. 13:12), when the earth will receive its long-waited and yearned-for rest, and when the promise of God to Enoch, the covenant made with Abraham, Hagar,[32] Isaac, Jacob, and many others, indeed, with all of humanity, and of which the Restoration is an explicit reminder, is fulfilled. We are invited to participate in the ongoing atonement that will lead to the fulfilling of this new and everlasting covenant. This covenant obligation to humanity and creation requires us to liberate the poor, exploited, and oppressed, to champion the voiceless and marginalized. It is to act in our capacity and calling as the living body of Christ in the world to "loose the bands of this temporal death" (Alma 42:11) from our suffering sisters and brothers. Indeed, it is to bear one another's burdens, mourn with those that mourn, and comfort those that stand in need of comfort. In a world of wars, exploitation, oppression, and suffering on a global scale, our steps may be small and faltering, but we must do what we can to "work out [our] own salvation with fear and trembling," secure in the knowledge that "it is God at work in [us]" (Philip. 2:12–13). The promised blessing of a present kingdom and salvation that can be realized only in the justice of living in consecration with one another rings out through the prophetic words of those Saints who consecrated and gave their all, even their very lives to this vision of covenant community at the birth of the Restoration:

> Fear not, and be just,
> For the kingdom is ours.
> The hour of redemption is near.[33]

---

32. Hagar is given many of the same covenant promises as Abraham, promises that are to be fulfilled through Ishmael and his descendants. This detail is often overlooked in our reading of this story, and it has far-reaching implications for our understanding and assertion of the unique covenant lineage and inheritance of the Christian and Latter-day Saint faith traditions. See Genesis 16:10; 21:18; and Janet Havorka, "Sarah and Hagar: Ancient Women of the Abrahamic Covenant," 147–66.

33. From a poem written by William W. Phelps and published in the first edition of *The Evening and The Morning Star* in Independence Missouri in June 1832. The poem would be known later as the hymn "Redeemer of Israel," Latter-day Saint Hymn #6.

Conclusion

Toward Restoration

We end this study where we began—in a Latin American country convulsed by a brutal military dictatorship. The country is Chile. The year is 1973. General Augusto Pinochet seized power from the democratically elected president Salvador Allende in a military coup. Allende's overthrow was planned (before he took office), funded, and carried out by the United States to protect their corporate interests from his government's program of land reform and nationalization.[1] Following the coup, with the support of US economists, Pinochet's regime enacted sweeping free-market economic reforms that privatized huge sectors of the economy and hollowed out public and social services. These reforms enriched corporations and the wealthy while decimating the working class.[2] By 1983, Pinochet's economic "shock treatments" had driven nearly half of Chile's population into poverty. During this same time, the regime embarked on a systematic campaign of repression and terror involving kidnapping, forced interrogations, torture, and killing of anyone suspected of harboring sympathies towards Allende's government, so-called "communists." Many simply "disappeared," never to be seen or heard from again.[3] Citizens were awakened in the night by pounding on the door and dragged from their homes to spend days, weeks, months, in clandestine government torture centers. The following illustrates a typical case:

> I was arrested about midnight on the 26th of December, 1975. Around 8 civilians arrived at my house, all armed with machine guns and small arms; after searching the house. . . . [T]hey handcuffed me together with my wife,

---

1. Stephen Kinzer, *Overthrow: America's Century of Regime Change from Hawaii to Iraq*, ch. 8; Tim Weiner, *Legacy of Ashes: The History of the CIA*, ch. 29.

2. Ricardo Ffrench-Davis, *Economic Reforms in Chile: From Dictatorship to Democracy*, 9–24. See also Donald G. Richards, "The Political Economy of the Chilean Miracle," 139–59.

3. Like many of her Central and South American contemporaries, much of the writing of Chilean author Isabel Allende (related to President Salvador Allende through her father and exiled to Venezuela after Pinochet overthrew the government) reflects the brutal realities of life under a repressive authoritarian regime. See Isabel Allende, *Of Love and Shadows*, for a powerful novel of political protest and resistance set in a fictional dictatorship similar to Pinochet's.

put tape over our eyes and dark glasses over that. . . . We were put in a private car . . . without any distinctive marks, and taken to Villa Grimaldi. They took us out of the car and immediately I was taken into the torture chamber. There they made me undress and with my hands and feet tied to the metal frame of the lower part of a bunkbed they began to apply electric current to me. This is the "grill." During the rest of the night they had me, applying electricity over my whole body, accompanied by blows with sticks, because of which I came out with several fractured ribs. While they applied electricity they threw water on my whole body.

It was already dawn when I was taken off the grill and thrown, with my feet and hands chained, on the patio of the Villa. During the day on several opportunities I was again taken to "interrogation," where I was beaten by various men with kicks, fists, and sticks. . . . Until the 31st of December I was taken to "interrogation" every day and every night.[4]

This example is only one of tens of thousands of cases of arrest and torture by the Pinochet regime. The casual brutality and dehumanization is difficult to process. What could the goal of such treatment be? In his extraordinary study of this historical moment, *Torture and Eucharist*, William T. Cavanaugh shows how the goal of the sustained and targeted campaign of arrest, torture, and terror by the Pinochet regime was to destroy the communal and social bonds of the nation, and to establish the state as the ultimate authority in the lives of the people: "to fragment the society, to disarticulate all intermediate social bodies between the individual and the state—parties, unions, professional organizations . . . where two or three are gathered, there is subversion in their midst."[5] Public gatherings were outlawed or watched carefully by secret police. Any communal bonds were a threat to the power of the state, and the seemingly indiscriminate and unpredictable torture turned the citizenry into fearful, suspicious, and compliant individuals without functional personal or social relationships.

In the face of this sustained and brutal campaign of terror and torture, the Catholic Church in Chile found itself at a loss as to how to respond. The bodies of its members were being destroyed by the state. Or rather, the communal body of the church, the body of Christ, was being dismembered. The church, however, found itself unable to act in the early days of the regime because of its desire to separate the spiritual from the political. The

---

4. William T. Cavanaugh, *Torture and Eucharist: Theology, Politics, and the Body of Christ*, 25–26.
5. Cavanaugh, 38.

1960s and 70s were a fraught political time in Chile and South America. Western governments and their corporate interests saw in the move toward justice and democracy the specter of communism and supported the violent overthrow of democratically elected governments, including that of Allende in Chile, which had swept into power promising revolutionary change. The church was being pressured by different factions of its membership to take an explicit political stand on various issues. It resisted, very aware of its imperial history and thinking that in doing so, it would fragment its membership and compromise its authoritative spiritual position. In its desire to maintain political neutrality, the church came to understand and articulate its responsibility as being solely over the souls of its members. It provided spiritual nourishment and sacraments and shepherded its members towards salvation in the next life. In a statement entitled "Christian Faith and Political Action," the Chilean Catholic bishops pushed back against explicitly political views of the good news of the gospel, stating,

> Liberation demands the construction of a better world within history, but it is projected also toward a Kingdom, which is the soul of that history and at the same time transcends it. This Kingdom, including in its historical dimension, is not identified with any this worldly process, economic structure or political regime.[6]

Thus, the Catholic Church came down firmly on the spiritual side, denying that politics had anything to do with its responsibility over the souls of its members. In staking its claim over the souls of the church, however, it had inadvertently ceded control of the bodies of its members to the state. When the bodies began to be brutalized, it had no authoritative position from which to act. Because these crimes against the citizens were "political" in nature, the church found itself hamstrung by its singular focus on the spiritual. Cavanaugh explains,

> The problem would begin to take shape when people began to knock at the Cardinal's door. In the days and weeks after the coup, tens of thousands of people were killed or taken prisoner. Bodies appeared in rivers, and the soccer stadiums were filled with supporters of the previous government, rounded up off the streets or hounded out of bed by furious troops. . . . Thousands were fired from their jobs and thousands more went into hiding or sought refuge at one of the many embassies willing to grant asylum. Amid great fear and confusion, the church was the only major civilian organization whose structure had survived the military siege.[7]

---

6. Cavanaugh, 79.
7. Cavanaugh, 87.

The Catholic Church began to be inundated with requests for help from desperate citizens. In the face of mounting atrocities, it began to make a few tentative statements against the regime, calling for greater freedom of the press, organization, and assembly. These increased in frequency and specifics, soon denouncing "the worst abuses of the military regime: torture, massive arrests, arbitrary decisions in the courts, economic discrimination, and lack of freedom of expression and assembly."[8] Church committees were established to watch over and support the scores of poor and marginalized people who were being terrorized by the regime, putting the church on a collision course with the government. The government demanded the dissolution of these committees, and when the church did not comply and continued denouncing the regime more forcefully in individual homilies and public statements, clergy were explicitly threatened by government officials: "We know that a lot of crazy people are running around out there. We are afraid that something could happen to you. It would be good if you took care of yourself"[9] was the warning issued by the head of the secret police to Cardinal Silva.

What became crystal clear to the Catholic Church in the early years of the regime was that "church-state conflict [was] the result of the church's defense of the poor and persecuted against the 'brute force' of the regime."[10] The church's identification with the poor and dispossessed placed them, according to the regime, in the ranks of the "communists" and political enemies of the state. When the regime virtually eliminated any opposing political parties or organizations through torture and disappearance in the first two years after the coup, many church clergy, nuns, and workers were discovered to have been collaborating and sympathizing with the opposition. The regime clamped down on church organizations that supported the poor, arresting and torturing dozens of their members and officers. Thus the church, after trying so hard to maintain political neutrality, found itself forced by its mission and mandate to the poor in firm and stark opposition to the regime. The boundary between the church and the state, the soul and body, so clearly entrenched in the church's religious consciousness, was shattered. The church had been shocked into awareness "that the regime's concerted attempts to silence, fragment, and

---

8. Cavanaugh, 90.
9. Cavanaugh, 91.
10. Cavanaugh, 98.

remove the church to a religious sphere must be met with the insistence of the church as a visible social body."[11]

The Catholic Church became "willing to give neither the souls nor the bodies of its members"[12] over to the regime. They started to fight back. The denunciations became more and more explicit and more and more political. The bishops spoke out not only against arrest and torture but also against violations of workers' rights to organize and the economic and educational policies that enriched the wealthy and immiserated the poor. The church fomented protests, and nuns and workers formed the vanguard. The junta raged against the church, arresting and exiling scores of clergy and workers. Bishops excommunicated known torturers in their congregations. The church began to fulfill its prophetic call to awaken society to the reality of their oppression and to help them envision a new reality, one of liberation and justice.

In opposition to the destruction of social and communal bonds that the regime instituted with torture and terror, the Catholic Church required something to reconstitute itself as a communal body. They found this in the Eucharist. For Catholic believers, the Eucharist, or communion, is the ritualistic practice by which the emblems are literally transformed into the body and blood of Christ, and the members are, in turn, literally reconstituted as his living body. In the context of the atomization that was taking place every day at the hands of the regime, this liturgy took on a critical significance. By reconstituting and rededicating the membership of the church as the living body of Christ, the church found the strength to band together and begin to resist the regime more forcefully.

This resistance took on a particularly temporal character. In addition to the increasing wave of denunciations and excommunications, the committees and organizations threw themselves into providing food for the poor, employment and training for workers, garden projects for food provision and distribution, and other efforts. Grassroots collectives, headed increasingly by women, became vocal and inventive critics. Handicrafts, sponsored by church sewing workshops, showed daily scenes of poverty, eloquent testaments to the brutality of the regime. Organized flash mob demonstrations against torture were deployed in public places, loudly decrying the violations of human rights and the government's silence on arrests and disappearances, making visible the corruption and atrocity perpetrated by the regime. These organizational efforts by the local Catholic

---

11. Cavanaugh, 111.
12. Cavanaugh, 111.

Church served to knit together communities that had been dissolved and decimated by the regime's program of torture and disappearance. Thus, the church embraced its role in the temporal salvation of its members and communities, refusing to relegate its responsibility to a spiritual or "religious" realm.

I suggest that this historical vignette serves as a microcosm of the position that The Church of Jesus Christ of Latter-day Saints finds itself in today. As discussed above, the forces and ideologies of the free market have atomized communities and destroyed the social and communal bonds upon which human relationship and covenant community is based. These systems, by their very nature, rely on and create individuals without social and communal attachments, pursuing their own interest without regard for anyone or anything else. They force us to compete for everything. For jobs, for goods, for prestige, for healthcare, for educational opportunities, for business acumen, for "likes" on social media. They rely for their survival on endless consumption, commodifying and monetizing all aspects of life. The globalization of capitalism is leading to expropriation, enclosure, neocolonialism, environmental destruction, poverty, misery, and death at an increasing pace. Underneath the Western myth of progress, the reality is generations of poor who have been and continue to be used up, sucked dry, and tossed aside as necessary costs in the search for never-ending profit. The world cries out for salvation. Who will answer?

The Church, although formed in (and I suggest, in response to) the crucible of the calamity which began with the Industrial Revolution, has doubled down on its responsibility as a primarily spiritual organization. We speak of preparing the world for the Lord's Second Coming, but our strategy to do so is far too often to remove ourselves from the world and circle the wagons, walling ourselves off in our "city on the hill."[13] We urge our members, and especially our youth, to shun "the world," to "keep the world out, keep Christ in,"[14] or to "love the sinner but hate the sin,"—injunctions that too often encourage, whether explicitly or implicitly, judgment, intolerance, and exclusion of anyone or anything outside of our strictly defined and socially enforced "gospel culture." Our evangelizing consists of a missionary program that has as its primary focus conversion of others to our faith. We spend huge amounts of money on construc-

---

13. See Patrick Q. Mason, *Restoration: God's Call to the 21st Century*, ch. 1.

14. This was the slogan shouted and chanted by several thousand youth at a For the Strength of Youth conference for Latter-day Saint teens attended by my daughter in 2020.

tion of temples, where we perform ordinances with the purpose of sealing together the entire human family in the next life.

At the same time, the Church urges and asserts political neutrality. It rarely makes political statements, and on the rare occasions that statements against injustice are made, they are often so general as to be devoid of any meaning, easily able to be used by those on all sides of the political spectrum to justify their own position. This equivocation has led to an alarming growth of extremist and separatist sympathies and alignment within the Church in recent years, including the organization of explicitly white-supremacist, nationalist, misogynist, and anti-LGBTQ+ movements founded in distorted doctrinal positions. These movements often leverage our (unfortunately) pervasive military religious vocabulary, metaphors, and sloganeering towards intolerant and hateful ends, even encouraging violence and societal cleansing of those who stand in the way of their political aim of a white patriarchal Christian theocracy. The popularity of these movements is increasing, and they draw tacit approval from the lack of explicit condemnation from Church leaders. The few times the Church has taken an explicit political stand, it has regrettably taken positions that contribute to, rather than alleviate, suffering, marginalization, exclusion, and injustice.[15] Our humanitarian efforts help millions but are viewed as secondary to the "work of salvation" that takes place in temples, made possible by exclusive priesthood authority. We rightly believe that in the ordinances of the Church "the power of godliness is manifest in the flesh" (D&C 84:20). Are we at risk, in our tallying of temple ordinances for living and dead—ticking the boxes for salvation in the next life—of forgetting or being blind to the particular historical and temporal character of "the flesh" that is crying out for the manifest power of God in our world? In our zeal to convert, have we forgotten that the small measure of leaven that causes the dough to rise does not change the entire loaf to yeast, thereby rendering it inedible, but merely helps it to realize its poten-

---

15. See D. Michael Quinn, "The LDS Church's Campaign Against the Equal Rights Amendment," 85–155; Neil J. Young, "The ERA Is a Moral Issue: The Mormon Church, LDS Women, and the Defeat of the Equal Rights Amendment," 623–44; Neil J. Young, "Mormons and Same-Sex Marriage: From ERA to Prop 8"; Joanna Brooks, *Mormonism and White Supremacy: American Religion and the Problem of Racial Innocence*; W. Paul Reeve, *Religion of a Different Color*; Matthew L. Harris and Madison S. Harris, "The Last State to Honor MLK: Utah and the Quest for Racial Justice," 5–21; Lester E. Bush Jr, "Mormonism's Negro Doctrine: An Historical Overview," 11–68.

tial as bread?[16] Are we so convinced of the universal necessity of our own particular "works of the law" that we have enforced boundary markers that compromise our ability to envision and create God's expansive and inclusive covenant community? Are we so enamored with our own narrow and culturally myopic collection of "absolute" and "eternal" truths that we have strayed into canonization of rigid, inflexible, alienating creeds that are an abomination in the Lord's sight?[17] How can the Church use its diplomatic influence and considerable wealth to call attention to worker, civil, and human rights abuses, particularly of indigenous people and women, and to stand with and champion the full humanity of the poor, abused, exploited, and marginalized throughout the world? What role should the Church have in political matters? Matters of economic policy? What should the "visible social body" of the Church look like?[18]

---

16. See Mason, *Restoration*, 21–26; Patrick Q. Mason and J. David Pulsipher, *Proclaim Peace: The Restoration's Answer to an Age of Conflict*, ch. 10.

17. Our usual reading of the Lord's condemnation of the Christian creeds of Joseph Smith's day is that they were an abomination because they weren't true statements about the nature of God, Christ, and God's plan for humanity. We assume that God then gave Joseph the true creeds. As demonstrated, however, by the prohibition on graven images in the Decalogue, the story of Job, the life and ministry of Jesus, Paul's letters to the saints, and Joseph Smith's own expansive and shifting revelations, the real abomination is absolutizing any construct or ideology of God that is inflexible and unresponsive to the real problems of history or the lived experience of people. Our religious tradition is not immune to such blasphemy. The challenge for authentic and living belief is to have faith in a God who has been revealed through historical acts of salvation while at the same time not constraining or universalizing our ideas or vision of God or God's present-day kingdom based on the character or cultural, religious, or political context of that same historical revelation. The "gods" revealed in this way cannot be adopted and applied wholesale to our current problems and circumstances. Claiming a privileged or monopolistic understanding of God or God's dealings with or plan for humanity denies the ongoing historical and therefore necessarily incomplete nature of the revelation of God that forms our own religious tradition's doctrine and worldview. Put another way, we must be willing and have the faith to "let God be God." This caution also applies to the discounting, minimizing, or denying of the messiness of our own Church history that permeates the idealized and sanitized narrative that we teach our members and use to proselytize.

18. As we contemplate these questions, we should ask, as does James Cone, "When does the Church cease to be the Church of Jesus Christ? When do the Church's actions deny the faith that it verbalizes? . . . What actions deny the Truth disclosed in Jesus Christ? Where should the line be drawn? Can the

These are questions the Church must grapple with as it embarks upon its third century. As we contemplate these questions, we would do well to remember what the prophet Joseph said at the beginning of the Restoration. In reference to the responsibility of members of the Church, he said they are to "feed the hungry, to clothe the naked, to provide for the widow, to dry up the tear of the orphan, to comfort the afflicted, whether in this church, or in any other, or in no church at all, wherever he finds them."[19] In the context of the present study, it is telling that this answer was in response to a question that explicitly addressed the obligations of those who owned property. The Prophet's response puts the onus on the wealthy and propertied to use their means to provide for the poor and needy, the oppressed and downtrodden—to empty themselves. His answer regarding what constitutes faithful membership should give us all pause as we consider the meaning of the gospel and its application in today's world. What does it mean to be the body of Christ? What does it mean to remember and to *re-member* the torn and broken body of Jesus in a suffering world?

In the throes of a brutal dictatorship, the Chilean church came to realize that the line between soul and body is an illusion. Joseph Smith had revealed this 150 years earlier: "the spirit and the body are the soul of man" (D&C 88:15). We cannot neglect the body and provide salvation to the soul. They are inextricably linked. The Lord clarifies, "To me all things are spiritual, and never at any time have I given a law that is temporal" (D&C 29:34). But this does not mean that we can content ourselves with viewing the world through spiritual eyes, dutifully avoiding or shunning interaction or engagement for fear of being tainted, waiting for Jesus to return to cleanse and change the earth. If we are truly to be leaven, we must purposely and conscientiously contact, mix with, and be absorbed by the world to effect its transformation. Indeed, we must lose ourselves. The cleansing will come through our efforts. The sanctifying will be accomplished by our consecration to doing, in the Lord's way, the work of the Lord—a work begun with a spiritual creation and ongoing in a tem-

---

Church of Jesus Christ be racist [or sexist] and Christian at the same time? Can the Church of Jesus Christ be politically, socially, and economically identified with the structures of oppression and also be a servant of Christ? Can the Church of Jesus Christ fail to make the liberation of the poor the center of its message and work, and still remain faithful to its Lord?" James H. Cone, *God of the Oppressed*, Kindle, loc. 916–17, 928–29.

19. Joseph Smith, "In Answer to the Above," 732.

poral history: "First spiritual, secondly temporal, which is the beginning of my work; and again, *first temporal, and secondly spiritual*, which is the last of my work" (D&C 29:32; emphasis added). What is our part in this work? To a general conference on October 5, 1856, Brigham Young said,

> Many of our brethren and sisters are on the plains with handcarts, and probably many are now seven hundred miles from this place, and they must be brought here, we must send assistance to them. . . .
>
> That is my religion; that is the dictation of the Holy Ghost that I possess, it is to save the people. . . . This is the salvation I am now seeking for. To save our brethren that would be apt to perish, or suffer extremely, if we do not send them assistance. . . .
>
> I will tell you all that your faith, religion, and profession of religion, will never save one soul of you in the celestial kingdom of our God, unless you carry out just such principles as I am now teaching you. Go and bring in those people now on the Plains, and attend strictly to those things which we call temporal, or temporal duties, otherwise your faith will be in vain.[20]

Young's words are as applicable to us today. There are scores of people suffering in our homes, pews, communities, nations, and the world, perishing or about to perish "on the plains." We must bring them in. It is not enough for us to claim the truth of the restored gospel as self-evident in some abstract theological sense outside of any particular historical reality or lived experience. It is not merely a divine ultimatum that demands unbending and unquestioning assent or assimilation. The truth and continued relevance of the gospel of Jesus Christ in our world depends on it being reshaped and reclaimed—indeed *restored*—as truly *good news* to those in the world who need it most.[21] As made clear by the French Jesuit priest Joseph Moingt, "We need constantly to be converted to the other, precisely to the other who suffers . . . the truth of yesterday, that same truth, has to become reality in history today."[22] Fulfilling our mission as a true and living Church of Jesus Christ today means more than modifying the design of our logo, retooling our public-relations and online campaigns, emphasizing the formal name of the Church, or making more frequent official proclamations or announcements of incremental changes in our "historic" semi-annual general conferences, which themselves often feel performative, insular, self-congratulatory, spiritually abstracted from

---

20. Brigham Young, October 5, 1856, *Journal of Discourses*, 4:113.
21. See Jon Sobrino, *Christ the Liberator: A View from the Victims*, ch. 13, for a similar discussion.
22. Joseph Moingt, quoted in Sobrino, *Christ the Liberator*, 255.

real-world issues and struggles, and fail to authentically engage with, or are dismissive of, or reactionary to the lived experience and faithful questions and difficulties of a growing number of members. It means more than joining our voices with those organizations and groups who decry the rise of "secularism" and the supposed threats to "religious freedom," a ploy used as cover by Christian nationalists to advocate for inscribing legal license to discriminate against and target hatred and intolerance towards LGBTQ+, Muslim, and other "non-Christian" groups. Rather, being a Church of Jesus Christ means acting in our covenant obligation as his living body to ease suffering in the world. It means continuing his ministry and mission of expanding the boundaries of the covenant community, especially to those who have been excluded and marginalized by social, political, or religious custom. It means being actively engaged in an ongoing "prophetic ministry of formation and reformation of alternative community."[23] It means recognizing and embracing the prophetic and liberative meaning, potential, and responsibility of the Restoration to reveal the reality of the economic and political ideologies, structures, and systems of oppression and exploitation in the world and to stand in solidarity with the poor and oppressed against those systems. It means "taking the crucified people down from the cross."[24] It means being willing to hear and respond to the historical and ongoing judgment and critique of our institutional doctrine, policy, practice, and culture given voice by the suffering reality of the poor, oppressed, and marginalized. It means imagining, and helping the world imagine and work towards, a new reality. It means building Zion.

To a kingdom steeped in exploitation, inequality, and idolatry, the prophet Micah said, "What does the Lord require of you but to do justice?" (Micah 6:8). To the prophet Isaiah, the Lord said, "Do justice, for my salvation is soon to come" (Isa. 56:1). To a group of terrified people on the shores of the Red Sea who were cowering before thundering Egyptian chariots, bent on their utter annihilation, Moses proclaimed, "Fear ye not, stand still, and see the salvation of the Lord" (Ex. 14:13 KJV). The salvation that was desperately needed and hoped for in these accounts was not a spiritual place in some far-distant heavenly kingdom after death, but a temporal, physical reality. Against all odds, the sea parted and the dumbfounded Israelites stepped as a body into the gulf between bondage

---

23. Walter Brueggemann, *The Prophetic Imagination*, 4.

24. These are the words of the Salvadoran martyr Ignacio Ellacuría. It is also the subject of an extended treatment and meditation by Jon Sobrino, *The Principle of Mercy: Taking the Crucified People from the Cross*. See also Sobrino, *Christ the Liberator*.

and liberation. They walked through on dry, solid ground toward a land promised to them by covenant.

Under a brutal colonial occupation, Jesus expanded the vision and meaning of God's covenant. He showed that the covenant was not to be fulfilled through divine or human violence, but through fellowship, inclusion, compassion, and reconciliation. He wore out, and in the end, gave his life for those who were vilified, hated, and marginalized. "In Jesus, the poor found someone who loved them and defended them, who sought to save them simply because they were in need."[25] He suffered with, and as, one of "the least of these" in order to save them "*in the human way, by showing solidarity with them,*"[26] and to show us in turn how to save one another. This is the covenant he revealed to his followers that was solemnized on Calvary's cross, and this is the new and everlasting covenant that is revealed and calls us from the crosses of the world today. *This is the meaning of the Restoration.* The ongoing reality of both the crucified Jesus and the risen Christ "breaking into history"[27] through the suffering and struggle of the poor and oppressed for the right to life against the powers of dehumanization and death reveals the hope and responsibility of a present, *this-worldly* kingdom and salvation. Indeed, the good news of the gospel points us toward a salvation realized and fulfilled through participation in the love of God manifest in the struggle for and liberation of humanity and creation. Toward a new day and new life for the crucified people of the world. Toward restoration of justice. Toward restoration of equity. Toward restoration of community.

Toward restoration. . .

---

25. Sobrino, *Christ the Liberator*, 211.

26. Sobrino, 88, emphasis in original.

27. Sobrino, *Christ the Liberator*; Jon Sobrino, *No Salvation Outside the Poor: Prophetic-Utopian Essays*.

Bibliography

Alexander, Bruce K. *The Globalization of Addiction: A Study in Poverty of the Spirit.* New York: Oxford University Press, 2010.

———. *The Roots of Addiction in Free Market Society.* Vancouver: Canadian Centre for Policy Alternatives, 2001.

Alexander, Michelle. *The New Jim Crow: Mass Incarceration in the Age of Colorblindness.* New York: The New Press, 2010.

Alighieri, Dante. *The Divine Comedy.* Translated by John Ciardi. New York: New American Library, 1961. Epub.

Allende, Isabel. *Of Love and Shadows.* Translated by Margaret Sayers Peden. Cambridge: Black Swan, 1994.

Almond, Philip C. *The Devil: A New Biography.* New York: I. B. Tauris & Co., 2014.

American Psychiatric Association. *Diagnostic and Statistical Manual of Mental Disorders, Version 5.* Washington DC: American Psychiatric Association, 2013.

Anderson, Sarah, Sam Pizzagati, and Brian Wakamo. *Executive Excess 2022: 28th Annual IPS Executive Compensation Report.* Washington, DC: Institute for Policy Studies, 2022.

Anselm of Canterbury. *The Major Works.* Oxford: Oxford University Press, 1998.

Applebaum, Anne. *Red Famine: Stalin's War on Ukraine.* New York: Doubleday, 2017.

Augustine of Hippo. *The Confessions.* Translated by Maria Boulding. New York: Vintage, 1998. Epub.

Barker, Margaret. *Temple Theology: An Introduction.* London: MPG Books Ltd, 2004.

Barone, Marco. *Luther's Augustinian Theology of the Cross.* Eugene: Resource Publications, 2017.

Barton, John. *A History of the Bible: The Story of the World's Most Influential Book.* New York: Viking Press, 2019.

Belnap, Daniel L., Gaye Strathearn, and Stanley A. Johnson, eds. *The Things Which My Father Saw: Approaches to Lehi's Dream and Nephi's Vision.* Salt Lake City: Deseret Book, 2011.

Benn, Ernest J. P. *The Confessions of a Capitalist.* London: Hutchinson & Co., 1925.

Benson, Ezra T. "Beware of Pride." *Report of the Semi-Annual Conference of the Church of Jesus Christ of Latter-day Saints*, April 1989. Salt Lake City: Church of Jesus Christ of Latter-day Saints, semi-annual.

Berlin, Adele, and Marc Zvi Brettler, eds. *The Jewish Study Bible.* New York: Oxford University Press, 2014.

Birch, Bruce C., Walter Brueggemann, Terrence E. Fretheim, and David L. Petersen. *A Theological Introduction to the Old Testament.* Nashville: Abingdon Press, 2005.

Bisharat, George. "Sanctions as Genocide." *Transnational Law and Comtemporary Problems* 379 (2001): 379–425.

Boersma, Hans. *Violence, Hospitality, and the Cross: Reappropriating the Atonement Tradition.* Ada: Baker Academic, 2006.

Bonhoeffer, Dietrich. *The Cost of Discipleship.* New York: Touchstone, 1995.

———. *Letters and Papers from Prison.* New York: Touchstone, 1997.

Borg, Marcus J., and John Dominic Crossan. *The Last Week: A Day-by-Day Account of Jesus's Final Week in Jerusalem*. New York: Harper Collins, 2006.
Brooks, Joanna. *Mormonism and White Supremacy: American Religion and the Problem of Racial Innocence*. New York: Oxford University Press, 2020.
Brown, S. Kent. "New Light from Arabia on Lehi's Trail." In *Echoes and Evidences of the Book of Mormon*, ed. Donald W. Parry, Daniel C. Peterson, and John W. Welch, 55–125. Provo: FARMS, 2002.
Brueggemann, Walter. *Isaiah 40–66*. Louisville: Westminster John Knox Press, 1998.
———. *Old Testament Theology: An Introduction*. Nashville: Abingdon Press, 2008.
———. *The Prophetic Imagination*. Minneapolis: Fortress Press, 2018.
———. *Theology of the Old Testament: Testimony, Dispute, Advocacy*. Minneapolis: Fortress Press, 2005.
———. *An Unsettling God: The Heart of the Hebrew Bible*. Minneapolis: Fortress Press, 2009.
Bush Jr., Lester E. "Mormonism's Negro Doctrine: An Historical Overview." *Dialogue: A Journal of Mormon Thought* 8, no. 1 (1973): 11–68.
Bushman, Richard L. "The Lamanite View of Book of Mormon History." In *By Study and Also By Faith*, ed. John M. Lundquist and Stephen D. Ricks, 2:52–72. Salt Lake City: Deseret Book, 1990.
Callister, Tad R. *The Infinite Atonement*. Salt Lake City, Deseret Book, 2000.
Calvin, John. *Institutes of the Christian Religion, Volume II*. Grand Rapids: Eerdmans, 1953.
Case, Anne, and Angus Deaton. *Deaths of Despair and the Future of Capitalism*. Princeton: Princeton University Press, 2021.
Cavanaugh, William T. *Torture and Eucharist: Theology, Politics, and the Body of Christ*. Hoboken: Wiley-Blackwell, 1998.
Chan, Jung, and Jon Halliday. *Mao: The Unknown Story*. New York: Anchor Books, 2006.
Charpin, Dominique. *Writing, Law, and Kingship in Old Babylonian Mesopotamia*. Translated by Jane Marie Todd. London: University of Chicago Press, 2010.
Clendinnen, Inga. "'Fierce and Unnatural Cruelty': Cortés and the Conquest of Mexico." *Representations* 33 (Winter 1991): 65–100.
Cohen, Donald, and Allen Mikaelian. *The Privatization of Everything: How the Plunder of Public Goods Transformed America and How We Can Fight Back*. New York: The New Press, 2021.
Colvin, Gina, and Joanna Brooks, eds. *Decolonizing Mormonism: Approaching a Postcolonial Zion*. Salt Lake City: University of Utah Press, 2018.
Cone, James H. *The Cross and the Lynching Tree*. Ossining: Orbis, 2011.
———. *God of the Oppressed*. Maryknoll: Orbis, 1997.
Cortés, Hernan. *Letters from Mexico*. Translated by Anthony Padgen. New Haven: Yale University Press, 1986.
Cosgrave, William. "The Theology of Liberation." *The Furrow* 37 (1986): 506–16.
Crawford, Neta C. *United States Budgetary Costs and Obligations of Post 9/11 Wars through FY2020: $6.4 Trillion*. Providence: Brown University, 2019.
Credit Suisse Institute. "Global Wealth Report 2022." Accessed February 1, 2023. https://www.credit-suisse.com/about-us/en/reports-research/global-wealth-report.html.
Crossan, John Dominic. *God and Empire: Jesus Against Rome, Then and Now*. New York: HarperCollins, 2007.
———. *Jesus: A Revolutionary Biography*. New York: HarperCollins, 1994.

Dahl, Larry E. "The Concept of Hell." In *A Book of Mormon Treasury: Gospel Insights from General Authorities and Religious Educators*, 262–79. Provo: Religious Studies Center, Brigham Young University, 2003.

Dalrymple, William. *The Anarchy: The East India Company, Corporate Violence, and the Pillage of an Empire*. London: Bloomsbury, 2019.

de las Casas, Bartolomé. *A Short Account of the Destruction of the Indies*. Translated by Nigel Griffin. London: Penguin, 1992.

de Sahagún, Fray Bernardino. *Florentine Codex: General History of the Things of New Spain: Book 12: The Conquest of Mexico*. Translated by Arthur J. O. Anderson and Charles E. Dibble. Salt Lake City: University of Utah Press, 1975.

del Castillo, Bernal Díaz. *The Discovery and Conquest of Mexico*. London: Routledge, 2004.

Dikötter, Frank. *Mao's Great Famine: The History of China's Most Devastating Catastrophe 1958–1962*. London, Bloomsbury, 2010.

Douglas, Mary. "Atonement in Leviticus." *Jewish Studies Quarterly* 1, no. 2 (1993): 109–30.

———. *Purity and Danger: An Analysis of the Concepts of Pollution and Taboo*. New York: Routledge, 1966.

Drinnon, Richard. *Facing West: The Metaphysics of Indian-Hating and Empire-Building*. Norman: University of Oklahoma Press, 1997.

Dunn, James D. G. *The New Perspective on Paul*. Grand Rapids: Eerdmans, 2007.

Eagleton, Terry. *Why Marx Was Right*. New Haven: Yale University Press, 2018.

Edward, Peter. "The Ethical Poverty Line: A Moral Quantification of Absolute Poverty." *Third World Quarterly* 27, no. 2 (2006): 377–93.

Eisen, Lauren-Brooke. *Inside Private Prisons: An American Dilemma in the Age of Mass Incarceration*. New York: Columbia University Press, 2017.

Ellacuria, Ignacio. "The Crucified People." In *Systematic Theology: Perspectives from Liberation Theology (Readings from Mysterium Liberationis)*. Edited by Jon Sobrino and Ignacio Ellacuria, 257–78. Maryknoll: Orbis Books, 1996.

Endō, Shūsaku. *The Samurai*. Translated by Van C. Gessel. Cambridge: New Directions, 1997.

———. *Silence*. Translated by William Johnston. New York: Taplinger Publishing Company, 1999.

Evans, C. Stephen. *Exploring Kenotic Christology: The Self-Emptying of God*. New York: Oxford University Press, 2006.

Fanon, Frantz. *The Wretched of the Earth*. New York: Grove, 2005.

Farnes, Sherilyn, and Mitchell K. Schaefer. "Myself . . . I Consecrate to the God of Heaven: Twenty Affidavits of Consecration in Nauvoo, June–July 1842." *BYU Studies Quarterly* 50, no. 3 (2011): 101–32.

Federici, Sylvia. *Caliban and the Witch: Women, the Body, and Primitive Accumulation*. New York: Autonomedia, 2004.

———. *Re-enchanting the World: Feminism and the Politics of the Commons,* Oakland: PM Press, 2019.

———. *Witches, Witch-Hunting, and Women*. Oakland: PM Press, 2018.

Ffrench-Davis, Ricardo. *Economic Reforms in Chile: From Dictatorship to Democracy*. London: Palgrave-MacMillan, 2010.

Finlan, Stephen. *Problems with Atonement: The Origins of, and Controversy About, the Atonement Doctrine*. Collegeville: Liturgical Press, 2005.

Fiorenza, Elizabeth Schüssler. *Bread Not Stone: The Challenge of Feminist Biblical Interpretation*. Boston: Beacon Press, 1995.

———. *In Memory of Her: A Feminist Theological Reconstruction of Christian Origins.* Freiberg: Herder, 1994.
Freire, Paulo. *Pedagogy of the Oppressed.* New York: Bloomsbury Academic, 2000.
Friedman, Milton. *Capitalism and Freedom.* Chicago: University of Chicago Press, 1962.
———. "A Friedman Doctrine: The Social Responsibility of Business is to Increase Its Profits." *The New York Times*, September 13, 1970, 17.
Froelich, Margaret. *Jesus and the Empire of God: Royal Language and Imperial Ideology in the Gospel of Mark.* London: Bloomsbury, 2021.
Galeano, Eduardo. *Open Veins of Latin America: Five Centuries of the Pillage of a Continent.* Translated by Cedric Belfrage. New York: Monthly Review Press, 1997.
Gathercole, Simon. *Defending Substitution: An Essay on Atonement in Paul.* Grand Rapids, Baker Academic, 2015.
Gibson, Joseph R. *How Europe and America are Still Underdeveloping Africa: Neocolonialism and the Scramble for Strategic Resources in 21st Century Africa.* Southfield, KITABU, 2012.
Girard, Rene. *I See Satan Fall Like Lightning.* Translated by James G. Williams. Maryknoll: Orbis Books, 2001.
———. *Violence and the Sacred.* Baltimore: The Johns Hopkins University Press, 1989.
Givens, Fiona and Terryl Givens. *The Christ Who Heals: How God Restored the Truth That Saves Us.* Salt Lake City, Deseret Book, 2017.
Givens, Terryl and Fiona Givens. *The God Who Weeps: How Mormonism Makes Sense of Life.* Salt Lake City: Ensign Peak, 2012.
Godfrey, Matthew C., et al., eds. *Joseph Smith's Revelations: A Doctrine and Covenants Study Companion from the Joseph Smith Papers.* Salt Lake City: Church Historian's Press, 2020.
Gottwald, Norman K. *The Hebrew Bible: A Socio-Literary Introduction.* Minneapolis: Fortress Press, 1987.
Grabbe, Lester L. *An Introduction to Second Temple Judaism.* London: T&T Clark, 2010.
Green, Joel B., and Mark D. Baker. *Recovering the Scandal of the Cross: Atonement in New Testament and Contemporary Contexts.* Westmont: IVP Academic, 2000.
Greenberg, James A. *A New Look at Atonement in Leviticus: The Meaning and Purpose of Kipper Revisited.* University Park: Penn State University Press, 2019.
Grimsrud, Ted. *Instead of Atonement: The Bible's Salvation Story and Our Hope for Wholeness.* Eugene: Cascade Press, 2013.
Gutiérrez, Gustavo. *On Job: God-Talk and the Suffering of the Innocent.* Translated by Matthew J. O'Connell. Maryknoll: Orbis Books, 1987.
———. *A Theology of Liberation.* Maryknoll: Orbis Books, 1988.
———. *We Drink From Our Own Wells: The Spiritual Journey of a People.* Translated by Matthew J. O'Connell. Maryknoll: Orbis Books, 2003.
Hagan, Kenneth. "Luther on Atonement Reconfigured." *Concordia Theological Quarterly* 61, no. 4 (1997): 251–76.
Hall, Douglas John. *The Cross in Our Context: Jesus and the Suffering World.* Minneapolis: Fortress Press, 2003.
———. *God and Human Suffering: An Exercise in the Theology of the Cross.* Minneapolis: Fortress Press, 1987.
———. *Lighten our Darkness: Towards an Indigenous Theology of the Cross.* Academic Renewal Press, 2001.
Han, Byung-Chul. *The Disappearance of Rituals: A Topology of the Present.* Translated by Daniel Steuer. Cambridge: Polity Press, 2020.

Hardy, Grant. *Understanding the Book of Mormon: A Reader's Guide*. Oxford: University Press, 2010.

Harris, James. *The Great Fear: Stalin's Terror of the 1930s*. Oxford: Oxford University Press, 2017.

Harris, Matthew L., and Madison S. Harris. "The Last State to Honor MLK: Utah and the Quest for Racial Justice." *Utah Historical Quarterly* 88, no. 1 (Winter 2020): 5–21.

Havorka, Janet. "Sarah and Hagar: Ancient Women of the Abrahamic Covenant." In *Astronomy, Papyrus, and Covenant*, ed. John Gee and Brian M. Hauglid, 147–66. Provo: Foundation for Ancient Research and Mormon Studies, 2005.

Hay, Douglas, Peter Linebaugh, John G. Rule, E. P. Thompson, and Cal Winslow. *Albion's Fatal Tree: Crime and Society in Eighteenth-Century England*. New York: Pantheon, 1975.

Hayes, John H. "Atonement in the Book of Leviticus." *Interpretation: A Journal of Bible and Theology* 52, no. 1 (1998): 5–15.

Heim, S. Mark. *Saved from Sacrifice: A Theology of the Cross*. Grand Rapids: Eerdmans, 2006.

Hennelly, Alfred T. *Liberation Theologies: The Global Pursuit of Justice*. New London: Twenty Third Publications, 1995.

Herzog, William R., II. *Jesus, Justice, and the Reign of God: A Ministry of Liberation*. Westminster: John Knox Press, 1999.

———. *Parables as Subversive Speech: Jesus as Pedagogue of the Oppressed*. Westminster: John Knox Press, 1994.

Hill, Christopher. *Reformation to Industrial Revolution: The Making of Modern English Society, Vol. 1 1530–1780*. New York: Pantheon, 1967.

———. *Winstanley: "The Law of Freedom" and Other Writings*. Cambridge: University Press, 2006.

———. *The World Turned Upside Down: Radical Ideas During the English Revolution*. London: Penguin, 1991.

Hilton, John III, and Joshua P. Barringer. "The Use of Gethsemane by Church Leaders, 1859–2018." *BYU Studies Quarterly* 58, no. 4 (2019): 49–76.

Hilton, Rodney. *Bond Men Made Free: Medieval Peasant Movements and the English Rising of 1381*. Oxfordshire: Routledge, 2003.

Hochschild, Adam. *King Leopold's Ghost*. Boston: Mariner Books, 1999.

Hodge, Charles. *The Orthodox Doctrine Regarding the Extent of the Atonement Vindicated*. London: B. Groombridge & Sons, 1846.

Holcomb, Justin S., ed. *Christian Theologies of Salvation: A Comparative Introduction*. New York: New York University Press, 2017.

Holland, Glenn S. *Gods in the Desert: Religions of the Ancient Near East*. New York: Bowman & Littlefield, 2009.

Hollenbach, Paul W. "Jesus, Demoniacs, and Public Authorities: A Socio-Historical Study." *Journal of the American Academy of Religion* 49, no. 4 (December 1981): 567–88.

Holmes, Stephen R. *The Wondrous Cross: Atonement and Penal Substitution in the Bible and History*. Milton Keynes: Paternoster, 2007.

Horsley, Richard A. *Covenant Economics: A Biblical Vision of Justice for All*. Westminster: John Knox Press, 2009.

———. *Galilee*. Minneapolis: Trinity Press International, 1995.

———. *Jesus and Empire: The Kingdom of God and the New World Disorder*. Minneapolis: Augsburg Fortress Press, 2003.

———. *Jesus and the Politics of Roman Palestine*. Columbia: University of South Carolina Press, 2014.

———. *The Prophet Jesus and the Renewal of Israel*. Grand Rapids: Eerdmans, 2012.

Hunter, James. *Set Adrift Upon the World: The Sutherland Clearances*. Edinburgh: Birlinn, 2016.

IPCC, 2022: *Climate Change 2022: Impacts, Adaptation, and Vulnerability*. Contribution of Working Group II to the Sixth Assessment Report of the Intergovernmental Panel on Climate Change. Cambridge University Press, 2022.

Isobe, Atsuhiko, et al. "A Multilevel Dataset of Microplastic Abundance in the World's Upper Ocean and the Laurentian Great Lakes." *Microplastics and Nanoplastics* 1, no. 1 (2021). https://microplastics.springeropen.com/articles/10.1186/s43591-021-00013-z.

Janzen, David. *Trauma and the Failure of History: Kings, Lamentations, and the Destruction of Jerusalem*. Atlanta: SBL Press, 2019.

Jeremias, Joachim. *New Testament Theology: The Proclamation of Jesus*. Charles Scribner's Sons: 1971.

Joelsson, Linda. "Exorcisms as Liberation: Trauma, Differentiation, and Social Systems in Luke." *Studia Theologic: Nordic Journal of Theology* 74, no. 2 (2020). https://doi.org/10.1080/0039338X.2020.1785934.

Joh, Wonhee Anne. *The Heart of the Cross: A Postcolonial Christology*. Louisville: Westminster John Knox, 2006.

Johnston, Sara Iles, ed. *Religions of the Ancient World: A Guide*. Cambridge: Belknap Press, 2004.

Jones, Robert P. *White Too Long: The Legacy of White Supremacy in American Christianity*. New York: Simon & Schuster, 2020.

Joseph, Peter. *The New Human Rights Movement: Reinventing the Economy to End Oppression*. Dallas: BenBella Books, 2017.

Josephus, Flavius. *The Jewish War; or, the History of the Destruction of Jerusalem*. Translated by William Whiston. London, 1737. Typescript available at http://penelope.uchicago.edu/josephus/war-pref.html.

Journal of Discourses. 26 vols. London and Liverpool: LDS Booksellers Depot, 1854–86.

Julian of Norwich, *Revelations of Divine Love*. Translated by Elizabeth Spearing. London: Penguin, 1998.

Katongole, Emmanuel M. *Mirror to the Church: Resurrecting Faith After Genocide in Rwanda*. Grand Rapids: Zondervan, 2009.

Kautsky, John H. *The Politics of Aristocratic Empires*. Chapel Hill: University of North Carolina Press, 1982.

Kendi, Ibram X. *Stamped From the Beginning: The Definitive History of Racist Ideas in America*. New York: Bold Type Books, 2016.

Kessler, R. "The Crimes of the Nations in Amos 1–2." *Acta Theologica Supp* 26 (2018): 206–20.

Kingsolver, Barbara. *The Poisonwood Bible*. London: Faber, 1999.

Kinzer, Stephen. *Overthrow: America's Century of Regime Change from Hawaii to Iraq*. New York: Times Books, 2007.

Kitamori, Kazoh. *Theology of the Pain of God: The First Original Theology from Japan*. Eugene: Wipf & Stock, 2005.

Kiuchi, Nobuyoshi. "Elijah's Self-Offering: 1 Kings 17,21." *Biblica* 75 (1994): 74–79.

Klein, Naomi. *No Logo*. Toronto: Vintage Canada, 2009.

———. *The Shock Doctrine: The Rise of Disaster Capitalism*. London: Penguin, 2007.

———. *This Changes Everything: Capitalism vs The Climate*. New York: Simon & Schuster, 2014.

Kolbert, Elizabeth. *The Sixth Extinction: An Unnatural History*. New York: Henry Holt and Co., 2014.
Kotsko, Adam. *Neoliberalism's Demons: The Political Theology of Late Capital*. Redwood City: Stanford University Press, 2018.
Lacocque, André. *The Book of Daniel*. Eugene: Cascade Press, 2018.
LaFeber, Walter F. *Inevitable Revolutions: The United States in Central America*. New York: W. W. Norton & Company, 1993.
Lebreton, L., et al. "Evidence that the Great Pacific Garbage Patch Is Rapidly Accumulating Plastic." *Scientific Reports* 8 (2018): https://doi.org/10.1038/s41598-018-22939-w.
Lenski, Gerhard E. *Power and Privilege: A Theory of Social Stratification*. Chapel Hill: University of North Carolina Press, 1984.
Leon-Portilla, Miguel, ed., *The Broken Spears: The Aztec Account of the Conquest of Mexico*. Translated by Angel Maria Garibay K. and Lysander Kemp. Boston: Beacon, 2006.
Lerner, Gerda. *The Creation of Patriarchy*. New York: Oxford University Press, 1986.
"Letter to Edward Partridge, 2 May 1833." The Joseph Smith Papers. Accessed December 25, 2021. https://www.josephsmithpapers.org/paper-summary/letter-to-edward-partridge-2-may-1833.
Li, Yiyun. *The Vagrants*. New York: Random House, 2009.
Linebaugh, Peter. *The London Hanged: Crime and Civil Society in the Eighteenth Century*. Cambridge: University Press, 1993.
———. *Stop Thief! The Commoners, Enclosure, and Resistance*. Oakland: PM Press, 2014.
Locke, John. *Two Treatises of Government*. Cambridge: University Press, 2003.
Luther, Martin. *Luther's Works Volume 34, Career of the Reformer IV*. St. Louis: Concordia Publishing House, 1960.
———. *Sermons of Martin Luther. Vol. 2. Sermons on Gospel Texts for Epiphany, Lent & Easter, Vol 2*. Albany: Ages Software, 1997.
Lynas, Mark. *Six Degrees: Our Future on a Hotter Planet*. London: Fourth Estate, 2007.
MacCulloch, Diarmaid. *A History of Christianity: The First Three Thousand Years*. London: Allen Lane, 2010.
MacQuarrie, Kim. *The Last Days of the Incas*. New York: Simon & Schuster, 2007.
Madley, Benjamin. "Reexamining the American Genocide Debate: Meaning, Historiography, and New Methods." *The American Historical Review* 120, no. 1 (February 2015): 98–139.
Mann, Michael E. *The Hockey Stick and the Climate Wars: Dispatches from the Front Lines*. New York: Columbia University Press, 2012.
Martin, Jamie. *The Meddlers: Sovereignty, Empire, and the Birth of Global Economic Governance*. Cambridge: Harvard University Press, 2022.
Marx, Karl. *Capital: Vol I: A Critique of Political Economy*. London: Penguin Classics, 1992.
Mason, Patrick Q. *Restoration: God's Call to the 21st Century*. Salt Lake City: Deseret Book, 2020.
Mason, Patrick Q., and J. David Pulsipher. *Proclaim Peace: The Restoration's Answer to an Age of Conflict*. Provo: BYU Maxwell Institute and Deseret Book, 2021.
McBride, Matthew, and James Goldberg, eds. *Revelations in Context: The Stories Behind the Sections of the Doctrine and Covenants*. Salt Lake City: The Church of Jesus Christ of Latter-day Saints, 2016.

McCarthy, Cormac. *Blood Meridian, or the Evening Redness in the West.* New York: Vintage, 1992.
McConkie, James W., and Judith E. McConkie. *Whom Say Ye That I Am: Lessons from the Jesus of Nazareth.* Salt Lake City: Greg Kofford Books, 2018.
McEwan, Joanne, and Pamela Sharpe, eds. *Accommodating Poverty: The Housing and Living Arrangements of the English Poor, c. 1600–1850.* London: Palgrave MacMillan, 2011.
McLaren, Brian D. *Do I Stay Christian? A Guide for the Doubters, the Disappointed, and the Disillusioned.* New York: St. Martin's Essentials, 2022.
Merchant, Carolyn. *The Death of Nature: Women, Ecology, and the Scientific Revolution.* New York: HarperOne, 1990.
Messadié, Gerald. *A History of the Devil.* New York: Kodansha, 1997.
Metz, Johannes Baptist. *Poverty of Spirit.* New York: Newman Press, 1968.
Mies, Maria. *Patriarchy and Accumulation on a World Scale: Women in the International Division of Labour.* London: Zed Books, 2014.
Miller, Adam S. *An Early Resurrection: Life in Christ Before You Die.* Salt Lake City: Deseret Book, 2018.
Moltmann, Jürgen. *The Crucified God: The Cross of Christ as the Foundation and Criticism of Christian Theology.* Translated by John Bowden and R. A. Wilson. Minneapolis: Augsburg Fortress, 1993.
Morrison, Toni. *Beloved.* New York: Vintage, 2004.
Mueller, John, and Karl Mueller. "Sanctions of Mass Destruction," *Foreign Affairs* 78 (1999): 43–53.
Neeson, J. M. *Commoners: Common Right, Enclosure, and Social Change in England 1700–1820.* Bristol: Past and Present, 1996.
Nibley, Hugh. *Approaching Zion.* Salt Lake City: Deseret Book Co., 1989.
———. *Lehi in the Desert, The World of the Jaredites, There Were Jaredites.* Provo: FARMS, 1988.
Nimmo, Paul T., and Keith L. Johnson, eds. *Kenosis: The Self-Emptying of Christ in Scripture and Theology.* Grand Rapids: Eerdmans, 2022.
Noll, Mark A. *The Civil War as a Theological Crisis.* Chapel Hill: University of North Carolina Press, 2006.
Novak, Michael. *The Spirit of Democratic Capitalism.* Lanham: Madison Books, 1982.
———. *Toward a Theology of the Corporation.* Washington DC: AEI Press, 1990.
O'Rourke, Lindsey A. "The Strategy of Covert Regime Change: US-Backed Regime Change Campaigns During the Cold War." *Security Studies* 29 (2020): 92–127.
Ostler, Blake T. "The Book of Mormon as a Modern Expansion of an Ancient Source." *Dialogue: A Journal of Mormon Thought* 20, no. 1 (1987): 66–123.
Pakenham, Thomas. *The Scramble for Africa: The White Man's Conquest of the Dark Continent from 1876 to 1912.* New York: Harper Perennial, 1992.
Park, Andrew Sung. *The Wounded Heart of God: The Asian Concept of Han and the Christian Doctrine of Sin.* Nashville: Abingdon Press, 1993.
Perelman, Michael. *The Invention of Capitalism: Classical Political Economy and the Secret History of Primitive Accumulation.* Durham: Duke University Press, 2000.
Pero, Cheryl, *Liberation from Empire: Demonic Possession and Exorcism in the Gospel of Mark.* New York: Peter Lang, 2013.
Platt, Tony. "US Criminal Justice in the Reagan Era: An Assessment." *Crime and Social Justice* 29 (1987): 58–69.

Polanyi, Karl. *The Great Transformation: The Political and Economic Origins of Our Time.* Boston: Beacon Press, 2001.

Potter, Kelli [R. Dennis]. "Liberation Theology in the Book of Mormon." In *Discourses in Mormon Theology: Philosophical and Theological Possibilities*, ed. James M. McLachlan and Loyd Ericson. Draper: Greg Kofford Books, 2007.

Prebble, John. *The Highland Clearances.* London: Penguin, 1969.

Quinn, D. Michael. "The LDS Church's Campaign Against the Equal Rights Amendment." *Journal of Mormon History* 20, no. 2 (Fall 1994): 85–155.

Ragusa, Antonio, et al. "Plasticenta: First Evidence of Microplastics in Human Placenta." *Environment International* 146 (2021): https://doi.org/10.1016/j.envint.2020.106274.

———. "Raman Microspectroscopy Detection and Characterisation of Microplastics in Human Breastmilk." *Polymers* 14, no. 13 (2022): https://doi.org/10.3390/polym14132700.

Rauschenbusch, Walter. *Christianity and the Social Crisis.* New York: MacMillan, 1920. Epub.

Reeve, W. Paul. *Religion of a Different Color: Race and the Mormon Struggle for Whiteness.* New York: Oxford University Press, 2015.

Richards, Donald G. "The Political Economy of the Chilean Miracle." *Latin American Research Review* 32 (1997): 139–59.

Rodney, Walter. *How Europe Underdeveloped Africa.* Washington DC: Howard University Press, 1981.

Romero, Oscar. "The Church Serves Personal, Communal, and Transcendent Liberation." The Archbishop Romero Trust. Accessed January 9, 2023. http://www.romerotrust.org.uk/homilies-and-writings/homilies/church-serves-personal-communal-and-transcendent-liberation.

———. *Voice of the Voiceless: The Four Pastoral Letters and Other Statements.* Maryknoll: Orbis Books, 1985.

Roy, Arundhati. *Capitalism: A Ghost Story.* Chicago: Haymarket Books, 2014.

Rozental, Alek A. "The Enclosure Movement in France." *The American Journal of Economics and Sociology* 16, no. 1 (October 1956): 55–71.

Rubenhold, Hallie. *The Covent Garden Ladies: Pimp General Jack and the Extraordinary Story of Harris's List.* London: Transworld, 2012.

Ruether, Rosemary Radford. *Sexism and God-Talk: Toward a Feminist Theology.* Boston: Beacon Press, 1993.

Savabieasfahani, M., et al. "Prenatal Metal Exposure in the Middle East: Imprint of War in Deciduous Teeth of Children." *Environmental Monitoring and Assessment* 188, no. 505 (2016): https://doi.org/10.1007/s10661-016-5491-0.

Savabieasfahani, M., F. Basher Ahamadani, and A. Mahdavi Damghani. "Living Near an Active U.S. Military Base in Iraq Is Associated with Significantly Higher Hair Thorium and Increased Likelihood of Congenital Anomalies in Infants and Children." *Environmental Pollution* 256 (2020). https://doi.org/10.1016/j.envpol.2019.113070.

Schlefer, Jonathan. *The Assumptions Economists Make.* Cambridge: Belknap Press, 2012.

Schmiechen, Peter. *Saving Power: Theories of Atonement and Forms of the Church.* Grand Rapids: Eerdmans, 2005.

Scholz, Susanne. *Sacred Witness: Rape in the Hebrew Bible.* Minneapolis: Fortress Press, 2010.

Schwager, Raymund. *Must There Be Scapegoats: Violence and Redemption in the Bible.* New York: Crossroad, 2018.
Schwartz, Robert F. "Inequality and Narrative in the Book of Mormon." *BYU Studies Quarterly* 61, no. 1 (2022): 31–75.
Schweitzer, Albert. *The Quest of the Historical Jesus.* Translated by W. Montgomery. Minneapolis: Augsburg Fortress, 2001.
Slobodian, Quinn. *Globalists: The End of Empire and the Birth of Neoliberalism.* Cambridge: Harvard University Press, 2018.
Smith, David Michael. "Counting the Dead: Estimating the Loss of Life in the Indigenous Holocaust, 1492–Present." Paper presented at the Twelfth Native American Symposium, Southern Oklahoma State University, 2017.
Smith, Joseph. "In Answer to the Above." *Times and Seasons* 3, no. 10 (March 15, 1842): 732.
Smith, Joseph, et al. *History of the Church of Jesus Christ of Latter-day Saints.* Edited by B. H. Roberts, 7 vols., 2nd ed. rev. Salt Lake City: Deseret Book, 1948 printing.
Smith, William Robertson. *Lectures on the Religion of the Semites.* Sheffield: Sheffield Academic Press, 1995.
Snell, Daniel C. *Religions of the Ancient Near East.* New York: Cambridge University Press, 2011.
Sobrino, Jon. *Christ the Liberator: A View from the Victims.* Translated by Paul Burns. Maryknoll: Orbis Books, 2001.
———. *Jesus the Liberator: A Historical Theological Reading of Jesus of Nazareth.* Translated by Paul Burns and Francis McDonagh. Maryknoll: Orbis Books, 1993.
———. *No Salvation Outside the Poor: Prophetic-Utopian Essays.* Maryknoll: Orbis Books, 2008.
———. "Poverty Means Death to the Poor." *CrossCurrents* 36 (Fall 1986): 267–76.
———. *The Principle of Mercy: Taking the Crucified People from the Cross.* Maryknoll: Orbis Books, 2015.
Soelle, Dorothee. *Suffering.* Minneapolis: Fortress Press, 1984.
Solzhenitsyn, Aleksandr. *The Gulag Archipelago 1918–1956.* New York: HarperCollins, 2002.
Song, C. S. *Jesus in the Power of the Spirit.* Eugene: Wipf & Stock, 2003.
———. *Jesus, the Crucified People.* Minneapolis: Augsburg Fortress, 1996.
Sowell, Thomas. *Black Rednecks and White Liberals.* New York: Encounter, 2005.
———. *Discrimination and Disparities.* New York: Basic, 2018.
Spencer, Joseph M. *For Zion: A Mormon Theology of Hope.* Salt Lake City: Greg Kofford Books, 2014.
———. *The Vision of All: Twenty-five Lectures on Isaiah in Nephi's Record.* Salt Lake City: Greg Kofford Books, 2016.
Stannard, David E. *American Holocaust: The Conquest of the New World.* Oxford: Oxford University Press, 1992.
Stendahl, Krister. "The Apostle Paul and the Introspective Conscience of the West." *Harvard Theological Review* 56, no. 3 (July 1963): 199–215.
———. *Paul Among Jews and Gentiles and Other Essays.* Philadelphia: Fortress, 1977.
———. "The Sermon on the Mount and Third Nephi." In *Reflections on Mormonism: Judaeo-Christian Parallels,* ed. Truman G. Madsen, 139–54. Provo: BYU Religious Studies Center, 1978.
Stewart, James B. "Thomas Sowell's Quixotic Quest to Denigrate African American Culture: A Critique." *The Journal of African American History* 91, no. 4 (2006): 459–66.

Suchocki, Marjorie Hewitt. *The Fall to Violence: Original Sin in Relational Theology*. New York: Bloomsbury Academic, 1995.

Swift, Charles. "Lehi's Vision of the Tree of Life: Understanding the Dream as Visionary Literature." *Journal of Book of Mormon Studies* 14, no. 2 (2005): 52–63.

Thomas, Hugh. *The Slave Trade: The Story of the Atlantic Slave Trade, 1440–1870*. New York: Simon & Schuster, 1997.

Thomas, Keith. *Religion and the Decline of Magic: Studies in Popular Beliefs in Sixteenth- and Seventeenth-Century England*. London: Penguin, 1973.

———. "Work and Leisure in Pre-Industrial Society." *Past & Present* 29, no. 1 (December 1964): 50–62.

Thompson, E. P. "History from Below." *Times Literary Supplement* 65 (1966): 275–80.

———. *The Making of the English Working Class*. New York: Vintage, 1966.

———. *Whigs and Hunters: The Origins of the Black Act*. New York: Pantheon, 1990.

Thurman, Howard. *Jesus and the Disinherited*. Boston: Beacon Press, 1996.

Todorov, Tzvetan. *The Conquest of America: The Question of the Other*. New York: Harper & Row, 1984.

Volf, Miroslav. *The End of Memory: Remembering Rightly in a Violent World*. Grand Rapids: Eerdmans, 2006.

———. *Exclusion and Embrace: A Theological Exploration of Identity, Otherness, and Reconciliation*. Nashville: Abingdon, 1996.

———. *Free of Charge: Giving and Forgiving in a Culture Stripped of Grace*. Grand Rapids: Zondervan, 2006.

Volluz, Corbin T. "Lehi's Dream of the Tree of Life: Springboard to Prophecy." *Journal of Book of Mormon Studies* 2, no. 2 (1993): 14–38.

Wallerstein, Immanuel. *Historical Capitalism with Capitalist Civilization*. New York: Verso, 2011.

Wallis, John. *The Bloody Code in England and Wales, 1760–1830*. New York: Springer International, 2018.

Weatherhead, Lesley D. *Psychology, Religion, and Healing*. Stewart Press, 1963.

Weiner, Tim. *Legacy of Ashes: The History of the CIA*. New York: Anchor Books, 2007.

Welch, John W., and Donald W. Parry. *The Tree of Life: From Eden to Eternity*. Salt Lake City: Deseret Book, 2011.

Whitehead, Colson. *The Nickel Boys*. New York: Doubleday, 2019.

———. *The Underground Railroad*. New York: Doubleday, 2016.

Whyte, Jessica. *The Morals of the Market: Human Rights and the Rise of Neoliberalism*. Brooklyn: Verso, 2019.

Wickham, Chris. *Framing the Early Middle Ages: Europe and the Mediterranean 400–800*. Oxford: Oxford University Press, 2005.

———. *Medieval Europe*. New Haven: Yale University Press, 2016.

———. "The Other Transition: From the Ancient World to Feudalism." *Past & Present* 103 (May, 1984): 3–36.

Widerquist, Karl and Grant S. McCall. *Prehistoric Myths in Modern Political Philosophy*. Edinburgh: University Press, 2017.

———. *The Prehistory of Private Property: Implications for Modern Political Theory*. Edinburgh: University Press, 2021.

Wilcox, Brad. *The Continuous Atonement*. Salt Lake City: Deseret Book, 2009.

Willey, Patricia Tull. *Remember the Former Things: The Recollection of Previous Texts in Second Isaiah*. Atlanta: Scholars Press, 1997.

Williams, James G. *The Bible, Violence, and the Sacred*. New York: HarperCollins, 1995.

Wink, Walter. *Engaging the Powers: Discernment and Resistance in a World of Domination*. Minneapolis: Fortress Press, 1992.

———. *Unmasking the Powers: The Invisible Forces that Determine Human Existence*. Minneapolis: Augsburg Fortress, 1986.

Witmer, Amanda. *Jesus, the Galilean Exorcist: His Exorcisms in Social and Political Context*. London: Bloomsbury, 2012.

Wright, N. T. *The Challenge of Jesus: Rediscovering Who Jesus Was and Is*. Westmont: Intervarsity, 1999.

Yinger, Kent L. *The New Perspective on Paul: An Introduction*. Eugene: Cascade, 2011.

Young, Neil, J. "The ERA Is a Moral Issue: The Mormon Church, LDS Women, and the Defeat of the Equal Rights Amendment." *American Quarterly* 59, no. 3 (September 2007): 623–44.

Scripture Index

Hebrew Bible

Genesis
Gen. 1:31 — 13–14
Gen. 3:12 — 180
Gen. 16:10 — 211
Gen. 21:18 — 211
Gen. 38 — 19

Exodus
Ex. 1:7 — 14
Ex. 2:23–25 — 15
Ex. 3:7–8 — 15
Ex. 6:6–7 — 16
Ex. 6:7 — 193
Ex. 6:9 — 16
Ex. 12:17 — 40
Ex. 14:13 — 223
Ex. 15–17 — 17
Ex. 18:13 — 17
Ex. 20:2–5 — 26
Ex. 21:2 — 18
Ex. 21:7 — 34n56
Ex. 21:13 — 18
Ex. 22:22–23 — 19
Ex. 23:9 — 19
Ex. 23:11 — 19

Leviticus
Lev. 4–6 — 20
Lev. 15:25 — 58
Lev. 16:21–22 — 22
Lev. 19 — 29
Lev. 19:9–10 — 19
Lev. 19:33–34 — 19
Lev. 25 — 19, 68

Numbers
Num. 27 — 19

Deuteronomy
Deut. 5:6–9 — 26
Deut. 15:7–11 — 19
Deut. 21–22 — 12n5

Joshua
Josh. 14–21 — 27

Judges
Judg. 3:7 — 25

1 Samuel
1 Sam. 8:11–18 — 28

1 Kings
1 Kgs. 2–3 — 28
1 Kgs. 4:20–21 — 29
1 Kgs. 5:13 — 29
1 Kgs. 7 — 29
1 Kgs. 9:19 — 29
1 Kgs. 11:1 — 30
1 Kgs. 11:6 — 30
1 Kgs. 12:4 — 30
1 Kgs. 12:14 — 30
1 Kgs. 13:33 — 30
1 Kgs. 17 — 23, 32n51
1 Kgs. 17:20 — 34
1 Kgs. 18 — 23, 24n39
1 Kgs. 21:2–3 — 31
1 Kgs. 21:19 — 32

2 Kings
2 Kgs. 2 — 23
2 Kgs. 23 — 24n38
2 Kgs. 4 — 32n51

2 Chronicles
2 Chr. 2:17–18 — 29

Nehemiah
Neh. 5:1–5 — 32
Neh. 5:10–12 — 32

Psalms
Ps. 10:7–9 — 33
Ps. 35 — 35
Ps. 69:1–3 — 35
Ps. 69:15 — 35

Isaiah
Isa. 1:11 — 76

Isa. 1:11–17 — 36
Isa. 2:7 — 36
Isa. 2:14–15 — 37
Isa. 5:8 — 37
Isa. 7:14 — 53
Isa. 49:14–15 — 40
Isa. 49:19–20 — 40
Isa. 56:1 — 223
Isa. 59:4 — 37
Isa. 59:7 — 37

Jeremiah
Jer. 5:27–28 — 37
Jer. 7:3–7 — 76
Jer. 7:11–14 — 77

Lamentations
Lam. 2:11–12 — 38–39
Lam. 3:22–24 — 39
Lam. 4:9–10 — 39
Lam. 5:21–22 — 39

Ezekiel
Ezek. 36:26 — 186

Hosea
Hosea 6:6 — 76

Amos
Amos 1:3–13 — 38
Amos 2:7 — 37
Amos 5:21 — 36, 76
Amos 6:2 — 38

Micah
Micah 2:1–2 — 37
Micah 3:1–3 — 37
Micah 6:8 — 223

New Testament

Matthew
Matt. 1:23 — 53
Matt. 4:3–4 — 52
Matt. 4:10 — 55

Matt. 5:43–44 — 183
Matt. 6:9–13 — 67
Matt. 6:24 — 55
Matt. 13 — 74
Matt. 17:14–16 — 60
Matt. 20:12–15 — 73
Matt. 21:13 — 76
Matt. 22:37–39 — 192
Matt. 25 — 75
Matt. 25:35–40 — 82
Matt. 25:40 — 192
Matt. 26:28 — 79
Matt. 27:46 — 179

Mark
Mark 1:14–15 — 43
Mark 2:5–7 — 55
Mark 2:9 — 57
Mark 2:11–12 — 55
Mark 3 — 61
Mark 5:1–9 — 62
Mark 5:15 — 65
Mark 5:19–20 — 66
Mark 5:24–34 — 58
Mark 10 — 155
Mark 10:23 — 156
Mark 12 — 76
Mark 12:43–44 — 200
Mark 15:40–41 — 78

Luke
Luke 1:46–55 — 44
Luke 1:65–79 — 45n1
Luke 4:16–20 — 43–44
Luke 6:20 — 147n18
Luke 9:40–44 — 60
Luke 10:37 — 82
Luke 11:20 — 60
Luke 13:31–32 — 66
Luke 16 — 75
Luke 16:19–26 — 145
Luke 16:26 — 144
Luke 17:20–21 — 56
Luke 20:10 — 74
Luke 20:15 — 74
Luke 21 — 76
Luke 23:34 — 184
Luke 24:21 — 79

John
John 1:17 — 84n2
John 9:1–3 — 60
John 11:50 — 77
John 14:8–9 — 173

Acts
Acts 4:32–35 — 87
Acts 5 — 87
Acts 8:1 — 87
Acts 9:1–2 — 87
Acts 10:9–16 — 88
Acts 11 — 88
Acts 13:46–47 — 88
Acts 23:1 — 104

Romans
Rom. 6:4 — 187
Rom. 6:5 — 210
Rom. 8:21 — 90
Rom. 13:13–14 — 93

1 Corinthians
1 Cor. 12:12–13 — 90
1 Cor. 13:12 — 211
1 Cor. 15:20 — 187

2 Corinthians
2 Cor. 8:9 — 204

Galatians
Gal. 2:10 — 190n2
Gal. 2:16 — 107
Gal. 3:28 — 90

Ephesians
Eph. 2:13–16 — 107
Eph. 6:12 — 181

Philippians
Philip. 2:2–8 — 203–4
Philip. 2:12–13 — 211
Philip. 3:6 — 104

Book of Mormon

1 Nephi
1 Ne. 1:20 — 140
1 Ne. 2:24 — 175
1 Ne. 4:2–3 — 140
1 Ne. 5:8 — 141
1 Ne. 7:11 — 141
1 Ne. 8:24 — 142
1 Ne. 8:27 — 142
1 Ne. 11:16 — 204
1 Ne. 11:26 — 204
1 Ne. 11:36 — 148
1 Ne. 12:16 — 144
1 Ne. 12:18 — 142, 147
1 Ne. 12:29 — 143
1 Ne. 14 — 209
1 Ne. 15:26 — 144
1 Ne. 15:28 — 142
1 Ne. 15:28–29 — 144
1 Ne. 15:30 — 142
1 Ne. 16–18 — 141

2 Nephi
2 Ne. 5:25 — 175
2 Ne. 10 — 194n4
2 Ne. 18:23 — 160

Jacob
Jacob 2:13 — 159, 162
Jacob 2:17 — 161

Mosiah
Mosiah 2:21 — 153
Mosiah 2:25 — 153
Mosiah 4:2–3 — 153
Mosiah 4:16–23 — 153
Mosiah 5:7–10 — 207
Mosiah 5:9 — 158
Mosiah 9:1 — 175n46
Mosiah 9–10 — 167
Mosiah 10:5 — 167
Mosiah 10:12–17 — 174–75
Mosiah 11–12 — 167–68
Mosiah 15:1–2 — 205
Mosiah 18:5–11 — 169
Mosiah 18:7 — 170
Mosiah 18:8–10 — 150
Mosiah 18:9 — 172
Mosiah 21 — 149
Mosiah 21:9–13 — 149
Mosiah 22 — 149
Mosiah 24:8–10 — 149
Mosiah 24:12–17 — 150
Mosiah 27:8–10 — 148
Mosiah 27:14 — 148
Mosiah 27:16 — 149

Alma

Alma 1:26–30 — 159
Alma 4:6 — 159
Alma 4:12–15 — 160
Alma 5:4–6 — 151–52
Alma 24:19–25 — 185–86
Alma 29:11–12 — 152
Alma 31:28 — 160
Alma 36:2 — 152
Alma 36:27–29 — 152
Alma 42 — 143
Alma 42:11 — 211
Alma 42:15 — 180
Alma 54:5–18 — 182
Alma 54:20–24 — 183

Helaman

Hel. 3:36 — 159
Hel. 6:18–24 — 163

3 Nephi

3 Ne. 6:10 — 159
3 Ne. 6:11–12 — 162
3 Ne. 17:5–10 — 171
3 Ne. 27:14 — 178, 207
3 Ne. 28:9 — 170n40

4 Nephi

4 Ne. 1:3 — 164
4 Ne. 1:24 — 160
4 Ne. 1:24–26 — 165
4 Ne. 1:25–26 — 137

Ether

Ether 13–15 — 181

Moroni

Moroni 8:27 — 158
Moroni 9 — 181

Doctrine and Covenants

D&C 1:17 — 109
D&C 2:2–3 — 190n1
D&C 29:32 — 222
D&C 29:34 — 195, 221
D&C 29:8 — 191
D&C 37:3 — 191
D&C 38:16–20 — 191
D&C 38:28 — 191
D&C 38:31–32 — 191
D&C 38:39 — 192
D&C 42:9 — 193
D&C 42:28–33 — 192
D&C 42:30 — 190n2, 193
D&C 42:34–39 — 193
D&C 44:6 — 194
D&C 49:19–20 — 194
D&C 49:20 — 9, 189
D&C 76 — 195
D&C 78:3–7 — 195
D&C 86:3 — 209
D&C 88:6 — 206
D&C 88:15 — 221
D&C 93:30 — 150, 203
D&C 97:21 — 210
D&C 104:4–6 — 196
D&C 104:13–18 — 196–97
D&C 121:39 — 54
D&C 130:8–9 — 196n8

Pearl of Great Price

Moses

Moses 4:18 — 180
Moses 7:18 — 9, 193
Moses 7:28–31 — 204
Moses 7:32–33 — 205
Moses 7:37 — 205
Moses 7:41 — 205
Moses 7:44 — 205
Moses 7:47 — 205
Moses 7:48–49 — 206
Moses 7:54–55 — 206
Moses 7:58–59 — 206
Moses 7:63 — 211

Subject Index

A

Abinadi, 168–69
Alexander, Bruce, 157
Allende, Salvador, 213
Alma the elder, 149–52
   at Waters of Mormon, 169–70
Alma the younger, 148–52
Amos, 37–38
Anselm of Canturbury, 97
apostasy, 135
Atlantic slave trade, 129
atonement, 22. *See also* reconciliation.
   Anselm's satisfaction theory, 97–98
   as building of covenant community, 187
   participatory, 206–7
   penal substitution theory, 100–102
   ransom theory, 97
   as reconciliation, 176–77
Augustine, 90–94

B

Benson, Ezra Taft, 164
Birch, Bruce, 15–16, 29
Black Act, 121
Black Death, 95
body of Christ, 221
bondage and captivity, 150–51
Book of Mormon, 138
   differing narratives, 175
   temporal deliverance in, 139–41
Borg, Marcus, 21, 76–77
Brown, S. Kent, 143
Brueggemann, Walter, 16, 23, 40–41, 223
burdens made light, 150
burned over district, 127

C

Calvin, John, 102
capitalism
   ethic of, 137
   horrors of, 208
   incompatible with covenant community, 137–38
Catholic Church, 214–17
Cavanaugh, William T., 213–17
Chile, 213
Christianity, early, 83–85, 87
Church of Jesus Christ of Latter-day Saints,
   fulfilling mission of, 222–23
   political neutrality of, 219
   role of, 219–20
   white nationalism in, 219
climate change, 134–35
Clinton, Bill, 165
colonialism, 122–31
Combination Act, 120
commons, 114–16
communism, 131–32
compassion, 171
Cone, James H., 18, 70, 220–21
conquistadors, 121–22
consecration, 199–203
corporate hegemony, 132–33
Cortés, Hernan, 124
covenant, 6, 8, 14–18, 27, 32, 36–41, 53–57, 68, 76–79, 83, 90, 103–6, 135–36, 139, 150–51, 161–69, 174–76, 180, 186, 190–99, 202, 207, 211, 224
   baptismal, 82
   code, 29
   community, 7–8, 36–37, 55–60, 66–68, 75, 79–80, 83, 90, 103, 107, 135–39, 161–67, 174–80, 187–94, 200–203, 209–11, 218–20, 223
   economics, 192–94
   justice, 47, 190n1
   obligations, 34, 36, 55, 68, 106, 107, 139, 160–64, 189, 202, 211, 223
   provides for the poor, 192–94
   relationship, 8, 16, 36, 106–8, 116, 138–39, 146–47, 162, 176, 180, 190, 193–96

cross
    fullness of jeong, 186
    as solidarity with poor, 179–80
    symbolism of, 178–80
Crossan, John Dominic, 11–21, 48, 59n26, 76–77
crucified people of the world, 80–82
cycle of violence, 181–83

D–E

Dalrymple, William, 130
Day of Atonement, 22
de Sahagún, Fray Bernardino, 125
demonic possession, 60–61
Dives, 197–98
Doctrine of Discovery, 122
Douglas, Mary, 21, 176
Drinnon, Richard, 127–28
Dunn, James, 105–6
earthly kingdoms and powers, 54
East India Company, 130
El Salvador civil war, 2–4
Elijah, 34
Ellacuria, Ignacio, 186
encomienda, 123
Endo, Shusaku, 172
enduring to the end, 210
Eucharist, 217
Exodus, The, 14–17
exorcisms, 60–67
exploitation, 113, 134

F–G

Fanone, Frantz, 64, 65
Feast of Toxcatl massacre, 125
Federici, Sylvia, 111
Finlan, Stephen, 86
Fiorenza, Elizabeth Schüssler, 78–79
Fraser, Nancy, 138n3
Gadianton robbers, 163
Galeano, Eduardo, 123
gathering of Saints, 191
globalization, 138
God
    Abba, 67–68
    character of, 16–17
    concern of, 18–19
    condescension of, 204
    emptying of, 205
    justice of, 146–47
    kingdom of, 56
    name, 15
    provision for the poor, 196–97
    righteousness of, 105–6
    weeping God of Enoch, 204–5
gospel, 1, 45
Gospels, 47
Grabbe, Lester, 50
great and spacious building, 147–48
Greenberg, James, 177
Grimsrud, Ted, 12n3, 14, 18, 20
gulf, 142–48
Gutiérrez, Gustavo, 43, 163n33

H–I

Hagar, 211
Hall, Douglas John, 171–72, 177
Han, Byung-Chul, 138
Harper, Stephen, 202
Hebrew Bible, 11–12
Herod Antipus, 48
Herod the Great, 48
Herzog, William, 46–47, 51, 57, 59, 71–74, 146, 155–56
highland clearances, 116–17
Hill, Christopher, 100
history from below, 112–13
Hodge, Charles, 102
Hogg, David, 97
Hollenbach, Paul, 62
Holmes, Stephen R., 98
Horsley, Richard, 61, 68
idolatry, 25–27
individualism, 99–100
indulgences, 96
internalized oppression, 70
Isaiah, 36–37
Israel
    monarchy, 27–29
    political and economic pressures on, 31
    new reality, 23–25
    suffering in Lamentations, 38–39

J

Janzen, David, 40n64
Jefferson, Thomas, 127–28
jeong, 186
Jeremiah, 37
Jeremias, Joachim, 67
Jesus
    advocates for equality of women, 78
    assault on the temple, 75–77
    assumes role of temple priest, 57
    changing ideas and titles, 84n2
    challenged by scribes, 57
    exorcisms by, 60–67
    expands covenant community, 58
    heals the paralytic, 55–57
    historical, 46–47
    historical context of, 48–49
    invokes Jeremiah, 76–77
    and kingdom of God, 55–56
    last supper, 79
    Lord's prayer, 67–68
    meaning of death, 78–79
    heals woman, 58–59
    parables of, 67–75
    pronouncement of ministry, 43–44
    refuses Satan's temptations, 51–55
    resurrection of, 79–80
    table fellowship, 59–60
    and the widow's mite, 76
Joh, Wonhee, 186
Josephus, Flavius, 62–63
Julian of Norwich, 187
justice of God, 146–47

K–L

kenosis, 203–4
King Benjamin, 153–57
King Noah, 167–68
kingdom of God, 56
LaCocque, André, 70
Law of Consecration, 194
Law of Moses, 18n20, 19n22
Legion, 64
Limhi, 149
Linebaugh, Peter, 120–21
Locke, John, 118–19
Luther, Martin, 99–105

M–O

MacCulloch, Diarmaid, 95–96
Marx, Karl, 113–14
Mary, 44
McCall, Grant S., 118
Metz, Johannes Baptist, 46, 83–86
Micah, 37
Moingt, Joseph, 222
Naboth's vineyard, 31–32
Native American genocide, 129
Neeson, J. M., 116
Nehemiah, 32
Nibley, Hugh, 143
Novak, Michael, 147n19
Old Testament, 11–12
ownership vs stewardship, 192

P

parables
    class juxtaposition, 71–72
    common reading of, 69
    laborers in the vineyard, 71–73
    relation to kingdom of God, 69
    scholarly reading of, 69
    sower, 74–75
    talents, 75
    unjust servant, 75
    wicked tenants, 73–74
Park, Andrew Sung, 177
Paul
    on the Body of Christ, 89
    conversion of, 87–88
    on creation, 90
    on justification, 89, 106
    legalist interpretation, 107–8
    metaphors of, 86
    mission to the Gentiles, 88
    new perspective on, 104–8
    on works of the law, 106
Pedro de Alvarado, 125
people of Ammon, 185–86
perpetual ordinances of remembrance, 39–40
Phelps, William W., 211
Pinochet, Augusto, 213
plagues, 16
Potter, Kelli, 156–57, 203, 207
Pratt, Orson, 197

predestination, 99n46
preferential option for the poor, 207–8
pride, 158–62
primitive accumulation, 112–14
privatization, 133
property
   in antiquity, 117–18
   crimes against, 119–22
   development of concept, 117–18
   private, 137
prophets
   response to oppression, 36–38
   role of, 23
Protestant ethic, 137
Psalms, 33–35
Purgatory, 94–95
purity prohibitions, 58–59

R

racism, 129
rape codes, 12–13
Reagan, Ronald, 165–66
reconciliation, 174, 183–84, 207
Requerimento, 123
Restoration, The
   as God's rejection of capitalist economic and social systems, 190–91
   significance of historical events, 189–91
   timing of, 109, 136
resurrection, 187
Riot Act (1715), 120
Roman Empire, 110
   conquest of Jerusalem, 48
   trauma inflicted on Galilee, 61
Romero, Oscar, 3–4

S

sacrament covenants, 82
sacrifice, 19–22
salvation
   afterlife, 1–2, 218
   changing definitions, 4–6, 83
   Hebrew word for, 13
   liberative approach, 8–9
   need for, 218
   in Old Testament, 12
   shift from historical to theological, 85
   temporal, 5
   working out our own, 211
Samuel, 28
scapegoat, 22
Scramble for Africa, 130
Second Coming, 206
Second Temple period, 48
serfs, 111–12
Sheol, 13
sin
   and contagion, 21–22
   as han, 177–78
   relational view, 178
   as systemic injustice and violence, 177
   and temple access, 56–57
   as wealth inequality, 194
sin offerings, 20
Smith, Joseph, 139, 194, 221
Smith, William Robertson, 21
Sobrino, Jon, 11, 78, 80–81, 187, 224
   on the body of Christ, 81
   on Israel's religion, 41
   on idolatry and oppression, 26–27
   on Jesus, 79, 82
   on salvation, 85
Soelle, Dorothee, 179, 208
Solomon, 28–30
Song, C. S., 51–52, 81–82
soul, 221
Stannard, David E., 122, 129
Steinbeck, John, 109
Stendahl, Krister, 104
stewardship, 196
Suchocki, Marjorie, 178, 184
suffering, 170–73

T–V

temple, 49–50
temporal deliverance, 11–41, 139–41, 191
Ten Commandments, 17–19
Tenochtitlan, 124–25
Thompson, E. P., 114–15
Thurman, Howard, 183
torture, 214
Transportation Act, 120
Tree of Life, 141
United Firm, 196

Unites States military action, 166
Vagrancy Act, 121
violent resistance, 75
Vold, Miroslav, 180, 184–85

W–Z

Walliss, John, 120
Washington, George, 127
wealth inequality, 194
Weatherhead, Lesley D., 63–64
Western civilization, 209
    interference in foreign governments, 134
    ruin of the Global South, 133

white nationalism, 219
Wickham, Chris, 113
Widerquist, Karl, 118
Willey, Patricia, 41
Williams, James, 33
Wink, Walter, 63
Witmer, Amanda, 45, 78
Workhouse Act, 120
world wealth distribution, 132
Wright, N. T., 187
Young, Brigham, 201–2, 222
Zion, 193, 210

Also available from
GREG KOFFORD BOOKS

For Zion: A Mormon Theology of Hope

Joseph M. Spencer

Paperback, ISBN: 978-1-58958-568-3

What is hope? What is Zion? And what does it mean to hope for Zion? In this insightful book, Joseph Spencer explores these questions through the scriptures of two continents separated by nearly two millennia. In the first half, Spencer engages in a rich study of Paul's letter to the Roman to better understand how the apostle understood hope and what it means to have it. In the second half of the book, Spencer jumps to the early years of the Restoration and the various revelations on consecration to understand how Latter-day Saints are expected to strive for Zion. Between these halves is an interlude examining the hoped-for Zion that both thrived in the Book of Mormon and was hoped to be established again.

Praise for *For Zion*:

"Joseph Spencer is one of the most astute readers of sacred texts working in Mormon Studies. Blending theological savvy, historical grounding, and sensitive readings of scripture, he has produced an original and compelling case for consecration and the life of discipleship." — Terryl Givens, author, *Wrestling the Angel: The Foundations of Mormon Thought*

"*For Zion: A Mormon Theology of Hope* is more than a theological reflection. It also consists of able textual exegesis, historical contextualization, and philosophic exploration. Spencer's careful readings of Paul's focus on hope in Romans and on Joseph Smith's development of consecration in his early revelations, linking them as he does with the Book of Mormon, have provided an intriguing, intertextual avenue for understanding what true stewardship should be for us—now and in the future. As such he has set a new benchmark for solid, innovative Latter-day Saint scholarship that is at once provocative and challenging." — Eric D. Huntsman, author, *The Miracles of Jesus*

The Liberal Soul: Applying the Gospel of Jesus Christ in Politics

Richard Davis

Paperback, ISBN: 978-1-58958-583-6

The Liberal Soul offers something lacking in LDS culture. That is the presentation of a different way for Latter-day Saints to examine the question of how to be faithful disciples of Christ and good citizens. It shows public policy decision-making regarding government role as the manifestation of the "liberal soul" rather than as the libertarianism advocated by past Mormon speakers and writers such as Ezra Taft Benson, Cleon Skousen, or Vern Andersen. It also takes a different approach from the less radical but still traditional economic conservative attitudes of well-known politicians such as Orrin Hatch or Mitt Romney.

Davis suggests that a Latter-day Saint can approach economic policy, war, the environment, and social issues with the perspective that society is basically good and not evil, tolerance and forbearance are desirable qualities instead of bad ones, and that government can and does play a positive role as a vehicle of society in improving the lives of citizens. He describes how Latter-day Saints can apply the Gospel of Jesus Christ to our roles at each of these three levels—individual, group, and society—rather than assuming the societal level violates the principles of the Gospel. The result is that Latter-day Saints can help bring about a Zion society—one where all benefit, the most vulnerable are aided and not ignored, inclusion is the rule and not the exception, and suspicion and fear are replaced by love and acceptance.

Praise for *The Liberal Soul*:

"Davis provides a thoughtful exploration into the principles of generosity, equality, and Christian discipleship and their important relationship to democratic government. This book clearly explains the strong connection between liberalism and Mormonism. I would recommend it to anyone who has ever asked me, 'How can you be a Democrat and a Mormon?'"
— U.S. Senate Majority Leader Harry Reid

Women at Church: Magnifying LDS Women's Local Impact

Neylan McBaine

Paperback, ISBN: 978-1-58958-688-8

Women at Church is a practical and faithful guide to improving the way men and women work together at church. Looking at current administrative and cultural practices, the author explains why some women struggle with the gendered divisions of labor. She then examines ample real-life examples that are currently happening in local settings around the country that expand and reimagine gendered practices. Readers will understand how to evaluate possible pain points in current practices and propose solutions that continue to uphold all mandated church policies. Readers will be equipped with the tools they need to have respectful, empathetic and productive conversations about gendered practices in Church administration and culture.

Praise for *Women at Church*:

"Such a timely, faithful, and practical book! I suggest ordering this book in bulk to give to your bishopric, stake presidency, and all your local leadership to start a conversation on changing Church culture for women by letting our doctrine suggest creative local adaptations—Neylan McBaine shows the way!" — Valerie Hudson Cassler, author of *Women in Eternity, Women of Zion*

"A pivotal work replete with wisdom and insight. Neylan McBaine deftly outlines a workable programme for facilitating movement in the direction of the 'privileges and powers' promised the nascent Female Relief Society of Nauvoo." — Fiona Givens, co-author of *The God Who Weeps: How Mormonism Makes Sense of Life*

"In her timely and brilliant findings, Neylan McBaine issues a gracious invitation to rethink our assumptions about women's public Church service. Well researched, authentic, and respectful of the current Church administrative structure, McBaine shares exciting and practical ideas that address diverse needs and involve all members in the meaningful work of the Church." — Camille Fronk Olson, author of *Women of the Old Testament* and *Women of the New Testament*

Whom Say Ye That I Am?
Lessons from the Jesus of Nazareth

James W. McConkie and Judith E. McConkie

Paperback, ISBN: 978-1-58958-707-6

"This book is the most important Jesus study to date written by believing Mormons for an LDS audience. It opens the door for Mormons to come to know a Jesus most readers will know little about—the Jesus of history." — David Bokovoy, author of *Authoring the Old Testament: Genesis–Deuteronomy*

"Meticulously documented and researched, the authors have crafted an insightful and enlightening book that allows Jesus to speak by providing both wisdom and council. The McConkies masterfully weave in sources from the Gospels, ancient and modern scholars, along with Christian and non-Christian religious leaders." — *Deseret News*

The story of Jesus is frequently limited to the telling of the babe of Bethlehem who would die on the cross and three days later triumphantly exit his tomb in resurrected glory. Frequently skimmed over or left aside is the story of the Jesus of Nazareth who confronted systemic injustice, angered those in power, risked his life for the oppressed and suffering, and worked to preach and establish the Kingdom of God—all of which would lead to his execution on Calvary.

In this insightful and moving volume, authors James and Judith McConkie turn to the latest scholarship on the historical and cultural background of Jesus to discover lessons on what we can learn from his exemplary life. Whether it be his intimate interactions with the sick, the poor, women, and the outcast, or his public confrontations with oppressive religious, political, and economic institutions, Jesus of Nazareth—the son of a carpenter, Messiah, and Son of God—exemplified the way, the truth, and the life that we must follow to bring about the Kingdom of Heaven.

www.ingramcontent.com/pod-product-compliance
Lightning Source LLC
Chambersburg PA
CBHW020225170426
43201CB00007B/324